Geographies of the Mind

John K. Wright on the Pinnacle, Lyme, New Hampshire (August 1968).
Photo courtesy of Philip W. Porter.

GEOGRAPHIES
OF THE MIND

ESSAYS IN HISTORICAL GEOSOPHY

In Honor of John Kirtland Wright

edited by

David Lowenthal and Martyn J. Bowden

with the assistance of Mary Alice Lamberty

published in collaboration with the
American Geographical Society, New York

New York

OXFORD UNIVERSITY PRESS

1976

GF
8
. G4

Contents

Geographies of the Mind

Introduction

THE LINEAMENTS OF THE WORLD we live in are both seen and shaped in accordance, or by contrast, with images we hold of other worlds—better worlds, past worlds, future worlds. We constantly compare the reality with the fancy. Indeed, without the one we could neither visualize nor conceptualize the other.

Each essay in this volume reflects some facet of this duality. They all show how our views of ourselves and our landscapes derive from our substantive environmental beliefs. The strength and consistency of these beliefs, and the extent to which we feel that others support them, affect all our attitudes toward, and behavior in, the world around us.

This book is a memorial to John Kirtland Wright and a reflection of his influence. Like most commemorative volumes, it is presumptuous and deficient. We—his friends, colleagues, and students—honor ourselves more than we commemorate Wright, by combining our efforts under the umbrella of his name. Nor can these essays begin to suggest the range, depth, and versatility of Wright's concerns.

Wright's own collection of essays, *Human Nature in Geography*, expressed with the gaiety, sparkle, and gentle modesty that were hallmarks of his style, is the best introduction to his many-faceted interests. Only a handful of the themes he explored there are developed here. But even *Human Nature in Geography* displays inadequately the full compass of Wright's work, nor can it convey how his work has come to permeate geographical scholarship. This

3

requires a review of the whole of his prodigious output (listed at the end of this volume), along with a picture of the man himself. The caliber of Wright's work and the quality of his personality are inseparable.[1]

For a geographer whose professional career was spent almost wholly in research and administration—his teaching was limited to a few seminars after he reached 65—Wright attracted an extraordinarily diversified and devoted following. The explanation lies in his personal ties and in the quality of his research.

Everyone who knew Wright can testify to the strength of his affections. He responded with infectious enthusiasm to anyone he liked or in whose work he took an interest. He had an unbounded capacity for stimulating and enduring relationships. When a piece of writing caught his attention he would at once seek out the author, not simply as a source of information but as a creative collaborator. Wright's unexpected letters of appreciation led to hundreds of fruitful friendships. Inquiries about his own work elicited detailed, meticulous responses. For those who sought enlightenment or encouragement, no effort on Wright's part seemed too great. And exchanges once begun were not easily allowed to lapse. Many of us can recall notes from Wright gently chiding us for letting so many months go by since we were last in touch and wondering how some project, dear to us both, was faring. Letters expressed and extended Wright in a fashion now almost obsolete.

Yet correspondence was only a part of Wright's personal influence. Still more did he enjoy seeing friends and colleagues. Perhaps partly because his scholarly life was perforce more solitary than most, he made hospitality a high art. Visitors to the American Geographical Society, to his home in Westchester and, after his retirement, in Lyme, New Hampshire, were not only treated as part of the family but also shared fully in Wright's innumerable enthusiasms, discussing sources and posing provocative or thorny or amusing propositions bearing on mutual research. No scholar was ever more generous with his time, more ready to explore with others what interested them.

Along with scholarly catholicity and camaraderie, Wright maintained a concern for the English language that made him an object lesson to his colleagues. His own editorial tasks never kept him from serving in an informal editorial capacity for his friends. All the contributors to this volume have benefited from, and been enlarged by, Wright's solicitous help, his scrupulous attention to draft after draft, his firm reminders about accuracy, precision, and the quality and meaning of language.

1. Brief surveys of Wright's life and work are Martyn J. Bowden, "John Kirtland Wright, 1891–1969," *Annals of the Association of American Geographers* 60 (1970):394–403; and David Lowenthal, "John Kirtland Wright, 1891–1969," *Geographical Review* 59 (1969):598–604.

Introduction

Because Wright so often gave more than he received as adviser and editor, to many of his friends he seemed the teacher, they the students. Yet no one was less mindful of formal distinctions of age or rank. Those who knew him only superficially sometimes found him formal and austere; but with friends of all ages he was simply himself, by turn somber and playful, yet always open and direct. As Wright grew older he more often recalled scenes, events, and people from the past; but his recountings were just as fresh and relevant to his juniors as to the contemporaries with whom he originally shared the experiences.

Wright's work, like his personality, endeared him to countless colleagues. It is too soon to assess his substantive legacy: he habitually developed enthusiasms for topics so fresh that tools were unavailable for their analysis, so that Wright himself had to invent and elaborate them. The substantive inquiry and the mode of investigation, coupled with his style of communication, were part of the same process. Categorizing medieval information about the world thus induced him to make not only a chronological but also a substantive classification of geographical data (in *Geographical Lore of the Time of the Crusades*). Similarly, the inadequacies of early census materials led him to devise cartographic techniques for weighting degrees of reliability (in "A Method of Mapping Densities of Population, with Cape Cod as an Example"). Thus one finds in Wright's work both new ideas and novel ways of assessing them.

Both ideas and techniques are characteristically expressed in a tone of infectious surprise. Wright's manner is not that of laying down definitive views or received truth but rather of saying, isn't it curious that this should be so, what can we make of it, how can we verify its truth or falsehood. The reader then asks his own questions and carries on, if he will, from where Wright has left off. Quizzical, tolerant, obsessively curious, always struck by anomalies, never dogmatic about sources or conclusions, Wright is infinitely seductive to his readers, who are flattered by the modesty of his manner and intrigued by the questions he poses.

Added to this is Wright's compelling readability. In these scientistic times it is sometimes hard to remember that humanism is not a matter simply of attitude and substance, but of communication, too. Wright was a master of English prose, with a style that is at the same time deeply personal and a model of clarity. It is noteworthy that a man whose reading and thinking encompassed so wide a range of abstruse materials was able to express himself in a fashion at once elegant and simple.

The matter as well as the manner of Wright's work stimulated colleagues. Not only was he consistently innovative and suggestive; the substance of what he said was and is of absorbing interest. In almost every essay he suggests a dozen new paths of inquiry. One reason for his stimulus is the dual perspective of most of Wright's work: he was simultaneously concerned both with evidence—true and false facts and hypotheses—and with the role it played in human thought and behavior. The interplay between experience and belief formed the substance and informed the quality of his scholarly achievement. It continues to animate his followers in the many realms he denominated "geosophy." His influence has been powerful and beneficent because the way he viewed relations between beliefs and acts encouraged the exploration of difficult themes with an open, humble, comparative eye.

The breadth of Wright's interests can be surveyed in the bibliography of his writings, published here for the first time. The smaller range of matter in *Geographies of the Mind* is nonetheless so multifarious as to frustrate any overview or generalization. What sensible statement can be made about a collection of papers that includes, among hundreds of other topics, devotion to sacred shrines in China and the renunciation of relics in America, Coronado's exploration of the Southwest and Harvard students' excursions to the White Mountains, attitudes toward presumed aridity in the Great Plains and ways of studying historical geography in universities? At first glance these might appear to have little in common beyond their joint dedication to Wright and, we hope, a Wrightian respect for the use of words. Yet six of them deal with landscapes and ideals that are specifically American and the other two—the essay by Tuan with which this volume opens and that by Porter and Lukermann with which it closes—with locales even more perfect and ideal than America.

A closer reading reveals substantial similarities of context if not of content, a joint focus on particular types of explanation and styles of inquiry. All eight papers deal with the impact of environmental ideas on thought and action, and ultimately also on the environment itself. All are concerned with habits of thought that condition what people learn about environment and environmental processes, how they change their minds, and how they persuade others to reject old, and adopt new, views. All the essays, strictly historical or otherwise, rely on the written record—traces of human attitudes left in the form of diaries, letters, textbooks, scholarly articles, novels, poems, and prayers. Each author expectably accords these sources varying prominence, since the nature of the evidence and the standards of demonstrable proof depend on intention as well as subject matter.

Within this framework of broad resemblances, patterns of purpose, structure, and content help to group these eight papers into several smaller clusters. The game of categories is one that any number can play, and those discerned here could be extended indefinitely. But some classification, however arbitrarily arrived at, may provoke useful discussion. Let me suggest one way these papers might be viewed as subsets in geographical methodology.

How we know what we do about the environment is the central preoccupation of two papers: that by Allen on exploration and that by Koelsch on the university milieu as a font of experience. Both papers provide a wealth of other data and insights, but their chief issues are essentially epistemological: What are the sources of our environmental information? What happens when we substitute one kind of evidence for another? How do we supplant inadequate or erroneous views and stereotypes?

Within this framework, Allen's particular concern is with a professional or semiprofessional type of specialist, the explorer, whose mission is to bring back accounts of the nature of newly found regions and to assess their potentialities. With illustrative material stretching over two millennia, he describes the sequence in which second-hand data are superseded by first-hand experience, and the impact of this replacement process on exploratory decisions. Koelsch, too, deals with the environmental information and images of a professional class—the American college community—but his concern is with the total educational experience of men of influence generally, and with the potential value of archival sources.

The principal theme of a second cluster of essays is the delineation of ideas about, and attitudes toward, particular types of place. The typology of places is itself culturally derived, shifting in character, affected by pressures from protagonists and entrepreneurs, and subject to changes in information and stereotypes, such as those discussed in the epistemological papers. Three papers exemplifying these themes are Tuan's on sacred places, Zelinsky's on cemeteries, and, in part, Bowden's on the Great American Desert.

The first two bear obvious affinities. Tuan explores geopiety as a cluster of feelings brought to bear on special types of environments, on the particular characteristics associated with home, and on the sense of rootedness that accompanies nationality. Sacredness depends on one or more of these linked attributes; and differences in the type, scale, and locus of reverence can be explained only by entire systems of value. Zelinsky's American afterworld is more specifically—indeed, more quantitatively—delineated in terms of its toponymy alone; its functions and boundaries are never in doubt. Yet the character of landscapes for the dead, no less than sacred places generally, is determined by the ever-changing mores and values of those who create them. But it would not do to press the similarity too far, for whereas Tuan emphasizes motive and affect throughout, Zelinsky's analysis is essentially descriptive; the deduction of aim and purpose is left to the reader.

Bowden's essay on the myth of the desert has one significant feature in common with the other two: it surveys a type of place whose nature and locale depend on changing stereotypes about function and appearance, use and utility. Bowden goes beyond Tuan in his concern with the motivations underlying environmental attitudes, and is more specific than Zelinsky in explaining changing views (how these qualities connect with other papers will emerge below). But Bowden resembles Tuan and Zelinsky in focusing on ideas about places felt to be destined for a particular use (or non-use), and for that reason set apart in people's minds from the surrounding landscape, if not from the rest of the world. If the papers by Koelsch and Allen are essentially epistemological in content, these three may be termed basically definitional: they deal with attempts to define, delimit, and describe landscapes of special importance to all people at all times (Tuan), to all Americans at some time (Zelinsky), or to some Americans in particular eras (Bowden).

Environmental and social ideals are the central concern of a third cluster of essays: Porter and Lukermann's and to some extent Lowenthal's and Zelinsky's. A major thematic component of these three papers is the nature of the world people would prefer to inhabit, as opposed to the world they actually do. The opposition is most explicit in Porter and Lukermann's utopias, where the authors show that the perfect world has changed both its locale and its character as the real world has itself been explored and altered. The shifting quality of utopian life reflects changes in real-world technology and society—changes that betoken the disenchantment reflected in dystopian literature.

Utopias bear comparison also with the particular localities studied in other papers—and especially with Tuan's sacred places, which both stimulate and emulate the utopian imagination. Zelinsky, again, provides a more specific gloss, viewing cemeteries as repositories of landscape virtues that the living desire for themselves if not for the departed. Place-names of the afterworld reveal it to be more manipulable than the real world. Lowenthal's essay on Americans' rejection of the past elaborates preferences for a wholly new world stimulated by the throwing off of Old World suzerainty, and shows how the man-made environment of nineteenth-century America, with its persistent emphasis on the future, reflected this preference. All three papers deal with types of future orientation—Lowenthal's with a national destiny meant to replace a sordid past, Zelinsky's with a personal future to replace the all-too-brief present, Porter and Lukermann's with a paradisaical future to replace an unsatisfactory contemporary world. Preferential values form the heart of the subject matter.

Occupation and alteration are processes central to the purpose of the final cluster of essays. How man changes milieus and the implications of these changes for environmental understanding are the primary themes of Mikesell's essay on sequent occupance and an important subsidiary theme for Allen, Bowden, and Lowenthal. What geographers have made of successive occupance by folk differing in economic organization and cultural equipment is the import of Mikesell's inquiry. The story of sequent occupance also has affinities with other essays that show how intellectual processes reflect environmental understanding and vice versa. Porter and Lukermann, and

8

Koelsch, are substantially concerned, like Mikesell, with the sociology of knowledge, and specifically with how a given social and intellectual climate influences scholarly interpretation.

This grouping classifies the papers in orientations that are primarily epistemological, definitional, value-preferential, and processual—four ways in which many other geographies of the mind might also be interpreted. But all these papers deal in one way or another with all four broad aspects of geosophy. Hence this classification may be little more than an arbitrary figment of this editor's imagination—one more misguided attempt to reduce to convenient order the bewildering multiplicities of the human mind that John K. Wright so rejoiced in showing up as "categorillas."

It remains to thank those who have helped to bring this project to fruition. We are proud that this book should be a publication of the American Geographical Society, to which Jack Wright devoted most of his scholarly career; and we are indebted to its present librarian, Lynn S. Mullins, and to Molly Laird, for searching out many fugitive Wrightian items for his bibliography. James J. Anderson of Oxford University Press has been patient and generous with us individually and severally, and we are grateful for his sustained interest. We are delighted to have had Mrs. Wright's support and her concern that her husband's insistence on quality be maintained. Thanks must go also to the authors of the essays included herein for their long travail and unstinting support. From the first submission to the final revision they mainly bore with tolerance the burdens placed on them by editorial requirements. Finally, our deepest gratitude goes to John K. Wright, without whom there would not only be no book but an unthinkable diminution in all our understanding and in the richness of our lives.

DAVID LOWENTHAL

1

Geopiety: A Theme in Man's Attachment to Nature and to Place

YI-FU TUAN

Like Mussorgsky, I shall present some "pictures at an exhibition" and not a sonata or symphony.

John K. Wright

ECOLOGY AND TERRITORIALITY are two themes that have captured the attention of both scientists and laymen in recent decades. Ecology is studied essentially as a problem in budgeting: of working out the energy exchanges between physical and biological systems if one be a scientist, of calculating long-range costs and benefits if one be a political economist. As for human attachment to place, a popular model is that of the animal's territorial behavior. Ecology and territoriality can be approached also through the byway of attitudes, beliefs, and values subsumable under the religious concept of geopiety. This is the route I shall take.

"Geopiety" is a term borrowed from John K. Wright to stand for a special complex of relations between man and nature.[1] "Geo" means earth; earth refers to the planet, the globe or its surface vis-à-vis heaven; it is also the soil and, by extension, land, country, and nation. "Piety" means reverence and attachment to one's family and homeland, and to

11

the gods who protect them. "Geopiety" covers a broad range of emotional bonds between man and his terrestrial home. The nature of the emotion is suggested by such related terms as "pity," "piety," the Roman *pietas,* and the Chinese *hsiao.* Reverence is the essence of the emotion, but other elements enter in varying degree: propitiation, pity, compassion, affection. People propitiate the strong and are compassionate toward the weak. It may seem strange that the single concept of reverence, or piety, should contain feelings that are opposed. The apparent incompatibility, however, disappears if we take in a broad time span rather than the moment, and if we remember that reciprocity lies at the core of piety.

In ancient Rome and China, a father's legal power over his children was absolute. Parents, however, are mortal and grow weak with age as their offspring gain strength; parents not only command but *need* service as well. Need is symptomatic of lack: filial piety calls for compassion as well as for reverence. The spirits that preside over nature have power over men, but they also need human offerings. Land supports men and at the same time requires human care. The term "piety" covers relations not only among men but also between man and the gods, and man and nature; in fact the three relations are closely interwoven. To be pious is to be dutiful to one's parents and gods. This is piety's primary meaning. As Fustel de Coulanges says, however, "the piety of ancients was love of country."[2] Piety is also the love of the fatherland, or patriotism. The Chinese term *hsiao* is usually, though not precisely, translated into English as filial piety or filiality. Here the sense of duty to parents and ancestors predominates. It is not the only duty: in the *Li Chi,* Tsang-Tze reports Confucius as saying, "To fell a single tree, or kill a single animal, not at the proper season is contrary to *hsiao.*"[3]

In this essay I shall develop some of the meanings of geopiety adumbrated above. A dominant theme is the worship of heaven and earth, of the Sky Father and the Earth Mother. At the local level are the sacrifices offered to the guarding spirits of place, at the grove, cave, spring, mountain, or river. The literature on this theme is rich and extensive. I shall touch on it lightly—using illustrations from the Greco-Roman world and from China—in part to remind us of our loss. By now nature is largely secularized: gods no longer inhabit the mountains and, as Khrushchev once bluntly told us, the Russian astronauts saw no sign of them even in heaven. Still, the study of geopiety is not solely an antiquarian exercise. The feeling persists. At the level of folk and youth culture, the current ecological movement seems to rest as much on geopious sentiment as on rational calculation. If only the genii could be restored to nature . . . but can they return without also resuscitating ancestor worship and fertility cults? Reverence or piety in the sense of awe toward a power that commands propitiatory rites has disappeared from the modern world. It is no great loss. We are left with the higher sentiment of compassion. The principle of reciprocal aid remains a viable concept in ecology. Moreover, geopious feelings are still with us as attachment to place, love of country, and patriotism.

The study of ecology and that of territorial behavior are scientific enterprises and, in the scientific purview, they encounter methodological difficulties whenever they involve human beings, their values and symbolic structures. The study of geopiety helps us to understand why these difficulties occur and offers, in addition, insights unique to the humanistic approach. It shows that the roots of certain modern concepts, such as that of reciprocation in nature, lie in profound human experiences that were given other (largely religious) expressions in the past. It leads us to see how human territoriality, in the sense of attachment to place, differs in important ways from the territoriality of animals unburdened by symbolic thought. It reveals the depth of the emotional bond between man and nature, man and place, in contrast with the cool calculations of modern ecological wisdom and the animal-behaviorist interpretation of human ties to place (though geopious practice can also include much amoral manipulation by ritualistic means). Finally, the study of geopiety, like all ventures into the history of ideas, may be an exercise in self-awareness—and this should shield us from the twin errors of excessive rationalism and excessive sentimentality.

PIETY AS RECIPROCITY

In Carl Kerényi's belief, the essential idea of Roman *pietas* is captured in the legend of the temple erected in Rome to the goddess Pietas. The story goes that on the site of the temple a mother had been imprisoned and was kept alive by the milk from her own daughter's breast. "The special thing which here stands out," he writes, "is something bodily and spiritual at the same time. Pietas here shows itself as a form of absolute reciprocity in nature, a completely closed circle of giving and receiving. In some variants of the story the mother's place is taken by the father. But the example thus revered is always this same natural circle of reciprocity."[4] The Roman legend should strike a familiar chord among the Chinese, for filial piety in China is exemplified repeatedly in stories of how the son or daughter uses his or her own flesh to make a nutritious broth for the sick mother.

The Confucian concept of *hsiao* is translated by some scholars as obedience rather than as filial piety.[5] The virtues it teaches were useful to the stratified society of Han times (206 B.C.–A.D. 220)—respect, docility, obedience, and subordination to elders and betters. The main idea behind *hsiao* is indisputably one-sided: it is obedience and reverence toward authority. Yet it has a penumbra of other meanings. In a broad sense the term connotes the principle of reciprocal duties felt to undergird universal harmony. In the *Hsiao Ching*, a work compiled sometime between 350 and 200 B.C., Confucius is made to say,

> Filiality is the first principle of heaven, the ultimate standard of the earth, the norm of conduct for the people. Men ought to follow the pattern of heaven and earth which leads them by the brightness of the heavens and the benefits of the earth to harmonize all under heaven.[6]

Hsiao includes the notion of duty of ruler to subject, parents to children; for without reciprocity there cannot be harmony. The recognition that duties and obligations are mutual extends beyond human relationships to nature. In old times (says the text) "the illustrious kings served heaven intelligently because they were filial in the service of their fathers. They served earth discreetly because they were filial in the service of their mothers. . . . Hence, because heaven was well served and earth honored, the spirits manifested themselves brilliantly."[7]

14

HEAVEN AND EARTH

Terra means both earth and soil. Similarly, the English word "earth" stands for a universal category—the surface counterpoised against heaven —and for something local, soil. The Chinese distinguish between *ti*, the consort of *t'ien* (heaven), and *t'u*, soil, the stuff of earth which has no evident paired opposition. Heaven, sky, or *t'ien* is a universal category. Even when heaven is anthropomorphized into a sky god, such as Zeus or Apollo, it easily breaks its tie with place to acquire the status of universal divinity. Earth gods, on the other hand, are local. Only sophisticated people conceive of Mother Earth as a world-wide entity. In practical worship, as Guthrie observes, "the Mother who broods over the scene is the Mother of each man's village or *pays*."[8] Chthonian deities antedate those of the sky. By Homeric times, however, the sky gods of Olympus were already well established. And in the course of the Chou dynasty (*ca.* 1027–256 B.C.) the Chinese crystallized the concept of *t'ien*, for which the *ti* (earth) was the counterpart, though of somewhat inferior status. *T'u* (soil) gods occupied still lower rank.

In prehistoric and protohistoric times chthonian deities were more important than sky deities in both the Mediterranean world and China. From the evidence of landscape and architecture in the Aegean basin, Vincent Scully traced the move from the worship of the earth goddess to that of the lordly Zeus of the sky. Unfortified Minoan sites nestled in the topographical hollows to benefit from close contact with the potent forces of the earth. The Mycenaeans worshiped the earth goddess and placed their houses and citadels below the protecting peaks, but their sites—unlike those of the peaceful Minoans—stood on low summits. The Dorians renounced the goddess and substituted for her their own thunder-wielding sky god. On Crete, Dorian strongholds were located on or under savage heights, not in nature's megara, the valleys.[9]

In the *Li Chi* a passage says,

> In the sacrifice at the Shê altars they [the illustrious kings of old] dealt with the earth as if it were a spirit. The earth supported all things, while heaven hung out its brilliant signs. They derived their material resources from the earth; they derived rules [for their courses of labour] from the

heavens. Thus they were led to give honour to heaven and their affection to the earth, and therefore they taught the people to render a good return [to the earth].[10]

The earth supports life and commands affection that is expressed in certain sacrifices performed at the *Shê* altars. Heaven, by contrast, is the source of regularity, of rules; and to heaven is due honor. Among human relationships the mother elicits love or affection, the prince honor or reverence; but the father commands both affection and reverence, according to the *Hsiao Ching*.[11] Heaven and earth are not equal in dignity; neither are the father and the mother.

GENIUS LOCI

Geopiety is directed to categories of nature that differ depending on one's religious sophistication and one's position in society. In China, only the emperor had the prerogative to sacrifice to Heaven and to Earth. He alone could claim to be a universal figure. The princes of the feudal states had no right to set their sights so high. They, like the emperor, had their ancestral temples and their altars to the gods of soil and crops. They performed rites to the spirits of rivers and mountains, but only to those within their territories. An idea of both the range of the nature gods worshiped and their hierarchical order is given in the *chi fa* (law of sacrifices) section of the *Li Chi*.

> With a blazing pile of wood on the grand altar they sacrificed to Heaven. . . . By burying the victim in the grand mound, they sacrificed to the seasons. With similar victims they sacrificed to the spirits of cold and heat, at the pit and the altar, using prayers of deprecation and petition; to the sun, at the altar called the royal palace; to the moon, at the pit called the light of the night; to the stars at the honoured place of gloom; to the spirits of flood and drought at the honoured altar of rain; to the spirits of the four quarters at the place of the four pits and altars; mountains, forests, streams, valleys, hills, and mounds, which are able to produce clouds, and to occasion winds and rain, were all regarded as dominated by spirits.[12]

Heaven stands at one end of the hierarchy, the spirits of the earth—identified with particular features—at the other. Mountains, forests, and streams require offerings because they have the power to affect weather, crop yields, and human fertility. In 566 B.C., when the state of Chêng was suffering from a great drought, officials were sent to placate the spirits of Mulberry Mountain. A few workers, however, cut trees on it and rain did not fall. A wise minister punished the despoilers and said: "When sacrifice is offered to a mountain, it is to make the trees grow. Cutting them down is therefore a great crime."[13] At harvest time, dances and music were performed in honor of, and to establish harmony with, all kinds of beings, animate and inanimate: creatures with feathers and without, creatures with scales and horns; stellar beings and heavenly gods; the spirits of rivers and lakes, mountains and forests, plains and uplands, the spirits of the earth.[14] In the early Chou period, seasonal festivals of a strongly emotional and sexual nature were held in the country near a mountain or beside the river. As part of the festival, young men and women waded across water, climbed hills, picked flowers, gathered wood, and engaged in song contests. Thereafter they paired off and participated in sexual rites.[15]

Greek and Roman gods, heroes, and spirits were unequal in status, and the places associated with them varied in degree of holiness. The Romans, moreover, distinguished between the *loca sacra* and the *loca religiosa*. *Sacer* is a legal term in ritual: it means that a place has been made over to the deity by certain formulas, accompanied with favorable auspices, under the authority of the state. Holy places not consecrated by the state came under the heading of *loca religiosa*: the shrines belonging to families and *gentes*, certain provincial temple sites, all burial grounds, and certain natural areas. A place struck by thunderbolt, for instance, became *religiosum*, and a low wall was erected to mark the holy spot where the bolt was believed to be buried. The sacredness of these places might not have received official recognition, but it was not to be violated.[16]

Gods and spirits inhabited the ancient Greek lands. In popular belief the rivers were holy. "An army did not cross a river without making a sacrifice to it," writes Nilsson, "and Hesiod prescribes that one should not cross a river without saying a prayer and washing one's hands in its water."[17] As in ancient China, the aid of rivers was sought for the fertility of both the land and human beings. Every river in Greece had its god, depicted in the shape of a bull or a horse. Centaurs were originally spirits of mountain torrents, representing the rough side of nature. Nymphs were almost everywhere: they dwelt in mountains, cool caves, groves, and meadows and by springs—especially by springs and in caves. They were beautiful and stood for the gentle side of nature. The ancient landscape was full of *numina* or local powers; the topographical ensemble itself had power and so did its parts. One could hardly move about in the countryside without meeting a shrine, a sacred enclosure, an image, a sacred stone, a sacred tree. The lowland at the mouth of the River Alpheus was described by Strabo as "full of temples of Artemis, Aphrodite, and the Nymphs, being situated in sacred precincts that are generally full of flowers because of the abundance of water"; and "there were numerous shrines of Hermes on the road-sides and temples of Poseidon on the capes."[18]

In the religion of pre-Hellenic and early Greek times, Artemis was a powerful earth goddess, the All-mother who promoted natural fertility, particularly in wild things but also in humankind. Later she became a sort of super-nymph who loved hills, groves, and well-watered places. A protector of wild animals, particularly young ones, Artemis was also the patron goddess of hunters. This may seem paradoxical, and yet hunting had its season and rules: it was not to be indiscriminate slaughter. "Perhaps the earliest example of a game preserve," to quote Guthrie, "is the grove of Artemis where Agamemnon slew the deer and was visited by the wrath of the divine gamekeeper. . . . Xenophon actually notes, in his work on hunting, that hares below a certain age are left alone as sacred to the goddess."[19]

As farmers the Roman people showed *pietas* toward woods, springs, and the earth. Literary evidence appears in the writings of Varro, Cato, and Horace, among others. Varro's book on farm management is a kind of practical handbook; religion plays no part, but the traditionally close relation between religion and agriculture is suggested in the dedicatory message to his wife. Cato was a conservative soldier and farmer who despised Greek ways and love of luxury. His work on agriculture, written in the second century before Christ, was meant to be practical; yet it contains a number of ritual prescriptions that reflect an older style of rural life more in tune with Cato's personal ideal than with the realities of his agricultural estate. Cato made use of slave labor to develop a new section of the country. His estate, advanced in agricultural techniques for its time, was largely isolated from family and community life.[20] Cato prescribed that expiatory rites be performed, but did so in language that sounds both formulistic and perfunctory.

> Harvesting leaves in a sacred grove should be done according to the Roman custom in the following manner. Offer a pig as atonement and use this form of words: "Whether thou art god or goddess"—to whom the sacred grove belongs—"as it is right to make thee an offering of a pig as atonement with a view to trimming this sacred grove and with a view to such and such uses"—provided the offering is made in due form, whether I make it or some one else makes it at my direction (is of no importance)—"with this purpose, then, in offering this pig as atonement, I make thee good prayers that thou be of good will and favorable to me, my house and household and my children; for these reasons be thou honored by the sacrifice of this pig as atonement."[21]

On digging up trees he wrote, "If you wish to dig up trees, offer a second atonement in the same way, and add this further expression: 'With a view to doing a piece of work.' As long as the work goes on, make the offering daily in parts. If you miss a day, or a festival of the state or one of the household intervenes, make another atonement."[22]

Rustic piety is more eloquently expressed in Horace's odes. Sacrifices were to be made to the Baudusian spring on his Sabine farm; and the water, clearer than crystal, was stained by the blood of a young goat "whose brow, swollen with budding horns, betokens both love and struggle." In another ode a pine tree is dedicated to Diana, virgin goddess and guardian of the hills and groves, who hears the cry of young mothers in their travail and rescues them from death. "Thine be the pine tree that rears itself above my country dwelling, so that gladly as each happy year comes round I may offer to it the blood of a young boar just beginning its slanting thrusts."[23]

FERTILITY, ANCESTORS, AND HEROES

Piety includes the sense of geopiety. Duty and reverence to family and ancestors extend to the spirits of dead ancestors and heroes, who become chthonian powers after burial and exert an influence on the living comparable to that of the spirits—more or less personified—of mountains, woods, waters, and earth. The direction of piety is toward the past, to parents and ancestors, and outward to groves and springs; nonetheless these reverential acts are performed for the benefit of living human beings and their future descendants. Cato offered prayers to sacred groves, but this did not prevent him—as Pliny was to point out—from cutting down the holy trees of his estate for mundane purposes.[24] Consider what Cato had to say about the rites to be performed on field borders.

> The lustration of the fields must be done as follows: Order the *suovetaurilia* (the sacrificial pig, lamb, and calf) to be led around, and say, "That with the help of the gods success may crown our labors. . . ." First offer a prayer, with wine, to Janus and Jupiter, and then say: "Father Mars, I pray and beseech thee that thou wilt be propitious and merciful to me, my house, and our household . . . that thou mayest keep away, ward off, and remove sickness . . . barrenness and destruction, ruin (of crops) and intemperate weather; and that thou mayest permit my harvests, my grain, my vineyards, my bushels to flourish and to bring forth abundantly; protect my shepherds and my flocks, and grant good health and strength to me, my house, and my household."[25]

This passage states explicitly how piety is necessary to the well-being of the narrow personal world of the sacrificer in both present and future. Elsewhere Cato gives a formula for the harvest offering. Before harvest a pig is to be offered to Ceres. The prayer Cato prescribes for the occasion is again in effect a supplication for private benefits: the gods are called on to bestow benefits on the person who sacrificed, his children, his house, and his household. Originally the offering was made to mother earth (*Tellus* or *Terra Mater*) and to the spirits of the departed buried in the earth. Spirits (gods) were propitiated lest a man unwittingly offended the earthly powers during the sowing, growth, and maturing of the grain. Such impiety to the dead, the *Di Manes* in the soil, would affect the crop.[26] Ceres, representing the ripened corn above ground rather than the seed buried in the bosom of the earth, gradually took her place side by side with Tellus; and in time the offering came to be more immediately concerned with the harvest than with the Manes. Cato gave the proper rites for the sacrifice, but he neglected to mention Tellus and the spirits of the dead.[27]

Landscapes and segments thereof were believed to emanate power. This power was personified in gods, goddesses, spirits, nymphs, dryads, centaurs. The deities were prayed to as though they dwelt in mountains, caves, groves, streams, or soil. Human beings, too, emanated power after death. Burial grounds were the *loca religiosa*, set aside from mundane uses. In Greek folk belief the *chthonioi* included both gods and heroes —that is, ancestors or other dead men raised to semidivine status. No clear distinction existed between the cults of heroes and of fertility gods; both kinds of spirit had power, and they had to be placated in order to ward off harm and ensure prosperity for the present and future occupants of the land. In ancient Greece, tombs of heroes and sanctuaries were common features in the landscape. Most heroes were anonymous or called only by an epithet such as "the leader." Heroes protected the soil and stood ready to help their fellow countrymen in all their needs. The bones and ashes of heroes continued to exert this power. Heroes thus provided a link between past and present.[28]

In China, popular belief personified the forces of nature in various ways. Aspects of the earth were perceived as different manifestations of the cosmic being. Thus, mountains were its body, rocks its bones, water the blood that ran through its veins, trees and grasses its hair, clouds and mists the vapors of its breath—the cosmic or cloud breath which is life's essence made visible. This is a fairly sophisticated view, since it requires a person to see unity—the cosmic being—underlying the appearances of nature. More specific, hence more pertinent to the immediate concerns of the farming populace, was the view that mountains, forests, and streams were themselves sacred powers (*shên*), capable of controlling weather and of regulating the seasons.[29] Mountains and rivers held lordly rank and titles corresponding to their power. In the universal hierarchy their positions apparently lay below that of the emperor. In the *Shi Ching*, for instance, all the spirits, including those of rivers and mountains, were submissive to the early kings of the Chou dynasty.[30] Aside from Heaven and Earth, the supreme deities of ancient China were the fertility gods of the soil and grain. They were personified, became heroes, and were given human pedigrees during the long mandate of the Chou dynasty. The god of the soil was known as *Shê* or *Hou-t'u* (lord soil) and described as a deified hero, Kou-lung, the son of Kung-kung. The god of grain, son of the hero-sage K'u, was known as *Hou-chi* (lord grain).

The point to note is that gods could become heroes and heroes gods; one's ancestors tended to be both heroes and semidivine. Man was surrounded by all kinds of forces, including ancestors, heroes, the gods of soil and grain, the lesser spirits of rivers and mountains. And he owed reverence to all; the piety he extended from parents to ancestors reached without break to the guardian spirits of nature.

Piety, as I have noted, included geopiety. In China, from remote antiquity to the modern period, the gods of soil and grain were worshiped side by side with the ancestors. In the capital of the emperor and in the residential compounds of feudal princes and lords, the Altar to Soil (*Shê chi tan*) stood next to the Temple of Ancestors near the palace. The god of soil (*Shê*) was propitiated down to the level of districts and villages. Similarly, ancestor worship was practiced throughout the kingdom, transcending distinctions of prince and peasant.[31] The two cults were maintained in close geographical proximity and may have grown out of one primary cult. The worship of a soil god required an altar in the open, a sacred tree, and a pole for which the technical term was *chu*; and *chu* was also a term for the ancestral tablet. As Bernhard Karlgren has shown, the primary cult was a form of phallicism for promoting human fecundity and the fertility of the fields. The evidence Karlgren adduces for this view hinges on the root meaning of words: it would seem that both the character *shê* and the character *tzu*, now meaning ancestor, were originally pictographs of the phallus; and that both the ancestral tablet and the *shê* pole (*chu*) were representations of the male organ.[32]

By middle and late Chou times, people who worshiped at the altar of soil and before the ancestral tablets probably no longer perceived the phallic content of their rites. Under Confucian teaching, piety had become an exalted ethic, governing men and, indeed, the universe. In the exegesis of literary canons, Confucian scholars not only ignored the phallicism but tended as well to minimize the impulse to placate unknown forces and manipulate them for the (material) benefit of the living. Among most people, however, this need to placate unknown forces has been a compelling motivation for the enactment of rites from antiquity to the present.

The spirits of the dead have power, the burial places of heroes and saints are holy ground. A grove is sacred because it belongs to some goddess; a mountain is sacred because it is the dwelling of the gods, and a piece of ground is sacred because the bones or ashes of a hero are buried in it. Gods, goddesses, and heroes differ in stature. In China the emperor was regarded as semidivine in his lifetime, and he retained this status after death. The land surrounding the tombs of the sacred emperors served as natural parks in which all living things partook of the holy character of the spirit of the deceased.[33] But the burial sites of lesser beings were and are perceived less as the source of power emanating from the countryside than as its conduit. This, then, is the principle of Chinese geomancy (*fêng shui*), which holds that (in March's words) "if a man is buried in a properly sited grave, his descendants will prosper; and that the siting of houses, cities, and whole regions similarly works good or ill for their inhabitants.[34]

Fêng shui is simultaneously a pietistic faith and a self-serving technique. Its purpose is to channel the powers in the landscape through the grave or house site for the benefit of the living inhabitants. *Fêng shui* is preoccupied with success. Notwithstanding the rites and rituals, morality plays no evident role in the principle of geomancy. The dead in their graves are not able to reward good conduct. Geomantic forces are amoral and can be manipulated to yield desirable results. The power of the site, derived from the special configuration of mountain, water, and plain, is not personified. In setting up a grave or house, however, men must placate the presiding deities of the place, seeking their protection.[35] A funeral prayer, noted by De Groot, opens with an address to the spirits of the water and mountains and ends with the supplication that the descendants of the dead may include many males, who will assume high office and become prosperous.[36]

PATRIOTISM AND ROOTEDNESS

Love of country, or patriotism, was an intense emotion among the peoples of ancient Greece and Italy. Attachment to one's native land, the place of one's birth, the hearth in which one was nurtured, the domicile of the deified souls of departed ancestors (*manes*) and of the gods, was so strong that the ancients could scarcely conceive a fate worse than exile, unless it be the destruction of the country itself. "Farewell, my home; farewell, you city-towers of fatherland!" a character in Euripides cries. "In anguish of despair I pass an exile from my bridal bowers."[37] In his play *Hippolytus*, Theseus refuses to impose the death penalty on Hippolytus for his alleged offense, the reason being that swift death is too light a punishment for so heinous a crime. Hippolytus must drain the bitter dregs of life as an exile on strange soil. This is the proper fate for the impious.[38]

The links binding a person to his hearth, to the family domain, and to his city were of a religious nature, as Fustel de Coulanges pointed out a century ago. No bond could be more important; to break it was an act of impiety. A mysterious relation existed between the soil and the gods, between the sacred fire of the family hearth and the cult of ancestors, between the communal hearth and the worship of heroes who protected the state. Fustel de Coulanges noted that the altar (family hearth) was the symbol of sedentary life. Once secured in a certain spot, the altar could not lightly be moved.[39] Moving the family god was permitted only under the constraint of necessity, such as war and soil exhaustion. The family hearth was holy to the household. On a larger scale every city had its hearth where the officials and a few specially honored citizens took their meals. A citizen thus had two fatherlands, the small one that was the family enclosure with its tomb and its hearth, and the great one— "the city with prytaneum and its heroes, with its sacred enclosure, and its territory marked out by religion."[40]

The piety of the ancient Greeks and Romans was the love of country. It rested on the sense of the country as one's native home, on the sense that one had sprung out of its soil and was nurtured by it, on the belief that one's ancestors since time immemorial were born in it. The autochthony of the Athenians was a common boast of Athenian poets and orators: "Our ancestors deserve praise," said Pericles in his funeral oration, for "they dwelt in the country without break in the succession from generation to generation, and handed it down free to the present time by their valor."[41] Isocrates argued forcefully for the value of autochthony. Athens was great for many reasons, but her clearest title to distinction lay in this:

> We did not become dwellers in this land by driving others out of it, nor by finding it uninhabited, nor by coming together here a motley horde composed of many races; but we are of a lineage so noble and so pure that throughout our history we have continued in possession of the very land which gave us birth, since we are sprung from its very soil and are able to address our city by the very names which we apply to our nearest kin; for we alone of all the Hellenes have the right to call our city at once nurse and fatherland and mother.[42]

In our time the bonds between person and person, and person and place, are regarded as strong if they are biological—that is, a matter of kinship in the one, and of birth and nurture in the other; but current religious beliefs hardly add to the strength of these ties. In ancient times, as among some nonliterate peoples, religion provided the ultimate sanction. This was so because, as we have noted, religion and the most intimate and immediate concerns of life were one. Not only did the gods play a central role in agriculture and in human fecundity but indeed the boundary between man and the gods was diffuse: human ancestors and heroes acquired semidivine status; many gods were anthropomorphized; and some became human heroes with human pedigrees. Furthermore, the ancients believed that their homeland was the dwelling place of household and communal gods, who lent sanction to their properties, traditions, and laws. When the Romans were about to raze Carthage to the ground at the end of the Third Punic War, a leading citizen made this eloquent plea:

> We beseech you, in behalf of our ancient city founded by the command of the gods, in behalf of a glory that has become great and a name that has pervaded the whole world, in behalf of the many temples it contains and of its gods who have done you no wrong. Do not deprive them of their nightly festivals, their processions and their solemnities. Deprive not the tombs of the dead, who harm you no more, of their offerings. If you have pity for us . . . spare the city's hearth, spare our forum, spare the goddess who presides over our council, and all else that is dear and precious to the living. . . . We propose an alternative more desirable for us and more glorious for you. Spare the city which has done you no harm, but, if you please, kill us, whom you have ordered to move away.

In this way you will seem to vent your wrath upon men, not upon temples, gods, tombs, and an innocent city.[43]

To this plea the Roman consul replied that the Carthaginians could establish hearths, temples, and a forum in another place that would in time be their country. After all, the Carthaginians had migrated from Tyre to Africa and learned to regard the new location as their home. The Roman reminded his defeated enemies that his own countrymen had caused their mother city, Alba, to change her abode to Rome for the common good, adding, "We consider *you* to be Carthage, not the ground where you live."[44] But the founding of Rome in fact showed that no abode could be changed without a risk of impiety against the sacred soil where the ancestors were buried. At the Palatine, Romulus and his companions performed various rites in order to be purified of all irreverence. They brought clods of earth from their homelands and threw them into the newly dug circular trench. Thereafter they could point to the site and say, This is the land of my fathers, for here are the *manes* of my family.[45]

The intense attachment to land based on the belief that the sacred soil is the abode of the gods waned as man acquired increasing control over nature and as Christianity spread to dominate the Western world. The impact of technology on the man-nature tie is a theme I cannot take up here. As to early Christianity, one of its express purposes was to loosen man's earthly bonds so that he might more easily enter the heavenly kingdom. "Let the dead bury the dead." Significantly, no grave could claim the body of Christ himself, and no place in Christendom was holy above all others. To be sure, saints' graves and shrines imparted a sacred aura to their surroundings, and to a degree the saints have substituted for the dead heroes and ancestors in the pagan world; but the long-term effect of the Christian doctrine was to denude nature of its spirits and mystery.

Patriotism in its modern form (that is, from about 1800 onward) continued, however, to use the rhetoric of the classical period. Men still speak of protecting their "sacred soil." There are no other gods than *la Patrie* herself. France's Legislative Assembly decreed on June 26, 1792, that "in all communes of the Empire an altar shall be raised, on which shall be engraved the Declaration of Rights with the inscription, 'the citizen is born, lives, and dies for *la Patrie.*' "[46] The lay religion for Revolutionary France was to be one in which the lawmakers were the preachers, the magistrates, the pontiffs; as Aulard has it, "the human family burns its incense only at the altar of *la Patrie,* common mother and divinity."[47] In the place of *manes,* gods, and saints were put the national heroes and their glorious battles, enshrined in monuments and history books.

The rhetoric of sacred soil was somewhat forced, especially when warring nations beseeched the same universal God to sanction their cause and to protect their soil. More attuned to immediate experience and less anachronistic was the idea of the fatherland or mother country that had given birth to and nurtured a people. "And you good yeomen, whose limbs were made in England; show us here the mettle of your pasture"[48]—thus Shakespeare had Henry V address his army on landing in France. The virtues of the land passed into the limbs of her sons. In World War I an English poet could exploit this sentiment in the famous lines:

> If I should die, think only this of me:
>   That there's some corner of a foreign field
> That is for ever England. There shall be
>   In that rich earth a richer dust concealed;
> A dust whom England bore, shaped, made aware,
>   Gave, once, her flowers to love, her ways to roam,
> A body of England's, breathing English air,
>   Washed by the rivers, blest by suns of home.[49]

The theme of birth and nurture is a commonplace of patriotic orations. "O France ô ma patrie! ô grand peuple, véritablement grand peuple!" declaimed Lazare Carnot on May 7, 1798. "C'est sur ton sol que j'eus le bonheur de naître; je ne puis cesser de t'appartenir qu'en cessant d'exister. Tu renfermes tous les objets de mon affection."[50] On June 5, 1794, in Westminster Hall, Edmund Burke said:

Next to the love of parents for their children, the strongest instinct, both natural and moral, that exists in man, is the love of his country: an instinct, indeed, which extends even to the brute creation. All creatures love their offspring; next to that they love their homes: they have a fondness for the place where they have been bred, for the habitations they have dwelt in, for the stalls in which they have been fed, the pastures they have browsed in, and the wilds in which they have roamed. We all know that the natal soil has a sweetness in it beyond the harmony of verse. This instinct, I say, that binds all creatures to their country, never becomes inert in us, nor ever suffers us to want a memory of it.[51]

The deep attachment that the Germans feel for their native land is captured by certain untranslatable words in their language. *Heimweh*, for example, is "homesickness" of a special intensity, a kind of hurt comparable to that of a lacerated skin; and *Elend*, one of the words for misery, is derived from *Ausland* (foreign country).[52] The common word *Heimat* is charged with emotion. By itself it usually refers to birthplace, but in different contexts it can also mean home, neighborhood, hometown, country of birth, or nationality. Leonard Doob has found (and translated) a superb example of *Heimat* sentimentality in a modern popular almanac, *Reimmichls Volkskalender*, of South Tyrol (1953).

> When we say this dear word "Heimat," then a warm wave passes over our hearts; in all our loneliness we are not completely alone and in all our sorrow we are not without comfort. What is Heimat? Heimat is first of all the mother earth who has given birth to our folk and race, who is the holy soil, and who gulps down God's clouds, sun, and storms so that together with their own mysterious strength they prepare the bread and wine which rest on our table and give us strength to lead a good life.[53]

A common figure of patriotic literature describes a people as rooted in the soil. Thus, a people's present attachment to land is secure because it has numerous ties with the deep strata of the past. Rootedness stems from genealogy—yes, but also from significant events shared by, or woven into, the myths of a people. The most important events are the battles fought by heroes in defense of the mother country. Blood sanctifies the soil; to shed it is a pious act, returning life to the soil whence it came. To quote again from the *Volkskalender*:

> Heimat is mother earth. Heimat is landscape. Heimat is the landscape we have experienced. That means one that has been fought over, menaced, filled with the history of families, towns and villages. Our Heimat is the Heimat of knights and heroes, of battles and victories, of legends and fairy tales. But more than all this, our Heimat is the land which has become fruitful through the sweat of our ancestors. For this Heimat

our ancestors have fought and suffered, for this Heimat our fathers have died.[54]

Rootedness in the soil is the steady increment of robust, unsentimentalized affections. The farmer and herder feel for the bit of earth they depend on and know so well. This warm feeling transcends specific religious and cultural contexts. Passages in the Old Testament psalms appear to reflect the sensual core of nature—nature seen with a real countryman's eyes and enjoyed almost as a vegetable might be supposed to enjoy it. "Thou art good to the earth . . . thou waterest her furrows . . . thou makest it soft with drops of rain . . . the little hills shall rejoice on every side . . . the valleys shall stand so thick with corn that they shall laugh and sing."[55] Chinese agricultural songs are more matter of fact and recognize no personal god; yet they convey the same kind of countryman's affection for weather, soil, and crops.

> A great cloud covers the heavens above,
> Sends down snows thick-falling.
> To them are added the fine rains of spring.
> All is swampy and drenched,
> All is moistened and soft,
> Ready to grow the many grains.[56]

ATTACHMENT TO PLACE AND MOVEMENT

In 1774, Lord Dunmore, Royal Governor of Virginia, wrote the Earl of Dartmouth, Secretary of State for the Colonies:

> I have learnt from experience that the established Authority of any government in America, and the policy of Government at home, are both insufficient to restrain the Americans: and that they do and will remove as their avidity and restlessness invite them. They acquire no attachment to Place: But wandering about seems engrafted to their Nature.[57]

The epic of the westward migration and settlement of the American continent is the antithesis of the sentiment and ideal of rootedness in native soil.

Americans, having no strong bond to place, were perhaps for that reason less averse to shifting the Indians from reservation to reservation.

What the Indians thought of the enforced moves was another matter. In 1867 at the Council of Medicine Lodge Creek, the Comanche Indian, Ten Bears, addressed white men with these eloquent words:

> You said that you wanted to put us upon a reservation, to build us houses and make us medicine lodges. I do not want them. I was born upon the prairie, where the wind blew free and there was nothing to break the light of the sun. I was born where there were no enclosures and everything drew a free breath. I want to die there and not within walls. I know every stream and every wood between the Rio Grande and the Arkansas. I have hunted and lived over that country. I live like my fathers before me and like them I live happily . . . why do you ask us to leave the rivers, and the sun, and the wind, and to live in houses?[58]

Attachment to place would not have found expression but for the fact of exile: home becomes vividly real only when juxtaposed against its contraries—foreign country and journey. Chinese poetry has frequently dwelt on the theme of longing for home. The exile might have been for personal reasons, such as when a woman leaves home to join her husband's household, or a young man goes to a strange city to take the civil service examination. Or the exile might have been occasioned by war, political banishment, military service at distant frontier posts. As suggested above, in classical antiquity (to the time of Cicero), banishment from one's native state or city was to be dreaded as much as, if not more than, the death penalty itself. During wars the threat of destruction to one's city provoked heart-rending cries of love for a material setting imbued with affecting memories and spiritual values. Death is the final exile confronting all men; the inexorable departure is so painful that in some cultures people seek consolation by seeing death as the return to the real home in another world.

Rootedness in the soil and the consequent growth of pious feelings toward it are not unexpected in traditional agricultural societies. But what of nomadic and nonagricultural peoples? Because they do not stay in one place and because their sense of land ownership is ill-defined, we might expect less attachment. On the other hand, we might expect a deeper, or at least a more consciously held, identification with place; for it is in enforced movement, in being compelled by nature or war to endure a foreign land, that the sentiment for home grows. In fact, herders and pastoralists reveal a wide range of feelings toward place and nature. According to Hoebel, land is the *sine qua non* of human existence, the most important single object of property; and with the exception of the Malayan sea gypsies all societies are territorially based.[59] The Eskimos, however, do not regard land as property: anyone may hunt where he pleases, and the idea of restricting the pursuit of food is repugnant to them. Their interest is in game, not in the land, even though each local group is identified by the territory in which it lives. Feelings of guilt about consuming animals (all of which, in the Eskimo view, have souls) are strong, but pious sentiment toward the earth seems to be minimal.

Geopiety, however, is compatible with a weakly developed sense of territorial boundary and land ownership. Reverence for the earth is common among American Plains Indians despite their migratory habits. For example, the nomadic Comanches change the location of their principal encampment from year to year; yet they worship the earth as mother. It is the receptacle and producer of all that sustains life; in honor it is second only to the sun. "Mother earth was implored to make everything grow which they ate, that they might live; to make the water flow, that they might drink; to keep the ground firm that they might walk on it."[60] The Lakota of the Northern Plains feel strongly about their country, particularly the Black Hills. A tribal legend describes these hills as a reclining female from whose breasts issue life-giving forces, and to them the Lakota go as a child to its mother's arms. The old people, even more than the young, love the soil; they sit or recline on the ground feeling close to a nurturing power.[61]

Some people may revere the sun, the earth, spring water, and striking topographical features such as the Black Hills. Others may become strongly attached to a place because it is their native land. Both pastoralists and hunter-gatherers can develop powerful feelings toward place. Consider, for example, the Nuer of the Sudan. The Nuer are cattle herders and small-time farmers. Their smallest political unit is the village, and their largest is the tribe. Intense loyalty is felt for both. As Evans-Pritchard notes:

> The people of a village have a feeling of strong solidarity against other villages and great affection for their site, and in spite of the wandering habits of Nuer, persons born and bred in a village have a nostalgia for it

31

and are likely to return to it and make their home there, even if they have resided elsewhere for many years.[62]

Loyalty toward tribal members and love for tribal country are both strong.

> Men who intend to leave the tribe of their birth to settle permanently in another tribe take with them some earth of their old country and drink it in a solution of water, slowly adding to each dose a greater amount of soil from their new country, thus gently breaking mystical ties with the old and building up mystical ties with the new.[63]

There can hardly be a more vivid expression of man's ties with the soil, even though the Nuer, primarily pastoralists, are not bound to the soil with the intimacy of farmers.

The Australian aborigines illustrate how intense the attachment to place can be for a people who depend on hunting and gathering and who are necessarily nomadic. Although they have no rules of landownership and no strict notions of territorial boundary, most Australian aboriginal groups distinguish two types of territory—estate and range. Estate is the traditionally recognized locus (country, home, dreaming place) of a patrilineal descent group and its adherents. Range is the tract or orbit over which the group ordinarily hunts and forages. Range is more important than estate for survival; estate is more important than range for social and ceremonial life. To natives, range is where they walk about or run; estate is where they sit down. Strong emotional ties belong to the estate: it is the home of ancestors, the dreaming place in which every incident in legend and myth is firmly fixed in some unchanging aspect of nature —rocks, hills, mountains, even trees, for trees can outlive many human generations.

In times of scarcity, which are frequent along the margins of the desert, the natives forage in other groups' ranges, but such trips are never of long duration.[64] As Gura of the Ilbalintja tribe explained to the anthropologist Strehlow, "Our fathers taught us to love our own country, and not to lust after the lands belonging to other men. They told us that Ilbalintja was the greatest bandicoot totemic centre amongst the Aranda people, and that, in the beginning, bandicoot ancestors had come from every part of the tribe to Ilbalintja alone and had stayed there for ever: so pleasing was our home to them."[65]

Landscape is personal and tribal history made visible; the native's identity—his place in the total scheme of things—is not in doubt, because the myths that support it are as real as the rocks, the waterholes, and the hills that he can see and touch. Strehlow, who knew the Australian aborigines both through his field work as an anthropologist and because he was raised among them, had this to say about the native's deep affection for his ancestral territory.

> Mountains and creeks and springs and waterholes are, to him, not merely interesting and beautiful scenic features in which his eyes may take a passing delight; they are the handiwork of ancestors from whom he himself has descended. He sees recorded in the surrounding landscape the ancient story of the lives and deeds of the immortal beings whom he reveres; beings, who for a brief space may take on human shape once more; beings, many of whom he has known in his own experience as his fathers and grandfathers and brothers, and as his own mothers and sisters. The whole countryside is his living, age-old family tree. The story of his own totemic ancestor is to the native the account of his own doings at the beginning of time, at the dim dawn of life, when the world as he knows it now was being shaped and moulded by all-powerful hands. He himself has played a part in that first glorious adventure, a part smaller or greater according to the original rank of the ancestor of whom he is the present incarnated form.[66]

GEOPIETY: AN EVALUATION

Piety is a word no longer normally used in discourse concerning relations among men or between man and nature. The term is rapidly becoming obsolete, though some of the ideas and feelings behind it are still meaningful; it can be argued that people would live more in harmony with nature could the sentiment be restored.

Piety is a feeling and an ethos characteristic of closed systems: parents give birth to and succor their offspring, who in turn honor their parents and care for them in their old age; nature nurtures men and men owe it reverence. The ecological doctrine that we should return to nature what we have extracted and the land ethos of a conservationist like Aldo Leopold are modern expressions of geopiety. The ideals of reciprocity and caring, of gratitude and respect, are not quite dead, but they have lost urgency since men learned to control the present and the future.

Piety is the compassionate urge to protect the fragile beauty and goodness of life against its enemies, not the least of which is time. Hence, care for old people as well as old buildings and the preservation of the past are acts of piety. Patriotism is geopiety; remove its exogenous imperial cloak and patriotism is compassion for the vulnerability of one's native soil. Roman patriotism was eloquent less in its pride of empire than when, in the third century before Christ, the Carthaginian threat aroused the Romans to a jealous love of their world. The British Empire was too large and abstract an entity to be the object of genuine affection and piety. England is more embraceable: England is this "happy breed of men," as Shakespeare's Richard II envisaged it, "this little world," "this blessed plot," guarded by the silver sea "against the envy of less happier lands."[67]

An intense attachment to the land of one's birth, rootedness in the soil, and respect for nature are uncommon today. How prevalent were they in the past? No summary answer will serve. It is, however, important to note that geopiety as a religious ideal was often perverted or ineffective in days gone by. Consider the sense of reverence toward nature in the ancient Mediterranean world and in China. The word "propitiation" is suggestive: nature has to be propitiated, sacrifices must be made, rites performed to coax her to yield her fruits. Nature and ancestor worship often go together: both are directed toward fertility and fecundity. Spirits of earth and of ancestors are called on—bribed by offerings and honors—to bestow prosperity on the family and to ensure its propagation. Cato's prescriptions for sacrifice to sacred groves and springs and to the land at critical stages of the agricultural year read like instructions in a technical handbook for gentleman farmers. His piety did not save the holy trees and groves from the axe. In China geomancy was and is essentially a technique to induce the forces of nature to yield material benefits. In the geomantic ceremony, an official reminds the earth god of all the victims sacrificed in his honor, and reminds him also that, however exalted, he still ranks below emperors and sovereigns. Moreover, the god is expected to feel honored by the high status of the officiant himself! Striking evidence of how little man's religious ideals control his acts are the vast transformations of Roman and Chinese landscapes: sacred groves—except for token plots—yielded continually to the exigencies of economic life.[68]

Piety toward one's kin and native land is a commendable sentiment; but it has an ungenerous side—exclusiveness and intolerance. Those who do not belong are beyond the law; foreigners and strangers, with their unassimilable ways, are viewed with suspicion and contempt. Isocrates claimed that Athenians were especially noble because they were autochthonous, "sprung from the very soil," unlike the Spartans, "a motley horde composed of many races." Australian aborigines are deeply loyal to their ancestral land and local group; they can also view condescendingly those who come from a different place and speak another dialect. It is not unusual to hear one group say of another: "We Southerners alone kept the Aranda tongue in all its purity as it has been handed down to us: the Western [Aranda] men have corrupted the speech of their forefathers."[69]

The form of geopiety called patriotism is easily distorted by abstractions. From an attachment to place based on intimate knowledge and memories, it is a short step to pride of empire or national state that is no part of one's direct experience. Pride in a mighty empire (Rome or the thousand-year Reich) takes the place of compassion for one's native city, which is vulnerable to enemies. In Europe since 1800 nationalism has been fostered at the expense of local piety. The influential pamphleteer and poet, Ernst Moritz Arndt, proclaimed that "the highest form of religion . . . is to love the fatherland more than laws and princes, fathers and mothers, wives and children."[70] Arndt also wrote a popular song, "Was Ist des Deutschen Vaterland?" with a clear message: abandon the local attachments, to places like Swabia or Prussia, places "where the grape grows on the Rhine" or "where sea gulls skim the Baltic's brine." The German's fatherland is none of these. "O no! more great, more grand / Must be the German's fatherland."[71]

Practice often falls far short of the ideal, and geopiety is no exception. But defects in geopious practice are human weaknesses; they are not inherent in the sentiment. The self-regarding *quid pro quo* attitude of the Romans toward their nature divinities was at odds with their own high ideal of *pietas*. Generosity that closes the circle need not be a mere matter of *do ut des* (I give so that you will give), a formula frequent in Roman prayers. Likewise, it is unnecessary for modern conservationists to argue their case solely on the ground of enlightened selfishness. Virtue can be its own reward, and intense loyalty to one's homeland does not necessarily lead to bigotry. The Greeks could mourn the Trojan Hector with Homer, and participate with Aeschylus in the agony of the Persians whom they had just defeated.

If the study of geopiety has any ethical lessons for us, they may well be these: (1) the fragility of goodness; (2) piety considered as reciprocity applies to relations between man and nature as well as between man and men; (3) piety toward a people and place can lead to intolerance and narrow pride, unless we remember that piety is also compassion. Compassion for our native soil does not preclude love for other lands. Compassion is for the frail and the circumscribed. It is incompatible with pride of empire, yet it does not conflict with our love of the earth itself, for the whole earth seen from a sufficient height is our native soil and only home—it is that "precious stone set in the silver sea," a fertile speck floating in the ocean of space.

NOTES

1. In "Notes on Early American Geopiety," John K. Wright states: "I have coined . . . *geopiety* (adj., *geopious*), in which Greek and Latin roots are unconventionally but perhaps not too unhappily married (Greek with Greek might be *geohosiety*)." See *Human Nature in Geography* (Cambridge: Harvard University Press, 1966, pp. 250–85). Wright uses the term to cover the natural theology and world systems of American "pietistic" scholars. The meanings I have given to the term in this paper differ from his.

2. N. D. Fustel de Coulanges, *The Ancient City* (Garden City, N.Y.: Doubleday, Anchor Books, n.d.), p. 199; first published as *La Cité antique*, 1864.

3. *Li Chi: Book of Rites*, trans. James Legge; ed. Ch'u Chai and Winberg Chai, 2 vols. (New York: University Books, 1967), 2:228.

4. Carl Kerényi, *The Religion of the Greeks and Romans* (New York: Dutton, 1962), p. 119.

5. Étienne Balazs, for example. See Arthur F. Wright's "Introduction," Balazs, *Chinese Civilization and Bureaucracy* (New Haven: Yale University Press, 1964), pp. xvi, 18.

6. *The Hsiao Ching*, trans. M. L. Makra (New York: St. John's University Press, 1961), p. 15.

7. Ibid., p. 35.
8. W. K. C. Guthrie, *The Greeks and Their Gods* (London: Methuen, 1950), p. 109.
9. Vincent Scully, *The Earth, the Temple, and the Gods* (New Haven: Yale University Press, 1962), pp. 27, 36–41.
10. *Li Chi: Book of Rites* 1:425.
11. *The Hsiao Ching*, p. 11.
12. *Li Chi: Book of Rites* 2:202–3.
13. *Tso Chuan*, Duke Chao, 16th year; *Ch'un Ts'ew* with the *Tso Chuen*, trans. James Legge, in *The Chinese Classics* (Hong Kong: Hong Kong University Press, 1960), 5, pt. 2, p. 665; Marcel Granet, *Fêtes et chansons anciennes de la Chine* (Paris: Librairie Ernest Leroux, 1929), p. 193.
14. *Chou Li* (*Le Tcheou-li*), trans. E. Biot (Paris: L'Imprimerie Nationale, 1939), 2:31, 32–33.
15. Granet, *Fêtes et chansons*, pp. 174–75.
16. W. Warde Fowler, *The Religious Experience of the Roman People* (London: Macmillan, 1911), pp. 36–37; G. Wissowa, *Religion und Kultus der Römer*, 2nd ed. (Munich: C. H. Beck'sche, 1912), pp. 408, 467–68, 477, 515.
17. Martin P. Nilsson, *Greek Popular Religion* (New York: Columbia University Press, 1940), p. 10.
18. *The Geography of Strabo*, book 8, 3:12, trans. H. L. Jones; quoted in Nilsson, *Greek Popular Religion*, p. 18.
19. Guthrie, *The Greeks and Their Gods*, p. 100; L. R. Farnell, "Artemis," in *The Cults of the Greek States* (Oxford: Clarendon Press, 1896), 2:425–86.
20. *Cato the Censor on Farming*, trans. E. Brehaut (New York: Columbia University Press, 1933), p. xli.
21. Cato, *De agricultura*, 139; in Brehaut, p. 119.
22. Cato, 140; in Brehaut, p. 119.
23. Horace, *Odes III*, 13, 22; in F. C. Grant, *Ancient Roman Religion* (New York: The Liberal Arts Press, 1957), pp. 165–66.
24. Pliny, *Natural History*, book 17, 267; cf. Brehaut, p. 120.
25. Cato, *De agricultura*, 141; in Grant, *Ancient Roman Religion*, pp. 36–37.
26. Wissowa, *Religion und Kultus*, p. 193, writes: "[es] ist eine heilige Handlung von doppelter Bedeutung, einerseits Einleitung der Ernte, andererseits zugleich ein Sühnopfer für eine etwa vorgefallene Verletzung des *ius manium*." Grant, *Ancient Roman Religion*, pp. 34–35, endorses this view.
27. Fowler, *Religious Experience of the Roman People*, p. 121.
28. Nilsson, *Greek Popular Religion*, pp. 19–21.
29. *Tso Chuan*, Duke Chao, 1st year, p. 580.
30. *Shi Ching*, trans. Arthur Waley as *The Book of Songs* (New York: Grove Press, 1960), p. 230. "He goes through his lands; May high Heaven cherish him! Truly the succession is with Chou. See how they tremble before him! Not one that fails to tremble and quake. Submission, yielding are all the Spirits, Likewise the rivers and high hills. Truly he alone is monarch." See Granet, *Fêtes et chansons*, p. 194.
31. E. Chavannes writes:

   . . . Besides these great divinities [Heaven and Earth] who eclipse all the others by their splendor, the ancient gods of soil, harvest, and ancestral temple continue to subsist, witnesses of the race's most entrenched beliefs. They represent the primitive feelings of the peasant farmer who, in his hard day-to-day work, counted on the supernatural support of his ancestors as would a child on his parent, and who implored the clemency of his natal soil so that unforeseen disasters should not come and ruin the tender crops. This local and familial cult lies at the root of religious thought in China: nothing is closer to the origins than the god of soil and the ancestral temple.

From the Appendix to "Le Dieu du sol dans la Chine antique," in *Le T'ai Chan* (Paris: Ernest Leroux, 1910), p. 525. See also E. Chavannes, *Les Mémoires historiques de Se-ma Ts'ien*, trans. of Ssu-ma Ch'ien's *Shi Chi* (Paris, 1898), 3:221.

32. B. Karlgren, "Some Fecundity Symbols in Ancient China," *Bulletin, Museum of Far Eastern Antiquities* (Stockholm), no. 2 (1930), pp. 1–21. *Tzu* (ancestor

祖) and *Shê* (the male god of the soil 社) are made up of the radical 示 ,

common in religious characters, on the left side, and of 且 (ancestral tablet)

and 土 (soil), respectively, on the right side. 且 and 土 can be traced back to

the phallic pictographs 且 ∩

33. The *yuan ling* (gardened tumulus) of the sacred emperors. See E. H. Schafer, "The Conservation of Nature under the T'ang Dynasty," *Journal of the Economic and Social History of the Orient* 5 (1962):280–81.
34. Andrew L. March, "An Appreciation of Chinese Geomancy," *Journal of Asian Studies* 27 (1968):253.
35. See Maurice Freedman, "Geomancy and Ancestor Worship," in *Chinese Lineage and Society* (London: Athlone Press, 1966), pp. 124–27.
36. See J. J. M. De Groot, *The Religious System of China* (Leiden: E. J. Brill, 1892), 1:223.
37. In *The Bacchantes*, 1368–70.
38. *Hippolytus*, 1047–50. See Ernest L. Hettich, *A Study in Ancient Nationalism* (Williamsport, Pa.: Bayard Press, 1933).
39. See Fustel de Coulanges, *Ancient City*, p. 62.
40. Ibid., p. 198.
41. In Thucydides, *The History of the Peloponnesian War*, book 2:36, trans. Richard Crawley (Chicago: The University of Chicago Press, Great Books, 1952), 6:396.
42. Isocrates, *Panegyricus*, 23–26, trans. George Norlin (Cambridge: Harvard University Press, 1928), 1:133.
43. *Appian's Roman History*, book 8, 12:84, trans. Horace White (London: Heinemann, 1912), 1:545.
44. Ibid., p. 555.
45. Fustel de Coulanges, *Ancient City*, p. 136.
46. Albert Mathiez, *Les Origines des cultes révolutionnaires* (1789–1792) (Paris: Georges Bellars, 1904), p. 31, quoted in C. J. H. Hayes, *Essays on Nationalism*

(New York: Macmillan, 1928), p. 103. Hayes translates *"l'Empire"* as "fatherland."

47. F. A. Aulard, *Le Culte de la raison et le culte de l'Être Suprême* (1793–1794) (Paris: Germer Baillière, 1892), p. 35, quoted in Hayes, *Nationalism*, p. 103.
48. Shakespeare, *Henry V*, act 3, sc. 1.
49. Rupert Brooke (1889–1915), *The Soldier*.
50. In *French Patriotism in the Nineteenth Century* (1814–1833), traced in contemporary texts, by H. F. Stewart and P. Desjardins (Cambridge: Cambridge University Press, 1923), p. 51.
51. *The Writings and Speeches of The Right Honourable Edmund Burke* (Boston: Little, Brown, 1901), 11:422–23.
52. See Leonard Doob, *Patriotism and Nationalism: Their Psychological Foundations* (New Haven: Yale University Press, 1964), p. 194.
53. Ibid., p. 66.
54. Ibid.
55. Psalm 65:9–14; quoted in C. S. Lewis, *Reflections on the Psalms* (London: Collins, Fontana Books, 1961), p. 67.
56. *Shi Ching:* The Book of Songs, Waley trans., p. 212.
57. Reuben Gold Thwaites and Louise P. Kellogg, eds., *Documentary History of Lord Dunmore's War* (Madison: Wisconsin State Historical Society, 1905), pp. 370–71.
58. Quoted in Ernest Wallace and E. Adamson Hoebel, *The Comanches: Land of the South Plains* (Norman: University of Oklahoma Press, 1952), p. 283.
59. E. Adamson Hoebel, *Man in the Primitive World* (New York: McGraw-Hill, 1958), p. 433.
60. Wallace and Hoebel, *The Comanches*, p. 196.
61. See Chief Standing Bear, *Land of the Spotted Eagle* (Boston: Houghton Mifflin, 1933), pp. 43, 192–93.
62. E. E. Evans-Pritchard, *The Nuer* (Oxford: Clarendon Press, 1940), p. 115.
63. Ibid., pp. 119–20.
64. W. E. H. Stanner, "Aboriginal Territorial Organization: Estate, Range, Domain and Regime," *Oceania* 36.1 (1965):1–26.
65. T. G. H. Strehlow, *Aranda Traditions* (Melbourne: Melbourne University Press, 1947), p. 51.
66. Ibid., pp. 30–31.
67. *Richard II*, act 2, sc. 1.
68. Y. F. Tuan, "Our Treatment of Environment in Ideal and Actuality,' *American Scientist* 58.3 (1970):244–49.
69. Strehlow, *Aranda Traditions*, p. 82.
70. Quoted in Hans Kohn, *The Mind of Germany* (New York: Charles Scribner's, 1960), p. 76.
71. Alfred Baskerville, trans., *The Poetry of Germany* (Baden-Baden and Hamburg, 1876), pp. 150–52; quoted in Louis L. Snyder, ed., *The Dynamics of Nationalism: Readings in Its Meaning and Development* (Princeton, N.J.: Van Nostrand, 1964), p. 145.

2

Lands of Myth, Waters of Wonder: The Place of the Imagination in the History of Geographical Exploration

JOHN L. ALLEN

> But know that in the Soule
> Are many lesser Faculties that serve
> Reason as chief; among these Fansie next
> Her office holds; of all external things,
> Which the five watchful Senses represent,
> She forms Imaginations, Aerie shapes,
> Which Reason joyning or disjoyning, frames
> All what we affirm or what deny, and call
> Our knowledge or opinion, she retires
> Into her private Cell when Nature rests.
> Oft in her absence mimic Fansie wakes
> To imitate her; but misjoyning shapes,
> Wilde work produces oft.
>
> *John Milton*, Paradise Lost

MAN IS INFORMED of the nature and content of his world, wrote Strabo, by "perception and experience alike," through habitation and exploration of the earth. Yet the world view of Strabo and his contemporaries was not confined to their recognized *oikoumene*. Images of unexplored areas were created by the rational application of arguments assuring

Strabo that "those places which our senses have not been permitted to survey" are similar to places well known and carefully studied.[1] Rational derivation of regional images for the unexplored parts of the world was a process inherent in Stoic philosophy, whose keystone (as Whitehead perceived) was abstract reasoning rather than observation.[2] Much of post-Hellenic scientific methodology, resting as it does on experiment instead of argument, has not been congruent with that approach,[3] and yet in thought about regions of the earth, the practices and predilections of the ancients have partly prevailed. Philosophers since Strabo have used geographical lore from the familiar world to create images of unperceived and unexperienced regions, and this use of knowledge obtained through actual observation and experience leads to conclusions about the characteristics of *terrae incognitae* which are not necessarily unsound in theory. The resulting geographical images, however, have often reflected inadequate and inaccurate conceptualizations of the world and its regions. At the roots of these faulty images is the fundamental character of geographical lore about the unknown lands.

For any region of the earth there exists a body of knowledge that results from attempts to define, describe, and classify that region and its particulars. When we deal with an area within the framework of human experience and perception, our attempts at definition and description are based on what we know about the region. But when efforts are made to describe *terrae incognitae*, extrapolations from the known become confused with the believed, conjectured, or desired. The white light of knowledge may be seen dispelling the shadows that have hidden the unknown lands from the sight of man. But geographical knowledge is not white light—it is a spectrum with wave lengths of differing sizes and values.[4] And in analyzing the spectrum it is difficult to separate what is truly known from what is thought to be known. Hence it is not only, as Strabo had it, experience and perception that combine to create the images men hold about lands outside the *oikoumene*: blending with these and often overshadowing them in impact on regional images is the transcendant force of the imagination.[5] "The Sirens' voices" call to men from lands beyond observation and experience, and, as John K. Wright knew, "upon all alike who hear their call they lay a poetic spell."[6] It is in the realm of poetry that man's imagination seats itself[7] and surpasses reason in the creation of images of the unseen. Imagination, then, must be viewed as critical for the processes of geographical exploration by which unknown lands are brought within the horizons of human experience.

When exploration is viewed as a process rather than as a series of distinct events, its major components—establishment of objectives, performance of operations to implement them, and the consequences of the operations—are clearly related to the imagination. No exploratory venture begins without objectives based on the imagined nature and content of the lands to be explored. Imagination becomes a behavioral factor in geographical discovery as courses of action are laid out according to preconceived images; later decisions based on field observations may be distorted by these images. The results of exploration are modified by reports written and interpreted in the light of persistent illusions and by attempts made to fit new information into partly erroneous systems and frameworks of geographical understanding.[8]

IMAGINATION AND THE OBJECTIVES OF EXPLORATION

"Explorers have seldom gone forth merely to probe about for whatever they may happen to discover," as Wright points out. "They have gone in quest of definite objectives believed to exist on the basis of such information as could be gathered from the geographical lore of their own and earlier times."[9] Indeed, use of the term "discovery" to describe the major event of an exploratory venture suggests pre-awareness of something to be discovered.[10] To assert that explorers go forth to discover things because they know of their existence is insufficient, however, since the process of knowing is so complex. The less that is known about an area, the more difficult it becomes to separate fact from fancy in its lore. Often the thinking and behavior of explorers have been influenced more by conjecture than by facts. The wide range of exploratory activity devoted to the search for the illusory and fantastic stands as witness to this.[11]

On the other hand, many exploratory objectives are derived from factual rather than mythical or fabulous lore. But such objectives are not necessarily more rational or objective than those based on pure fiction,

43

since interpretations of factual geographical lore may also be biased. We tend to evaluate the geographical lore of a particular place and time as a coherent and unified body of knowledge from which explorers could have drawn information and established exploratory goals. But lore has seldom been either coherent or unified, and motives of exploration have been modified by the general cultural, intellectual, and environmental background of the explorers themselves and by the hope, desire, and ambition that always color geographical images.[12] Explorations as widely separated in space and time as those of Pytheas, Columbus, and Lewis and Clark illustrate how the imagination conditions exploratory goals.

In the fourth century before Christ the Greek astronomer-adventurer Pytheas journeyed from his native Massilia through the Pillars of Hercules that bounded his Mediterranean world on the west.[13] His exploratory goals evolved in part from vague awareness of the general location of the "Tin Islands" (Great Britain), which had been supplying the Mediterranean with tin for centuries; but they stemmed also from the conditioning given that awareness by the commercial desire for the potentially profitable trade between those distant islands and Massilia. Similarly, the goals of Columbus prior to his first voyage were based on the conception of a spherical earth and the limited knowledge of lands to the west—both part of European geographical lore at the end of the fifteenth century.[14] But, as Samuel Eliot Morison shows, for Columbus and his contemporaries such lore and the goals derived from it were modified by other stimuli: the widely-read accounts of Oriental travelers, the rise of exploring zeal on the Iberian peninsula, the desire of European merchants for easier commercial routes to the East, and the widening cultural and scientific horizons of Renaissance men. All these factors combined to produce geographical theories that favored exploration, and from these theories Columbus derived the sailing directions which he supposed would carry him to Zaiton, greatest port of Cathay.[15]

For their part, Meriwether Lewis and William Clark, early nineteenth-century American explorers, sought a water passage to the Pacific through North America. As with Pytheas and Columbus, the objectives of Lewis and Clark were drawn in part from objective geographical lore, made available by eighteenth-century explorers, on the nature and content of the western interior as far as the Rocky Mountains.[16] More

44

important for Lewis and Clark, however, were their sponsors' interpretations of that lore and the imaginary geography of theoreticians. Europeans had believed in a water passage across North America ever since they had realized that the continent barred their path to the riches of China. Those who planned the Lewis and Clark venture and wrote the contemporary geographies tempered the sketchy lore on the interior with belief in that passage, in order to create the geographical feature which, although imaginary, was the goal of Lewis and Clark. As I have elsewhere recounted, this feature was the short portage through a pyramidal height-of-land, connecting the Atlantic and Pacific drainage systems and providing a commercially profitable water passage across North America.[17] Lewis and Clark went west in search of an imaginary objective.

In each of these examples the motives and goals of the explorers appear to have been based on some combination of real and imaginary geography—in other words, on two entirely different types of geographical knowledge. The first type may be termed "empirical knowledge," and it can be evaluated in the light of what modern geographers accept as geographic reality. In John K. Wright's classification, empirical knowledge can be of the highest quality, contributed by commercial, diplomatic, military, scholarly, or clerical enterprise; it can be of intermediate quality derived from the sketchy accounts of a few travelers and from hearsay; or it can be of the lowest quality, acquired through rumor and conjecture.[18] Regions of interest to explorers are seldom entirely well known; most regions are either only partly known or virtually unknown. Usually the well-known part of a region—the zone for which the highest-caliber information is available—is its peripheral area; farther into the interior lies the partly known zone for which only lore of intermediate quality obtains; the bulk of the interior is a zone virtually unknown.[19]

This gradation is seen clearly in the empirical lore on the interiors of Australia and Africa before the great inland explorations of those continents in the nineteenth century. In both cases, knowledge graded downward from the continental margins, accurately described and charted by generations of seamen, through inland areas contacted intermittently by traders, slavers, and missionaries, and, ultimately, into interior *terra incognita*.[20] But when, in the opening years of the nineteenth century, government officials and geographical societies began to explore into the interiors, their goals were based less on what empirical knowledge was available than on nonempirical lore.

Nonempirical, or imagined, lore is usually assessed in terms of how the explorers themselves evaluated the subjective and imaginative elements that flavored their images of the lands to be explored.[21] Like empirical lore, nonempirical knowledge can be zoned into areas of perceived degrees of reliability. The spatial differences between the zones of nonempirical lore and empirical knowledge are of fundamental importance for interpreting the objectives of explorers. The areas imagined as well known or partly known by explorers who are evaluating nonempirical lore are more spatially extensive than are the similar zones of empirical knowledge. Likewise, areas imagined as totally unknown are, in the minds of explorers, consistently either small or entirely absent. Because imaginary geographical features play a dominant role in establishing goals of exploration, explorers often believe that they know a great deal more about the regions to be investigated than they actually do. The explorers of the African and Australian interiors sought objectives known primarily through nonempirical lore. The nonempirical images of the unknown lands were often highly detailed. Thus, according to E. W. Bovill, before Mungo Park found the Niger River he already believed that a mighty river flowed along an east-west axis somewhere in the interior.[22] And for Charles Sturt, who discovered the Murray and Darling rivers, the pre-exploratory image of Australia contained great rivers that should have existed on the basis of nonempirical lore.

IMAGINATION AND EXPLORATORY BEHAVIOR

At the outset of an exploratory venture, as I have noted in another essay, field behavior and operations are based at least in part on the explorer's initial pattern of beliefs about the area.[23] Routes are chosen, supplies are acquired, and other logistical decisions are made on the basis of preconceived notions about the nature and content of the lands to be investigated. As an expedition proceeds, the explorer may begin to recognize inadequacies and inaccuracies in his original images. He may modify his

behavior accordingly, thus adding to the chance of his expedition's successful negotiation of unknown territory and to the fulfillment of its
objectives; or he may realize that the objectives are ill-conceived or illusory. Conversely, an inability to realize the discrepancy between a preconceived image and an emerging reality may render an explorer unable
to modify his behavior and may therefore cause his expedition to fail.

Often an exploring party will pass from a region about which empirical knowledge is reliable into a region about which the available information is for the most part nonempirical lore. Yet, because explorers often
consider as equally accurate their images of both the empirically known
and nonempirically known areas, they may not immediately recognize
the transition and will continue to accept their pre-exploratory knowledge as accurate. When explorers finally perceive the inadequacy of
their original knowledge, they shift from confidence in pre-exploratory
data to reliance on detailed local lore obtained from natives and field
observations. A shift from faith in preconceived ideas to confidence in
data obtained and evaluated empirically may take place several times,
whenever a discrepancy is found between a prior image and conditions
actually met.

These shifts and the accompanying behavioral changes make it possible to view expeditions in terms of operational zones. Just as empirical
and nonempirical knowledge can be graded and zoned in terms of reliability, so explorers' behavioral reactions to knowledge and images can be
classified areally. Thus, an expedition passes through several operational
zones, with transitional areas near the points where preconceived images
begin to be recognized as inconsistent with reality. The width of the
transitional area, and the time lag between recognition and rejection of
inadequate data and its replacement by new, more realistic forms, are
critical. The farther an explorer travels between the point at which his
preconceived image begins to break down and the point at which he
makes changes in his expedition's operational behavior, the greater his
chance of failure.[24] Often the successful explorer is the one who recog-
nizes the inadequacy of his preconceived image quickly and modifies his
decision-making and behavior directly thereafter. An example, drawn
from the annals of North American exploration, illustrates the signifi-

cance of the interaction between image and reality for the nature and outcome of the exploratory process.

Iberian folklore tells of an archbishop and six bishops who fled westward across the Atlantic after the Moorish invasion of Spain and built seven Christian cities.[25] It was not known where the Seven Cities lay but, by the fourth decade of the sixteenth century, Spanish exploration had made it clear that they were neither in Mexico nor in the Caribbean. They were still believed to exist, however; and as rumors of Indian villages were sifted and combined with empirical lore the Seven Cities came to rest in the western interior of the American Southwest.[26]

Speculation on the location of the Seven Cities was crystallized by the reports of Cabeza de Vaca, survivor of an ill-fated expedition seeking the fabled province of gold.[27] Although de Vaca had wandered across the northern parts of Mexico and the southwestern United States for six years, he had learned remarkably little about the major features of the interior. But he knew a great deal about the "golden cities" to be found there and said he had seen "hawkbells" of copper, superbly decorated cotton cloaks, and arrowheads made of pure emeralds. Since the cities from which these must have come were supposed to lie north of the lands he had traversed and north of the well-known lands of Mexico, de Vaca was believed. According to nonempirical lore, the Seven Cities existed, and if they were not in Mexico and if de Vaca had not seen them in his travels, it was only logical to think that they could be found farther in the interior of North America. In response to this logic Don Hernando de Soto and his party wandered for months through the American Southeast in search of those cities where, as he hoped, "there was so much gold . . . that the people wore golden hats."[28] And Antonio de Mendoza, viceroy of New Spain, dispatched a Franciscan friar and a black slave into what was later New Mexico to find those cities "seven in number" whose very streets were paved with gold.[29]

Neither de Soto nor Fray Marcos discovered the Seven Cities of Gold. But Estevan the Moor followed directions given him by Indians and pushed northward across Sonora and into Cibola (New Mexico), a province Fray Marcos termed "the finest in the world." Cibola contained seven great cities, and farther north there "were still other provinces all greater than that of the Seven Cities."[30] The inhabitants of Cibola were unfriendly, however, and Estevan was slain. Fray Marcos, who had followed his trail, caught only a glimpse of the City of Gold before he was forced to flee. A glimpse was enough. "It is situated in a plain," he reported, "and seems to be handsomer and more important than any city yet seen and even larger than Mexico. . . . It is said to be the smallest of the Seven Cities and . . . Tontonteac is still larger and finer."[31] From the account of Fray Marcos a detailed image of the Seven Cities and the way thither from Mexico developed. On the basis of that image Francisco de Coronado, governor of New Galicia in Mexico, secured for himself a grant from the Viceroy to "explore and conquer" the Seven Cities of Gold.[32]

In the spring of 1540 a company bound for the conquest of Cibola set forth from Culiacán and wound its way through the mountainous terrain of western Mexico into the rugged country of southeastern Arizona. Guided by assurances from Fray Marcos, who accompanied the expedition, that the roads through the mountains were level and easy and that ample forage for horses, mules, and cattle existed everywhere along the route to Cibola, Coronado advanced with confidence toward the first of the Seven Cities. His faith in the available geographical information flagged little despite the obvious distortions in the friar's data on forage and water. Even though the bellies of both men and animals were caved in with hunger by the time they reached the mountains of Arizona, Coronado evidently still trusted the image and lore.[33] His faith was rewarded when, in July, his starving *caballeros* and foot soldiers espied, across a heat-shimmering plain, towers that glittered in the sun.

The towers which were supposed to be gold were only mud pueblos some four stories high, and there was no gold. The desperate Spaniards, partly in hunger, but more in anger and frustration, launched an attack on the Zuñi and after a brief battle, Cibola was conquered. The "city" was a shock to minds that had come prepared to find rooms filled with gold and emeralds. Cibola was only a collection of Zuñi pueblos and the fabled Tontonteac only the mud apartments of the Hopi. Fray Marcos found it prudent to depart immediately for Mexico with the words of his commander ringing in his ears: "He has not told the truth in a single thing he said."[34] With the realization of the discrepancy between the preconceived image and observed reality, Coronado was on the border of a new zone of operation. Decisions could no longer be made on the basis of the information with which he had left Culiacán; a new framework of decision-making had to be developed.[35]

Although the earlier information had proven faulty, the Cities of Gold concept was still strong enough to influence exploratory behavior within the new operational zone. But the system for gathering data was altered radically. With the rejection of older lore came a need for information of a different character, and Coronado turned to data gathered locally. This shift in reliance led to questioning the Indians extensively about the surrounding territories. Most importantly, however, the change in emphasis made new patterns of exploratory behavior necessary. Thus, Coronado divided his command and dispatched four reconnaissance parties to obtain data on the true location of the expedition's central objective, while he proceeded into the valley of the Rio Grande to spend the winter of 1540–41 and await the return of his scouts.[36]

One of the scouting parties made a crucial discovery. Pushing eastward across the Rio Grande and into the valley of the Pecos, this force received information from a captured Indian named the Turk that toward the northeast lay the new Peru and the new Mexico—cities of gold so rich that their lords were lulled to sleep under trees hung with little golden bells, and sailed in boats with prows of solid gold. In this new province of Gran Quivera even the common people "had their ordinary dishes of wrought plate, and the jugs and bowls were made of gold."[37] A new myth had arisen to fill the gap left by the disappointment of Cibola. Even though other Indian captives told the Spanish that the Turk was lying, they were not believed; for the Turk had only repeated what the conquerors had always known to be true. In the spring of 1541 Coronado and his men left the Rio Grande valley for Gran Quivera.

Coronado's army moved across the southern reaches of the Rockies, pushed past the Staked Plains of New Mexico and Texas and beyond, until, somewhere in the vastness of the southern Great Plains, the commander of the army of conquest realized that he had been misled. It is impossible to say at what point this recognition came, but it was an important awakening because it meant still another shift in field behavior.

Coronado ordered the main body of the army to return to the winter quarters on the Rio Grande. The Turk was placed in chains and a new guide was selected from among the Indian captives. Although this new guide avowed that he himself was from Quivera and that it was anything but a fine and rich city, the Spanish were driven by the ingrained lore of several centuries to go and see. Coronado, with a hand-picked detachment capable of greater mobility and speed than the entire command, moved northward as far as the Smoky Hill River of Kansas. Here, the new guide told him, was Quivera. But there were no noble lords lolling under the music of tinkling bells and no pieces of golden tableware. There were only the poor grass huts of the Wichita Indians. So the attempt to discover the Cities of Gold ended.

Facing his failure, Coronado had the Turk, whose lies had led the Spaniards to grass huts rather than golden towers, garroted. He then obtained directions from the Wichitas for a shorter and more direct route back to his winter camp on the Rio Grande and returned by that route. The earlier decision to pare his forces to increase ease of movement had been a wise one; the decision to follow a shorter route back and waste no more time in searching for an illusion was wise also. That such decisions were made, that the expedition returned successfully from a land which, although still only partly understood, was empirically better known than it had been before, was the result of Coronado's ever-increasing ability to replace the old nonempirical lore with newer and more reliable data.

Coronado's expedition had failed in its central objective—the discovery of the Seven Cities of Gold. But in other ways the Coronado story was one of success. Unlike many other large forces that have entered almost completely unknown lands, his returned with a minimum loss of life, a feat accomplished by having achieved a high degree of efficiency in negotiating *terrae incognitae*.[38] Throughout the course of the expedition, Coronado had remained aware of what he was doing and where he was. It was primarily because of his ability to shift from one source of geographical data to another and correspondingly to change his field decisions and behavior that he and his men were able to traverse thousands of miles of unknown territory and emerge with a more accurate image of it.

Before Coronado, the interior had been filled with myth and rumor, and images of the territories north of Mexico were highly inaccurate. After Coronado, men still sometimes dreamed of Quivera, and their dreams were filled with the things that were to be found in other dreams of the time. But in the reports of Coronado's travels are found geographical features of astonishing clarity—the nature of the pueblo tribes of the Southwest, of the mountains and plateaus of northern Mexico, Arizona, and New Mexico, and of the Great Plains with their nomadic tribes and their endless herds of bison. After Coronado there was more empirical data and less myth. The central function of exploration—the expansion of geographical knowledge—had been achieved.

IMAGINATION AND THE
RESULTS OF EXPLORATION

Exploration has far-ranging historical consequences for commercial patterns and processes, land settlement, and political and military relations among nations. These consequences, as John K. Wright remarks, grow out of the expansion of geographical horizons and the addition of new geographical lore to the general fund of knowledge.[39] Like other things related to geographical discovery, however, the results of exploration are subject to the interpretations, modifications, and inventions of those faculties of the human mind that are collectively called "the imagination." To say that geographical information is available as the result of exploration is not to say that a region is known empirically. As Wright says, whatever the quantity and quality of empirical knowledge for an area, "there seems practically no limit beyond which the mind cannot produce knownness"[40]—cannot, in other words, obtain more precise data. If empirical and nonempirical lore about a region differ before exploration, empirical and nonempirical lore will differ following the exploration as well. Disjunctions between the actual and imagined lore nearly always exist and are responsible for much of the subjectivity in the writing and interpretation of exploratory accounts.

The difficulty of assimilating exploratory accounts into the general store of knowledge results from problems of fitting the new information into recognized geographical frameworks. If an explorer returns with information that contradicts or subverts strong and generally accepted concepts, his data may have little immediate effect in creating more accurate regional images. For example, despite the failure of mariners to discover a sea-level passage through the poleward margins of the North American land mass, late sixteenth- and early seventeenth-century theoretical geographers and mathematicians continued to hold to the concept of what Peter Martyr called "indrawing seas . . . great straits which provide a passage for the waters flowing from east to west,"[41] and persisted in using astronomical computations to prove that such a passage existed between the Atlantic and Pacific oceans. And despite "increasingly convincing evidence" about the true character of the Arctic Ocean provided by explorers during the nineteenth century, many reputable and intelligent scholars remained obdurate in their belief in an "open polar sea."[42] In both instances geographical theories delayed acceptance of knowledge resulting from exploration; these theories, although inconsistent with new exploratory information, were too prevalent in geographical thought to be drastically or rapidly changed.

The power of imagination over experience in the expansion and consolidation of geographical knowledge is exemplified also by the persistence of myths that constantly retreat into still unknown territory. Such mythical geographical features change remarkably little over time and continue to dominate geographical lore despite the generations of explorers who failed to find them. When the features on which the myths might have been based become known, they are not recognized for what they are; and the search for the fabled and legendary continues. Unlike the Seven Cities of Gold, which disappeared rather quickly from geographical lore after the Coronado exploration, many myths have had a durability that has stimulated protracted exploration. Much of this exploration, although failing to dispel the myth itself, has contributed significantly to empirical geographical knowledge. Two strikingly similar examples may be seen in the search for the Kingdom of Prester John in Asia and Africa and in the quest for the South American land of El Dorado.

The first references to Prester John, a Christian priest-king who ruled over a vast realm of unparalleled splendor somewhere in Asia, appeared in European literature in the mid-twelfth century. After the circulation of "the Letter of Prester John," purportedly from the legendary monarch to the Pope, the Kingdom of Prester John became an exploratory objective that consumed the energies of travelers and adventurers for more than two centuries.[43] Initial investigations into the Asian interior and India failed to find the fabled realm, but few were discouraged. When the visits to Asia by the Polos and their successors gradually lifted the veils of ignorance about Asia from European eyes, the Kingdom shifted its locale. The reports of explorers who had failed to find the mythical ruler and his glorious lands had not removed the myth from geographical lore but had only transferred it in space. By the mid-fourteenth century, it was believed that the lands of Prester John would finally be discovered in Africa, in "India Ethiopie"; and the reports of Italians and Portuguese who traveled in East Africa did little to demolish faith in the existence of the mythical kingdom.

In the fifteenth century Prince Henry of Portugal began a concerted effort to find the Christian monarch. By the end of that century, when Portuguese explorers had made contact with the ancient Coptic Kingdom of Ethiopia, Prester John was, so far as the Portuguese were concerned, finally found.[44] Yet realization of this fact was long in coming for many other Europeans. Even after the establishment of Portuguese relations with Ethiopia, men from England, Holland, Italy, and Spain searched elsewhere for the Kingdom, persisting in believing in a mythical land that experience had repeatedly shown did not exist.

The consequences of the quest for Prester John were far-reaching; geographical knowledge about eastern Africa, much of the African coast including the route around the Cape, and a good part of Asia between the Mediterranean and Cathay, was added to European lore. The search for Prester John finally died out in the New World along the mighty Orinoco, about which Columbus had expressed the hope that this might be the River of Paradise flowing from the center of Prester John's realm.[45] As the quest faded, however, it was supplanted by the search for El Dorado, an imaginary place whose central imagery stemmed directly or indirectly from the legend of Prester John.

El Dorado, the land of the Golden Man, entered geographical lore in the early part of the sixteenth century, when, after the conquest of Peru, tales began reaching Spanish ears from lands to the north.[46] These tales described religious ceremonies in which a king of immense wealth covered himself with gold dust and, after dumping vast treasures in gold and silver into a lake, washed the dust from his body and thereby purified his spirit and that of his subjects. The fabled lake of El Dorado, as the Spanish had received the tale, was located originally in the Bogotá region. But as exploration into the Colombian highlands failed to uncover the civilization of the Golden King, the myth shifted location, and, growing in intensity and elaboration until for many it took on a splendor rivaling the Old World's Prester John, came to rest in the tangled interior of Venezuela and Guiana.

A frenetic search by Spaniards, Germans, and Englishmen opened up the northwestern parts of the Amazon Basin, made known much of the Orinoco Basin, cleared up many mysteries about the eastern slope of the Andes, and was responsible for the first descent of the Amazon.[47] By the middle of the seventeenth century, however, no one had come any closer to El Dorado. Yet, despite the fact that explorers had been able to show only where El Dorado was *not*, the myth remained firm in geographical lore. As late as the mid-nineteenth century, European mapmakers represented the lake of gold, silver, and emeralds on their maps of South America, and governments continued to dispatch explorers in search of El Dorado; even some twentieth-century explorers have sought the lands of the Golden Man.[48] And although its seekers have been drawn by the lure of imaginary features, their explorations, like those of their forebears who struggled through the unknown lands of Asia and Africa in search of Prester John, have helped to expand geographical lore.

Many inaccurate images based on ill-founded theories persist; many myths are long-lived; and many explorations are of little immediate consequence for geographical knowledge. But the persistence of inaccurate images or myths does not result exclusively from the fact that those who read the accounts of exploration either refuse or are unable to use those accounts to enrich geographical awareness or to erase myth and legend from world or regional images. In many instances the failure of an exploratory account to improve geographical knowledge stems from the nature of the information contained in it, information that may support rather than break down long-standing concepts and images or may create new but inaccurate geographical ideas. Reflections on what was seen in the field are colored by strongly held preconceptions. Columbus, for example, frequently noted that he had seen many things that, in Wright's words, "to him betokened the nearness of Marco Polo's Cathay."[49]

Preconceptions are not alone responsible for the failure of an exploration to augment the accuracy of geographical knowledge or for the creation of new but misleading images. In many cases the transmission and interpretation of exploratory data may be distorted by a desire for personal gain or by national pride. And, as Howard Mumford Jones demonstrates, such distortions in promotional literature, descriptive geographies, popular writings, and the arts are responsible for the preservation of old theories and myths and for the creation of new and fanciful regional images.[50] "I will promise these things that follow and [I] know to be true," wrote Sir Walter Raleigh, animated by a combination of personal ambition and nationalism in describing the northern coast of South America: "Commanders and Chieftains . . . shall find there more rich and beautiful cities, more temples adorned with golden images, more sepulchres filled with treasure, than either Cortes found in Mexico, or Pizarro in Peru."[51] A teleological faith in the English nation as chosen of the Lord induced Sir Thomas Mitchell to report the discovery in the heart of Australia of a bountiful land "typical of God's providence," an area described by later observers as "utterly unknown to man and as utterly forsaken by God."[52] And it may have been frustration in having his "continuall paines and travaile" ignored by the Spanish crown that prompted Captain Pedro Fernandez de Quirós, discoverer of the New Hebrides archipelago, to refer to his find as "the fifth part of the Terrestriall Globe . . . twice greater in Kingdoms and Seignories, than all that which . . . doth acknowledge subjection and obedience unto your [Spanish] Maiestie."[53]

But an explorer need not have ulterior motives for distortions to taint geographical knowledge. However honest, objective, and accurate the reports of exploration, imagination modifies the accounts of discovery. Explorers may present a partial picture of an area by describing only what they have actually witnessed. Those who interpret their reports may have difficulty in adjusting the size of observed features to the scale of pre-exploratory *terrae incognitae*. Distortions may occur in translating what was seen on the ground (the landscape view) into an aerial perspective (the mapped view). What exploration makes known may expand in the imagination to encompass what remains unknown. Blank spaces are intolerable to the geographical imagination, and people are tempted to fill them with imaginative extrapolations. It is doubtful, for example, whether any American in the last half of the 1840s could have viewed the charts showing Frémont's tracks across the western interior of the United States without consciously or unconsciously filling the spaces between the traverse lines. Indeed, can we read the accounts of Frémont's travels without shaping images that may not be fully congruent with reality, as understood either in the mid-nineteenth century or today? No exploration in any part of the world (or, now, out of it) can be fully assessed without reference to that agency of the human mind which, "misjoyning shapes, Wilde work produces oft."

IMAGINATION AND EXPLORATION

A new approach to the study of geographical exploration was outlined more than a quarter-century ago by John Kirtland Wright.[54] Following Wright, I have undertaken to show how imagination conditions the objectives of exploration and the behavior of explorers, and how this bears on the development of geographical knowledge. This essay has suggested a means of evaluating the role of the imaginative element in geographical thought as it affects exploration. Although objective empirical lore is important in establishing exploratory goals, subjective nonempirical lore is at least equally important. Disparities between empirical lore and nonempirical lore are significant for interpreting exploratory behavior, since explorers in the field are often affected by contradictions between conditions actually encountered and preconceived lore. Imagination further distorts the consequences of exploration in both the writing and the interpretation of exploratory records, however empirically derived and logically analyzed.

The process of exploration is conditioned by the imagination, and thus the study of exploration should focus on imagination's influence. Exploratory enterprises might be grouped on the basis of certain apparent similarities in the way the imagination has shaped their goals, experiences, and results. The imagination evokes certain responses and elicits certain activities from those who would explore. Thus, goals imaginatively set forth influence explorers in many different areas and periods as they search for imaginary objectives, despite the failure of others to find them. The search continues even in the face of facts that conflict with preconceptions about the existence of exploratory objectives. During that search, pre-exploratory images are only partially modified, and disparities between empirical and nonempirical lore survive. Generations of explorers have devoted their careers to imaginary objectives—to the search for a Prester John, for a Passage to India, for the Lake of the Golden Man or a Golconda or an Ophir. These objectives, the lands of myth and waters of wonder, have themselves conditioned exploratory behavior and modified exploration's consequences.

NOTES

1. Strabo, *Geography*, book 1, 1, 8.
2. Alfred North Whitehead, *Science and the Modern World* (New York: Macmillan, 1932), pp. 7–19.
3. See James O. Thomson, *History of Ancient Geography* (Cambridge: Cambridge University Press, 1948), p. 94.
4. Bernard DeVoto, *Course of Empire* (Boston: Houghton Mifflin, 1952), p. 51.
5. Aristotle, *Politics*, book 1, 5.
6. In "*Terrae Incognitae:* The Place of the Imagination in Geography," *Annals of the Association of American Geographers* (hereafter *Annals* AAG), 37 (1947): 1–15; reprinted in Wright, *Human Nature in Geography* (Cambridge: Harvard University Press, 1966), pp. 66–88.
7. Francis Bacon, *Advancement of Learning*, book 2, 1, 1.
8. John K. Wright, "Where History and Geography Meet: Recent American Studies in the History of Exploration," *Proceedings of the 8th American Scien-*

tific Congress 9 (1943):17–23; reprinted in *Human Nature in Geography*, pp. 24–32.

9. Ibid., p. 27.
10. See Edmundo O'Gorman, *The Invention of America* (Bloomington: Indiana University Press, 1961), p. 9.
11. The literature is too voluminous to cite, but a good point of departure is Boies Penrose, *Travel and Discovery in the Renaissance, 1420–1620* (Cambridge: Harvard University Press, 1952).
12. David Lowenthal, "Geography, Experience, and Imagination: Towards a Geographical Epistemology," *Annals AAG* 51 (1961): 241–60.
13. See Rhys Carpenter, *Beyond the Pillars of Hercules* (New York: Delacorte, 1966), pp. 143–98.
14. See George E. Nunn, *The Geographical Conceptions of Columbus* (New York: American Geographical Society, 1924), pp. 54–90.
15. *Admiral of the Ocean Sea* (Boston: Little, Brown, 1942), pp. 54–78.
16. DeVoto, *Course of Empire*, chaps. 1–9; A. P. Nasatir, *Before Lewis and Clark: Documents Illustrating the History of the Missouri* (St. Louis: St. Louis Historical Documents Foundation, 1952); John L. Allen, "Geographical Knowledge and American Images of the Louisiana Territory," *Western Historical Quarterly* 2 (1971):151–70; idem, *Passage Through the Garden: Lewis and Clark and the Image of the American Northwest* (Urbana: University of Illinois Press, 1975), chaps. 1–6.
17. John L. Allen, "Pyramidal Height of Land: A Persistent Myth in the Exploration of Western Anglo-America," *International Geography* (Toronto: University of Toronto Press, 1972), 2:395–96.
18. See *Geographical Lore of the Time of the Crusades* (New York: American Geographical Society, 1925), pp. 256–57.
19. Different types of information—physical lore, cultural-ethnological lore, and the like—can exist at different levels; thus, while the physical lore of a zone might be of high quality, the cultural-ethnological lore for the same zone might be of lesser quality.
20. See Percy Sykes, *A History of Exploration* (New York: Harper Torchbook, 1961), p. 211; and J. H. L. Cumpston, *The Inland Sea and the Great River* (London: Angus and Robertson, 1965), p. 56.
21. John L. Allen, "An Analysis of the Exploratory Process," *Geographical Review* 62 (1972): 13–39.
22. In *The Niger Explored* (London: Oxford University Press, 1968), pp. 1–4.
23. In "Analysis of the Exploratory Process," p. 16.
24. Ibid., pp. 17–20.
25. Stephen Clissold, *The Seven Cities of Cibola* (New York: C. W. Potter, 1961), p. 24.
26. Garcilaso de la Vega, *The Florida of the Inca*, trans. and ed. John Grier Varner and Jeanette Johnson Varner (Austin: University of Texas Press, 1951), p. 7.
27. See Cleve Hallenbeck, *The Journey and Route of Alvar Núñez Cabeza de Vaca* (Glendale, Calif.: Arthur H. Clark, 1940).

28. In "The Narrative of the Expedition of Hernando de Soto by the Gentleman of Elvas," ed. T. H. Lewis, in F. W. Hodge, ed., *Spanish Explorers in the Southern United States, 1528–1543* (New York: Charles Scribner's Sons, 1907), p. 154.

29. "Report of Fray Marcos," in George P. Hammond and Agipito Rey, eds., *Narratives of the Coronado Expedition* (Albuquerque: University of New Mexico Press, 1940), pp. 60–61.

30. Ibid., p. 66.

31. Ibid., p. 79.

32. In "Appointment of Coronado as Commander of the Expedition to Cibola," in Hammond and Rey, *Narratives of Coronado Expedition*, pp. 83–86.

33. "Narrative of the Expedition to Cibola . . . by Pedro de Casteñada," in Hammond and Rey, *Narratives*, pp. 204–5.

34. "Letter of Coronado to Mendoza," in Hammond and Rey, p. 170.

35. The transition was quite rapid in this case. Normally, the passage of time would be greater before one operational framework was completely abandoned for another.

36. See "Letter of Coronado to Mendoza," p. 176.

37. "The Narrative of the Expedition of Coronado," in Hodge, *Spanish Explorers*, p. 314.

38. DeVoto, *Course of Empire*, pp. 45–47.

39. In "Where History and Geography Meet," p. 30.

40. In "Introduction to the Torchbook Edition," in Sykes, *History of Exploration*, p. xxiii.

41. In *De Orbe Novo*, cited in Tryggvi J. Oleson, *Early Voyages and Northern Approaches* (Toronto: McClelland and Stewart, 1964), p. 132.

42. See John K. Wright, "The Open Polar Sea," *Geographical Review* 43 (1953): 338–65; reprinted in *Human Nature in Geography*, pp. 89–118.

43. The Prester John legend is discussed in Malcolm Letts, *Sir John Mandeville: The Man and His Book* (London: Batchworth Press, 1949), pp. 76–87.

44. Penrose, *Travel and Discovery*, pp. 60–64, 173–76; J. H. Parry, *The Age of Reconnaissance* (New York: New American Library, 1964), chap. 7.

45. Letter from Columbus to Ferdinand and Isabella, October 18, 1498, in R. H. Major, trans. and ed., *Select Letters of Christopher Columbus* (London: Hakluyt Society, 1847).

46. See Earl Parker Hanson, *South from the Spanish Main* (New York: Delacorte, 1967), pp. 223–35.

47. Penrose, *Travel and Discovery*, pp. 141–49.

48. Leonard Clark, *The Rivers Ran East* (New York: Funk and Wagnalls, 1953).

49. In "Where History and Geography Meet," p. 28.

50. In "The Colonial Impulse: An Analysis of the Promotion Literature of Colonization," *Proceedings of the American Philosophical Society* 90 (1946):131–61.

51. Quoted in Hanson, *South from the Spanish Main*, p. 250.

52. Quoted in Ernest Scott, ed., *Australian Discovery by Land* (London: J. M. Dent, 1929), pp. 189 and 279.
53. In *Terra Australis incognitae, or A New Southerne Discoverie,* trans. and ed. Carlos Sanz (Madrid: Ministry of the Interior, 1963), p. 3.
54. See "Where History and Geography Meet," pp. 24–32.

3

Terrae Incognitae and Arcana Siwash: Toward a Richer History of Academic Geography

WILLIAM A. KOELSCH

JOHN K. WRIGHT, reflecting on his lifelong contributions to what he called "foolrushery—what fools do when they rush in where angels fear to tread," observed that "interdisciplinary cross-fertilization is as indispensable to the balance of scholarship as the bees are to the balance of Nature."[1] Homage to the ideal of interdisciplinary research and teaching is a recurring ritual on the American campus. Yet the institutional and intellectual history of the American college and university—the arena in which such interdisciplinary experiences have traditionally been sought (by and for students as well as scholars)—has lagged behind the city, the nation-state, and a great many other subjects as an object of scholarly concern.

Like the organized analysis of life of the campus, the history of geography has been haltingly pursued since Wright's "extrepid implorings" for its cultivation, half a century ago. In 1925 Wright had perceived the history of geography as a realm of ideals or images of things geographic created by minds responding to geographical stimuli. This realm of intellectual activity, as Wright first formulated it, comprised a central core, the history of scientific geography, and a secondary domain of what he originally called "non-scientific" geographical ideas.[2] By 1946, in Wright's Presidential address to the Association of American Geographers, this peripheral area had been captured by the shock troops of epistemology, feeling, behavior, imagination, metaphor, subjectivity, and idiosyncrasy, and incorporated into an extended region that Wright somewhat reluctantly termed "geosophy."[3]

Beginning with the indisputable fact that geography, scientific or otherwise, has been taught in some colleges and universities and with the hope that some geography has even been learned there, we might ask how the history of American geography and the history of American higher education can profitably be cross-fertilized. More directly, as Wright might have put it, how do we map the geosophy of Siwash?[4] To seek to do so is to aspire to the triple crown of historian, geographer, and archivist, and perhaps thereby to stand in the grand tradition of Wrightian foolrushery.[5]

HISTORIES OF AMERICAN GEOGRAPHY

While there are numerous histories of American historical activity and several general histories of higher education, no substantial history of American geography exists. Charles C. Colby's 1935 Presidential address to the Association of American Geographers, "Changing Currents of Geographic Thought in America,"[6] is still suggestive as an outline of the field. Nearly twenty years later, another of the Association's presidents, J. Russell Whitaker, termed concentrated, mature, and productive scholarship in "the record of geographic thought, including the history of geographers themselves," a major need within the profession.[7] Yet his prophecy of "notable progress" in this area was not to be fulfilled during the next two decades.[8]

Scientific geography in the United States, except for the work of individuals such as Jedidiah Morse and George Perkins Marsh, has been carried on under the sponsoring shelter of governments,[9] of learned societies and private research foundations,[10] and of academic institutions. The history of geographical activity in each of these categories needs to be systematically examined; within them, the biographical approach has been the one most cultivated in recent years.

A geographer eminent enough to be elected to the National Academy of Sciences eventually becomes the subject of an illuminating biographical memoir.[11] The *Dictionary of American Biography* has brief but scholarly sketches of twenty-one geographers (not all academic), one of whom met an untimely end through wandering in an intoxicated condition in front of a saluting-gun as it was about to be fired. The four supplements to the *Dictionary* so far completed contain another dozen entries.[12] Also under way is the elaborate biobibliographical project organized by the International Geographical Union's Commission on the History of Geographical Thought, which will include studies of a number of prominent American academic geographers, together with basic bibliographies.[13] The availability of these brief accounts should stimulate research on a larger scale.

The first substantial biographical and/or critical perspective on an academic geographer was afforded by Leonard Chester Jones's *Arnold Guyot et Princeton* (1929).[14] Almost all the biographies,[15] dissertations,[16] and shorter scholarly studies of individual geographers or aspects of their work[17] have been published within the last twenty-five years. While all of them, and others not yet completed, in effect respond to Whitaker's call for "dispassionate study of our forebears as individuals," they are still too limited in number.[18] Certainly if it be conceded that there is merit in studying "the careers of individual geographers as bearing on the larger progress of geography," as Wright suggested over a quarter-century ago, then we could profit from further biographical monographs of major academic and other professional geographers on a scale comparable to recent works on J. Russell Smith, Mark Jefferson, Ellsworth Huntington, and William Morris Davis.

Histories of college geography curricula, of college textbooks, and of geography study in specific institutions and departments are even scarcer than biographies. A few early articles in the geographical literature make passing reference to geography in the American college before a full-scale, independent geography department was established at the University of Chicago in 1903, but they are unreliable in detail.[19] Materials for a history of American academic geography in the Colonial period were surveyed in Warntz's *Geography Now and Then*.[20] Notes for Barrows's course in the historical geography of the United States at the University

William A. Koelsch

of Chicago and the syllabus for Rostlund's cultural geography course at the University of California at Berkeley have been published;[21] syllabi and manuscript notes of other courses doubtless exist in various university archives, as yet unstudied or even uninventoried.

Research on the history of geography textbooks has almost entirely neglected the college level.[22] Geography at Harvard has been studied in a dissertation, and geography's role in teacher education has been examined in two other dissertations.[23] Brief essays by Alice Foster and Charles C. Colby recount the history of the geography department at Chicago to its semicentennial celebration in 1953;[24] my more extended history of the second fully staffed independent graduate department, the Graduate School of Geography at Clark University (1921–71), is still in progress. Information on academic geography can be gleaned also from Wright's history of the American Geographical Society and, prospectively, from Preston James's projected history of the Association of American Geographers.

AMERICAN GEOGRAPHY IN COLLEGE HISTORIES

The works cited thus far have been produced largely by geographers or geographic educators, who have examined the history of academic geography in the context of professional geography. If we would seek signs of a concern with geography in the general context of higher education, we must turn to the historiography of college and university history. The beginnings of scholarly interest in the history of higher education coincided with the rise of the American graduate school in the 1870s and 1880s when Herbert Baxter Adams and historians he trained at The John Hopkins University produced histories of education as part of a general quest to understand all social institutions.[25] Most of these men, however, did not sustain their research interest, and so, for a long time thereafter, the burden of researching educational history was assumed by less well qualified investigators. Their studies turned up new materials in a variety of special areas, but too often the results were weakened as history either by their focus on a current problem, issue, or action, or by the necessity of appealing to alumni in tone and content.

66

Since about 1930, however, increasing numbers of professional historians have turned to college and university history. Samuel Eliot Morison had shown that it was possible to write the history of one institution, Harvard University,[26] in a non-parochial way; his example was followed in several case histories at a high level of historical scholarship. Comparative institutional studies in the 1950s and 1960s have further illumined our understanding of the place of higher education in American life.[27]

It is rare, however, that either these well crafted works or their less successful institutional companion volumes yield much information useful to the historian of academic geography. Examination of a hundred histories of both all-male and coeducational institutions from Akron to Yeshiva, selected from Clark University collections, disclosed that only fifteen made index reference to geography, and most of those references were quite trivial. A novice searching the indexes of other histories in the selected group of one hundred would be unable to discover that geography had been taught at such well-known centers of geographical research as the universities of California, Chicago, Minnesota, Missouri, North Carolina, Washington, and Pennsylvania State University.

Of course, lack of index reference to geography may simply be a sign of poor indexing (and yet scanning sample volumes seldom disclosed additional information). It may indicate also that geography is perceived by the institution's historian to be of minor importance. In institutions with major departments of geography, the lack of an entry for it may betray either a failure of communication within the institution or disinterest on the part of geographers in the preservation of departmental records from which institutional histories might be written. Clearly the geographers at such institutions and the institutional historians might profit from some Wrightian "interdisciplinary cross-fertilization."

RECENT RESEARCH TRENDS

During the late 1950s and the 1960s, new currents were stirring in America in both the history of education and the history of geographical ideas. Critics felt that the history of education had previously been lim-

ited too narrowly to the study of ideas, themes, and goals from the writings of great educational reformers, abstracted out of their social context
and influence. Such topics as the common schools, it was alleged, had
been seen too often in a rhetorical and political context, as the supposed
"foundation of American democracy," rather than as functioning intellectual and social systems. The Fund for the Advancement of Education's Committee on the Role of Education in American History,
formed in 1954, tried to redirect the history of education by posing a
simple but fundamental question: "What actually has the pattern of
educational experience been in the United States?"[28] The Committee's
historians differed over whether the history of education should be limited to deliberate, purposeful attempts to instruct particular persons or
groups, or should seek to study, in Bernard Bailyn's felicitous phrase,
"the entire process by which a culture transmits itself across the generations."[29] Both paths, however, led the history of education beyond the
institution and the professional educator; its scope was now to be "the
life of the young as they move toward maturity."[30]

As we have seen, Wright's 1946 Presidential address set the stage for
a similar liberation from the traditional categories, data, and methods of
the history of geography. Wright used the term "geosophy" to charac-
terize the study of the geographical ideas, true or false, of all people,
from all points of view.[31] Geosophy was linked with the humanities by
its concern with subjective experience and imaginative expression.
Wright's address reinforced Derwent S. Whittlesey's earlier contention
that only the limits of man's sense of (terrestrial) space bound the outer
extent of this new territory, and anticipated Ralph H. Brown's dictum
that "men at all times have been influenced quite as much by beliefs as
by facts."[32] In short, research in geography had, thenceforth, to take
cognizance of relations among environmental phenomena, perception,
cognition, and behavior.[33]

The new mode of thinking initiated by Wright, Whittlesey, and
Brown was not fully appreciated until the 1960s,[34] by which time
Wright had retired and Whittlesey and Brown were dead. David Lowenthal extended Wright's ideas more systematically toward the social and
behavioral sciences in his 1961 essay "Geography, Experience, and

Imagination: Towards a Geographical Epistemology."[35] Other geographers were working fruitfully along geosophical lines throughout the decade.[36] By the time of Wright's death in 1969, the ideas he had expressed in 1925 and 1946 were beginning to be seen as seminal antecedents of an intellectual movement that has since been termed the "cognitive reformation" in American geography.[37]

These developments in the history of education and the history of geography (historical geosophy) show certain similarities. The scope of both fields has broadened to include the whole process of acculturation: in education, the acculturation of the young as they move toward maturity; in geosophy, the acculturation of every man as he moves toward what Wright called "geographical awareness" in all its variety. The data sources have expanded as the methodological focus of each has shifted from traditional emphases on the perceptions of leaders (methodological innovators, educational theorists and the like) toward a new concern with ordinary, day-to-day processes affecting greater numbers of previously unstudied groups of people. The activities of classroom teachers, students, the family, inmates of social welfare and penal institutions concerned with children; of "farmers and fishermen, business executives and poets, novelists and painters, Bedouins and Hottentots" (in Wright's litany[38]) all came within the purview of these newly enlarged fields.

Within the narrower sphere where history of higher education and history of geography overlap, however, the newer currents in educational history and in geography have thus far had little impact. Most of the exciting new research in the history of education concerns pre-college and non-school populations, though a few signs of ferment are appearing in studies of higher education. In geography the "cognitive reformation" has begun to play a significant role in the formulation of man-environment theory, but in a historical context it has thus far been limited largely to the study of popular attitudes, to the perceptions of non-academic intellectuals, and to other groups outside the college-university world. I know of no substantial current research in the history of academic geography (including my own) which is not following fairly traditional historiographical patterns, intellectual and institutional.

Yet in principle the American college and university should provide numerous advantages as a laboratory in which to combine the new geosophy and the new educational history. Within this institutional framework we can observe the relations between scientific and popular forms of geosophy, and between teacher and student. The setting is characterized by high visibility and a highly articulate membership; one would expect it to yield an abundance of source materials to help answer a variety of geosophical questions. Such questions would range from the specific (What were New England undergraduates' perceptions of Africa before the Civil War?) to the general (What changes in man-environment theory have taken place as a result of the work of academic geographers in America?). Any trace of geosophical activity in the academy should be set in the context of explanation: What does such activity say about societal expectations for the young or about the changing college population or about the process of image formation? What, in short, does it mean?

As the proportion of the population attending college has risen, professors and students have increasingly served as a bridge between the intellectual and the "common man." Yet even before the advent of mass higher education in the mid-twentieth century, students and teachers exercised a social influence disproportionate to their numbers. The geosophies of such groups are worth examining if only because they are the perceptions of a significant group of decision-makers, either as professional academics or as college-trained folk. If this assumption is valid, and if we are to proceed in some order of priority, then the geosophy of the academy might well assume greater importance among the research tasks ahead.

ARCHIVES AND ACADEMIC GEOGRAPHY

One prerequisite to research in the geosophy of higher education is the geographer's mastery of bibliographical tools and his increasing understanding of the special nature of archives.[39] "An archive is a *terra incognita*, a mysterious island, more mysterious than a library," mused John K.

Wright as he reviewed his early identity with the help of his family's papers at Dartmouth.[40] But, as Geoffrey Martin has suggested, geographers until recently have remained largely ignorant of the interior of such archival islands, and even of their coastlines.[41]

A college or university archive consists of those official records of the institution deemed to be of lasting value. Ideally, it should contain also personal papers of teaching and administrative officers, curricular material such as course syllabi and notes, records of student and alumni organizations, and the like. The archive often preserves the ribbon copies of doctoral dissertations, duplicate sets of university publications, and a collection of secondary historical works relating to the institution. These diverse materials, which may contain information useful for the solution of geographical questions, may be called the institution's arcana, the "secret or mysterious knowledge or information known only to the initiate." Truly a college or university archive contains, in Wright's phrase, "a veritable archipelago of mysterious islands."[42]

College and university archives vary widely in quality, organization, and operation. The oldest, largest, and most complex university archive in the United States, housing more than a hundred thousand items, is that of Harvard University,[43] organized in its present form only in the 1930s. The Harvard model has stimulated the development of professional standards among college and university archives in America,[44] but few institutions have the staff, money, or space to do as good a job of collecting and making available research materials. Periodic surveys made by the Society of American Archivists have disclosed a sharp increase in the number of institutions reporting the existence of an archive, from eighty-four in 1950 to nearly six hundred in 1966, of which only eleven had staffs of three or more people.[45] Still, the signs are hopeful; more and more colleges and universities, many with geography departments, are making their official records and other historical materials available and developing reporting and retrieval mechanisms for the benefit of researchers.

Late in 1971 the Association of American Geographers established an Advisory Committee on Archives and Association History. The initial mandate of this committee—to make recommendations concerning the archives and history of the Association itself—soon expanded to include the broader field of the archives of American geography. In April 1974 the Council of the Association approved a set of Committee recommendations which, when implemented, will greatly expand the resources available for the historian of American geography. One major part of the plan will establish a central Archives of American Geography, to consist of the Association's own archives and other manuscript and printed materials relating to the history of American geography. Another part of the proposal will establish programs of assistance and encouragement for the preservation in appropriate repositories of the archives of geographical societies, the personal papers of American geographers, and the records of geography departments in colleges and universities. These programs should further stimulate archival awareness throughout the profession, as well as increasing the number of studies of academic geography and academic geographers. We may even dream, with Wright, of some future when professorships of geosophy will be established in our leading universities.

THE GEOSOPHY OF STUDENTS: A NEW FRONTIER?

On entering the territory where geosophy and the new history of education meet, one may be temporarily at a loss for guidance into material concerned with student cognition and behavior.[46] There is no good general history of student life in America. The standard reference on student customs was completed in 1900, and deals largely with student organizations.[47] A few of the better histories of individual institutions give some attention to students, or at least to their geographical origins and their games, fraternities, and disorderly conduct. As Frederick Rudolph reminds us, however, the neglect of students in the writing of college and university history has become a significant tradition in its own right. Rudolph's dictum that "unquestionably the most creative and imaginative force in the shaping of the American college and university has been the students"[48] need not be accepted uncritically. Yet we still must come to terms with the question of what geosophy was learned at Siwash, as well as what was conceived and taught there by its professional geographers—or, perhaps, what Siwash's geographers believed they had taught.

With what considerations should we approach the geosophy of students? We should avoid the narrow identification of what is learned with what is purposefully taught. The lectures and course assignments of professional geographers are clearly intended to acculturate the young into consensual geographical perceptions of the world, and therefore we need to study textbooks and course syllabi. A more paideocentric view,[49] however, would assume that "the channels of purposeful instruction or indoctrination" are only a part, perhaps a small part, of what is learned. Wright's suggestion of 1925 that "the image . . . is determined very largely by the nature of the mirror"[50] means, in an educational context, that there is also an autonomous selection process on the part of the student. One corollary of such a process is that the student, for one reason or another, may "tune out" the channels over which we are attempting to broadcast. Another is that students will create and follow their own interests, build their own interdisciplinary, cross-fertilizing synthesis, operate on their own wave lengths. "For a few years the college is their oyster," says Rudolph, "and they will have it served up exactly as they wish it."[51]

To trace the geosophical interests of students, then, means examining evidence from less fully elaborated notions than those contained in the more scientific geography of their mentors. It means examining the student culture outside the curriculum, as well as formal classroom, library, and laboratory experiences. Recent work in historical geosophy has expanded the range of our knowledge of cultural-geographic perceptions by examining "folk" images,[52] in sources and through a methodology which has some direct relevance to student populations. But geosophical studies in general have seldom directly addressed the central methodological problem of the relationship of environmental perception to behavior in the context of the past. One geographer, perhaps despairing of linking these two burgeoning fields, prefers to *brusquer* the issue by asserting that "how men behave in the world may be the best clue as to how they view the world."[53]

To understand the geosophy of students we must examine what they think in part by observing what they do. Michael Oakeshott asserts that the concept of activity should be central in historical writing, and that it is necessary to look beyond narrowly specified, premeditated activity to more artless forms. "Activities emerge naïvely," writes Oakeshott, "like games children invent for themselves."[54]

The notion is useful in the context of the geosophy of the academy. The concept of activity links perception (more properly, cognition) and behavior. By identifying traces of activity among the documents, we can sometimes reconstruct, in part, the content of environmental imagery not otherwise directly available to us from the testimony of the witness. We can track a student to Neuschwanstein Castle, for instance; and even though he did not write an article for the campus literary magazine about it, we can reconstruct from other testimonies, including that of artifacts, what his probable image was, and even, through cautious extrapolation, the "consensual image" of whole student populations of the period.

Conversely, as we examine literary remains revealing environmental imagery, we can validate the content of the image by setting it against the broader, sometimes quantifiable pattern of behavior (relative number of visits to alternative sites, for instance, as a measure of the power of the image). Both the physical experience of the place and the mental constructs registering that experience are aspects of the same cognitive process. Yet Oakeshott's emphasis on the naïve and artless character of activity expands our conventional understanding of process beyond the structured and purposeful. Activity in this sense serves as a unifying concept that allows us to see the geosophical phenomena of the academy as occurring across a wide spectrum. The relatively unsystematic pursuits of the student and the professional activity of the academic geographer become equally worthy of study. Indeed, examination of student efforts, simply because of the number of cases and the new methodological work being done in the history of education, may be even more likely to lead us to advances in man-environment theory.

THE GEOSOPHY OF STUDENTS: A CASE STUDY

About a dozen years ago I began a study that would apply some of Wright's insights and some of the then new perspectives in educational history to aspects of Harvard University before the Civil War.[55] I chose antebellum Harvard for a variety of reasons, including some that had nothing to do with geography. Yet it seemed possible at the time to get at critical questions similar to those J. A. Jakle has more recently and more sharply posed: "How did persons in a past society perceive their place in the temporal and spatial sense, and undertake decision-making accordingly? To what extent did the timing and spacing of persons, objects and events in past environments influence the management of human affairs?"[56]

The character of its student population and the institution's place in the history of American higher education suggested the intrinsic importance of beginning at Harvard. Another reason was the abundance, indeed superabundance, of Harvard materials for the period. Yet during that period at Harvard there were no professional geographers and no courses in geography as such. Given that circumstance, what geosophical perceptions existed had to be sought in naïve or at least in nonprofessionally geographical activity. This meant examining diverse materials in order to establish general patterns of student activity. About a third of the printed material I examined proved to contain traces of "geosophical" activity as Wright defined it, much of it naïvely pursued.

Geosophical activities in the Harvard environment of the 1840s and 1850s were extremely varied. They normally began with an entrance examination, testing among other things the applicant's formal geographical knowledge, through such questions as how Indiana was bounded, what the principal divisions of Palestine were, and whether Amsterdam was or was not north of London. Although no formal courses in geography were offered at Harvard until the 1870s, students gained insight into foreign cultures through language and literature courses and association with the increasing number of faculty members who had traveled or studied abroad. The lectures of Louis Agassiz and Asa Gray offered a theoretical and practical acquaintance with zoogeography and plant geography, and Agassiz introduced field observations and excursions into Harvard's curriculum in biology and geology. Some surveying and map-making (including a map of Harvard Yard) were carried on during the late 1850s in Charles W. Eliot's mathematics course. The library provided copies of great geographical works such as

Varenius's *Geographia generalis*, Peter Heylyn's *Cosmographia*, Mercator's and Ortelius's atlases, and accounts of voyages and travels, including the Ebeling collection of books, maps, and charts.

Some historical geography and map work were required by the classicists and historians, although unfortunately George Perkins Marsh, who undoubtedly would have stimulated such pursuits, declined the McLean professorship of ancient and modern history at Harvard in 1855. Assigned topics for the Bowdoin Prize essays, the public "exhibitions" in spring and fall, and Commencement "parts" frequently had a geographical content, as evidenced in such titles as "The History of the United States as Influenced by Their Physical Geography," "Travellers in the Middle Ages," "The Opening of the Amazon," "European Travel Considered as Part of an American Liberal Education," "Ancient Greek Settlements in the Crimea" (relevant enough in 1855!), "The Prospects of Australia," "Humboldt's Aspects of Nature," and "The Influence of Natural Scenery on the Poetical Literature of the North and of the East."

Beyond these faculty-defined student tasks, students were employed in meteorological and magnetic observations at the Harvard Observatory, in efforts to determine an American prime meridian, and in geographical survey work under government auspices. The student societies, with their up-to-date and accessible libraries, were heavily patronized, and their essays and debates suggest some student-generated geosophical interests, as do reviews of the work of Thoreau, Buckle, and Von Humboldt, among others, in the student literary magazine. A few students, particularly those in the Scientific School, had contact with the Swiss geographer Arnold Guyot during the five or six years he lived in Cambridge; Daniel Coit Gilman made his home with Guyot while pursuing his own advanced reading in 1853. Some students read Guyot's *Earth and Man* either before or during their college years. Students sometimes traveled on summer surveys, collecting expeditions, or field trips with Agassiz, with the chemists Eben N. Horsford and Josiah Parsons Cooke, and with the anatomist Jeffries Wyman. There was also some student interest in polar exploration.

More clearly student generated were summer vacation walking trips in the White Mountains and other scenic areas of the Northeast.[57]

Francis Parkman (A.B. 1844) dignified such recreational activity through his concern to organize in an explanatory historical framework the ensuing discoveries about the varying character of places. During and immediately after their Harvard period, a few young men each year participated in overseas mercantile and maritime activity as supercargoes, factors, or, like Richard Henry Dana, as ordinary seamen. Hundreds of students—perhaps a third of each graduating class in the early and mid-1850s—traveled to Europe either before graduation or within five or six years afterward, commonly in company with classmates or other Harvard men. Some visited Alexander von Humboldt, some attended Carl Ritter's lectures at the University of Berlin. One Harvard man, the Reverend William L. Gage (A.B. 1853), was so taken by Ritter's lectures that he translated them into English and wrote a biography of that Christian *savant*. At the other extreme, geographical experience for many students was almost pure sensation: the stimulus of being on a moonlit night on the spot where Socrates, Plato, Zeno, and Aristotle had trod the groves of Academe, for example, or the pleasure of climbing unexplored and badly mapped territories in the White Mountains "without compass or guide . . . , all for the love of adventure and the honor of Old Harvard," as one student wrote in 1859.[58]

The resulting images might be relatively unorganized, they might be erroneous, they might be useful (or useless), they might be serendipitous. But to discover them we must look beyond formal instruction, beyond scientific geography, to the realm of lore. To understand what geographical learning is taking place among the undergraduates, we must look at student life in its totality. We shall soon find evidence of Rudolph's contention that "the most sensitive barometer of what is going on at a college is the extra-curriculum . . . [since] it records the demands of the curriculum, or the lack thereof."[59] In antebellum Harvard, though the students lacked formal instruction in geographical ideas, they (or some of them, at least) carved what they could out of the opportunities available and created modes of dealing with the natural and human environment—and these may have been livelier, more imaginative, and more personally satisfying than what many a professor might have organized for them.

In retrospect, I see the Harvard study as having raised, by implication

77

at least, a number of methodological, structural, and literary problems: how does one discern (or fashion) coherence from the ideas and actions of hundreds of individuals whose common root may be little more than institutional affiliation in time and space? How does one assign weights to the scattered traces, organize the results, and discern (or devise) relations between those diverse experiences we call geographical and other experience? What effect, if any, does formal instruction have on subsequent behavior? Can links between perception and decision-making ever be convincingly demonstrated for human beings in past societies? Can we ever really comprehend the significance of timing and spacing, and their interrelations, when reconstructing past events? In concentrating on the difficult task of piecing together traces of activity, I gave less than adequate thought and space to content analysis of images. On the other hand, examining "the actual pattern" and translating it into categories based on forms of activity exposed a fresh dimension of student-generated learning experiences which, generalized and given broader meaning, helped to clarify emerging thought about the history of education.[60]

Nineteenth-century Harvard, although an important place in a period when Americans were reaching out to explore their own and other *terrae incognitae,* was but one geosophical environment at one time. Study of a single institution may serve, however, as a heuristic device for the geosophical exploration of other academic institutions in differing space-time situations. Yet a more fruitful approach might be to isolate one activity, such as the geographical surveys (seen as internship activity), or the Grand Tour (seen as cognitive and affective environmental learning), or the college entrance requirement in geography (seen as a measure of societal expectation for the young), and examine that activity in multi-institutional, comparative studies. Such studies might then link content analysis of images with explanatory frameworks drawn from the social sciences, and in the process simplify some of the literary problems of unity, coherence, and emphasis in regard to which my Harvard study is, in retrospect, notably deficient.

MAPPING THE GEOSOPHY OF SIWASH

The history of academic geography, even as traditionally conceived, is still *terra incognita* in America. Beyond the range of scientific college and university geography lies further unexplored territory, toward which the Wrightian spirit beckons. Thanks to recent developments in historical geosophy and in the history of education, and to increasing archival awareness among geographers, we can begin to explore and even to cultivate that territory, and to give form to its lore. Untapped sources, unarticulated relations, and newly framed questions are always alluring, and among the arcana of Siwash we encounter them at every hand. In the course of mapping the geosophy of Siwash, we learn new meanings for old terms like geography, education, and institution; we try to make old concepts intelligible in fresh ways. The lore of the Academy is, after all, our heritage as students and teachers, just as the scientific traditions and literature of our profession belong to us as professional geographers. We need to explore the possibilities of both the lore and the letter.

NOTES

1. "Introduction," *Human Nature in Geography* (Cambridge: Harvard University Press, 1966), p. 10.
2. J. K. Wright, "The History of Geography: A Point of View," *Annals of the Association of American Geographers* (hereafter *Annals* AAG) 15 (1925):192–201; and "A Plea for the History of Geography," *Isis* 8 (1926):477–91, reprinted in *Human Nature in Geography*, pp. 11–23.
3. In 1946 Wright defined geosophy, or earth knowledge, as "the study of geographical ideas from any and all points of view"; historical geosophy was his comprehensive term for the history of all types of geographical knowledge, and thus he reconciled the scientific-nonscientific dichotomy of 1925. See his "*Terrae Incognitae*: The Place of the Imagination in Geography," *Annals* AAG 37 (1947):1–15, reprinted in *Human Nature in Geography*, pp. 68–88, esp. pp. 85–88; see also Martyn J. Bowden, "John Kirtland Wright, 1891–1969," *Annals* AAG 60 (1970):394–403; and David Lowenthal, "John Kirtland Wright, 1891–1969," *Geographical Review* 59 (1969):598–604. Although the fields Wright described were indeed white unto the harvest, the laborers were few; in 1956 and 1961 only about fifteen members of the Association of American Geographers listed the history of geography or of geographical thought as a special

79

interest, a number increased to thirty-three by 1967 and to eighty-four by 1971. See *Handbook-Directory*, 1956 (Washington: Association of American Geographers, 1956); *Handbook-Directory*, 1960 (ibid., 1961); and personal communication, Terry Rich to William A. Koelsch, Dec. 2, 1971. The figures given here exclude historical cartographers and also historical geographers properly so-called. Geosophy has not yet been recognized by the Association as a specialty code.

4. The title of this paper is the product of cross-fertilization of two other titles, Wright's *"Terrae Incognitae"* and Thomas LeDuc's "Arcana Siwash: The Function and Needs of a College Archives," *American Archivist* 9 (1946):132–35. "Siwash" is defined in one standard dictionary as "a small college regarded as typical of its class," and in another as "a small usu. inland college that is notably provincial in outlook." Siwash is also a subjective, partly imaginary environment, constructed from memory, legend, and the lore of many individual colleges. See the preface to George Helgeson Fitch's novel, *At Good Old Siwash* (Boston: Little, Brown, 1911 and later editions).

5. In the present essay I limit myself to a discussion of American geography and American higher education, since I know the literature of those fields best. Parallel essays might be written on other national traditions of historiography, geography, and archival practice.

6. In *Annals AAG* 26 (1936):1–37. An address by William Morris Davis, "The Progress of Geography in the United States," ibid., 14 (1924):159–215, is similarly suggestive.

7. J. Russell Whitaker, "The Way Lies Open," *Annals AAG* 44 (1954):237–38. See also a similar comment by Carl O. Sauer, in his "Foreword to Historical Geography," ibid., 31 (1941):4.

8. Preston James's broad survey, *All Possible Worlds: A History of Geographical Ideas* (Indianapolis: Bobbs-Merrill, 1972), contains several chapters on professional geography in America, with useful bibliographies.

9. See, e.g., A. Hunter Dupree, *Science in the Federal Government: A History of Policies and Activities to 1940* (Cambridge: Harvard University Press, Belknap Press, 1957); Nathan Reingold, ed., *Science in Nineteenth-Century America: A Documentary History* (New York: Hill and Wang, 1966); William D. Pattison, *Beginnings of the American Rectangular Land Survey System, 1784–1800* (Chicago: University of Chicago, Department of Geography, 1957); *Geographers in Government* (New York: American Geographical Society, 1968); James, *All Possible Worlds*, chap. 14.

10. See J. K. Wright, "The Field of the Geographical Society," in Griffith Taylor, ed., *Geography in the Twentieth Century* (New York: Philosophical Library, 1951), pp. 543–65; Wright, *Geography in the Making: The American Geographical Society, 1851–1951* (New York: American Geographical Society, 1952); Ralph S. Bates, *Scientific Societies in the United States*, 3rd ed. (Cambridge: M.I.T. Press, 1958).

11. James D. Dana, "Memoir of Arnold Guyot, 1807–1884," *Biographical Memoirs*, National Academy of Sciences, 2 (1886):311–47; William Morris Davis, "George Perkins Marsh, 1801–1882," ibid., 6 (1909):73–80; Reginald A. Daly,

"William Morris Davis, 1850–1934," ibid., 23:263–303; John K. Wright and George F. Carter, "Isaiah Bowman, December 26, 1878–January 6, 1950," ibid., 33 (1959):39–64.

12. Allan Johnson and Dumas Malone, eds., *Dictionary of American Biography*, 20 vols. (New York: Charles Scribner's Sons, 1928–36); Harris E. Starr, ed., *Dictionary of American Biography*, Supplement One (ibid., 1944), Robert L. Schuyler, ed., *Dictionary of American Biography*, Supplement Two (ibid., 1958); Edward T. James, ed., *Dictionary of American Biography*, Supplement Three (ibid., 1972); John A. Garraty and Edward T. James, eds., *Dictionary of American Biography*, Supplement Four (ibid., 1974).

13. Philippe Pinchemel, "Les Geographes," *Bulletin de l'Association des Geographes Françaises* (Paris) 411–12 (1973):687–92.

14. In "Université de Neuchâtel, Recueil de Travaux Publiés par la Faculté des Lettres" 14 (1929). Jones's briefer study in English, "Arnold Henry Guyot," may be found in *Faculty Papers of Union College*, 1.1 (January 1930):31–57 (Union College *Bulletin* 23.2 [1930]).

15. See, e.g., Virginia M. Rowley, *J. Russell Smith, Geographer, Educator, and Conservationist* (Philadelphia: University of Pennsylvania Press, 1964); Geoffrey J. Martin, *Mark Jefferson, Geographer* (Ypsilanti: Eastern Michigan University Press, 1968); idem, "The Ellsworth Huntington Papers," *Yale University Library Gazette* 45 (1971):185–95; idem, "Ellsworth Huntington and 'The Pace of History,'" *Connecticut Review* 5 (1971):83–123; and idem, *Ellsworth Huntington: His Life and Thought* (Hamden, Conn.: Archon Books, 1973); also Richard J. Chorley and others, *The History of the Study of Land Forms*, vol. 2, *The Life and Work of William Morris Davis* (London: Methuen, 1973).

16. Examples include John E. Chappell, "Huntington and His Critics: The Influence of Climate on Civilization," Ph.D. diss., University of Kansas, 1968; Paul F. Griffin, "Richard Elwood Dodge: His Life and Contributions to Geography," Ph.D. diss., Columbia University, 1952; George A. Knadler, "Isaiah Bowman: Backgrounds of His Contribution to Thought," Ed.D. diss., Indiana University, 1958; and Vera E. Rigdon, "The Contributions of William Morris Davis to Geography in America," Ph.D. diss., University of Nebraska, 1934.

17. E.g., J. K. Wright, "Daniel Coit Gilman: Geographer and Historian," *Geographical Review* 51 (1961): 381–99, reprinted in *Human Nature in Geography*, pp. 168–87; idem, "Miss Semple's 'Influences of Geographic Environment': Notes toward a Bibliobiography," *Geographical Review* 52 (1962):346–61, reprinted in *Human Nature in Geography*, pp. 188–204; Lawrence E. Gelfand, "Ellen Churchill Semple: Her Geographic Approach to American History," *Journal of Geography* 53 (1954):30–41; Arthur J. Hawley, "Environmental Perception: Nature and Ellen Churchill Semple," *Southeastern Geographer* 7 (1968):54–59; William A. Koelsch, "The Historical Geography of Harlan H. Barrows," *Annals AAG* 59 (1969):632–51; Robert Anstey, "Arnold Guyot, Teacher of Geography," *Journal of Geography* 57 (1958):441–49; H. Phillip Bacon, "Fireworks in the Classroom: Nathaniel Southgate Shaler as a Teacher," *Journal of Geography* 54 (1955):349–53.

18. Among works in progress are Robert Anstey's biography of Guyot and Allen Bushong's biography of Semple, who has been studied also by Judith Bronson in a dissertation in history at St. Louis University; Geoffrey Martin and Shirley Wightman have each embarked on a biography of Bowman; and Robert E. Dickinson is preparing an American companion to his *Makers of Modern Geography* (London: Routledge & Kegan Paul, 1969).

19. See Charles Redway Dryer, "A Century of Geographic Education in the United States," *Annals AAG* 14 (1924):117–49, esp. p. 143; Huldah Winstead, "Geography in American Universities," *Journal of Geography* 10 (1911–12):311–16; and Raphael Pico, "Geography in American Universities," *Journal of Geography* 40 (1941):291–301.

20. William Warntz, *Geography Now and Then: Some Notes on the History of Academic Geography in the United States* (New York: American Geographical Society, 1964).

21. Harlan H. Barrows, *Lectures on the Historical Geography of the United States as Given in 1933*, ed. William A. Koelsch (Chicago: University of Chicago, Department of Geography Research Paper no. 77, 1962); Erhard Rostlund, *Outline of Cultural Geography* (Berkeley: California Book Co., 1955, 1963).

22. In addition to references listed in Jurgen Herbst's bibliography, *The History of American Education* (Northbrook, Ill.: A.H.M. Publishing Corp., 1973), see Albert Perry Brigham and Richard E. Dodge, "Nineteenth Century Textbooks in Geography," in Guy M. Whipple, ed., *The Teaching of Geography*, 32nd yearbook, National Society for the Study of Education (Bloomington, Ill., 1933), chap. 1; James F. Chamberlin, "Early American Geographies," *Yearbook of the Association of Pacific Coast Geographers* 5 (1939):23–29; John R. Sahli, "Student Interest Appeals in Early American Geography Textbooks," *Journal of Geography* 53 (1954):20–24; Stephen B. Weeks, "Confederate Textbooks, 1861–65," U.S. Commissioner of Education, *Report, 1898–1899* (Washington: Government Printing Office, 1900) 1:1149–51. There are also several dissertations in this area.

23. Rita Mary Morris, "An Examination of Some Factors Related to the Rise and Decline of Geography as a Field of Study at Harvard, 1638–1948," Ed.D. diss., Harvard University, 1962; Edna Arundel, "The Evolution of Human Geography in Teacher Education," Ph.D. diss., Yale University, 1942; Lorin Kennamer, Jr., "The Development of Methods in Teaching School Geography," Ed.D. diss., George Peabody College for Teachers, 1952. See also J. Russell Whitaker, "Historical Geography in School and College," *Peabody Journal of Education* 27 (1949):3–15; W. L. Mayo, *The Development and Status of Secondary School Geography in the United States and Canada* (Ann Arbor: University Publishers, 1965), and Katheryne Thomas Whittemore, "Celebrating Seventy-Five Years of the Journal of Geography, 1897–1972," *Journal of Geography* 71 (1972):7–18.

24. Foster, "The New Department in Its Setting," in *A Half-Century of Geography —What Next?* (Chicago: University of Chicago, Department of Geography, 1955), pp. 1–7; Colby, "Narrative of Five Decades of Geography," ibid., pp. 8–20.

25. Comments in this paragraph are based on Frederick Rudolph, "Historiography of Higher Education in the United States," in his *The American College and University: A History* (New York: Alfred A. Knopf, 1962), pp. 497–516.
26. Samuel Eliot Morison's histories of Harvard include *The Development of Harvard University, 1869–1929* (Cambridge: Harvard University Press, 1930), which has a section on geology and geography by William Morris Davis and Reginald A. Daly; and three other works, *The Founding of Harvard College* (1935), *Harvard College in the Seventeenth Century*, 2 vols. (1936), and the more popular *Three Centuries of Harvard, 1636–1936* (1936). Morison's work on early Harvard has been criticized in Winthrop S. Hudson, "The Morison Myth Concerning the Founding of Harvard College," *Church History* 5 (1939): 148–59.
27. Jurgen Herbst's *The History of American Education* contains numerous college and university references. Also valuable for higher education references are the reviews of the history of education literature appearing occasionally since 1936 (regularly about every three years since 1952), in *Review of Educational Research* and, more recently, in the bibliographies and reviews in *History of Education Quarterly*.
28. The principal methodological statements are: Committee on the Role of Education in American History, *The Role of Education in American History* (New York: Fund for the Advancement of Education, 1957), and *Education and American History* (ibid., 1965); Wilson Smith, "The New Historian of American Education," *Harvard Educational Review* 21 (1961):136–43; Bernard Bailyn, *Education in the Forming of American Society* (Chapel Hill: University of North Carolina Press, 1960); and Lawrence Cremin, *The Wonderful World of Ellwood Patterson Cubberley: An Essay on the Historiography of American Education* (New York: Columbia University, Teachers College, 1965). I am especially indebted in these paragraphs to Robert L. Church, "History of Education as a Field Study," *Encyclopedia of Education* 4 (New York: Macmillan, 1971):415–23. The bibliographical essay in Cremin, *American Education: The Colonial Experience, 1607–1783* (New York: Harper and Row, 1970) is basic, as is the content of the book, first of a projected three volumes. See also David Tyack, "New Perspectives on the History of Education," in Herbert J. Bass, ed., *The State of American History* (Chicago: Quadrangle Books, 1970); Lawrence R. Veysey, "Toward a New Direction in Educational History: Prospect and Retrospect," *History of Education Quarterly* 9 (1969):343–59; and Daniel J. Boorstin, "Universities in the Republic of Letters," *Perspectives in American History* 1 (1969): 369–79.
29. In his *Education in the Forming of American Society*, p. 14.
30. Quoted from *Education and American History*, p. 8.
31. As Wright pointed out in a communication to the *Annals AAG* 39 (1949): 47, Charles R. Dryer had, in 1919, quoted Henry Wilson's use of the term "geosophy" earlier to mean the geography of thought, or what in 1946 Wright called "sophogeography." See Dryer, "Genetic Geography: The Development of the Geographic Sense and Concept," *Annals AAG* 10 (1920):13, and Henry

Wilson, "The Geography of Culture and the Culture of Geography," *Geographical Teacher* 9 (1918):196. Dryer's essay needs rereading in the light of current developments in geosophy.

32. Whittlesey, "The Horizon of Geography," *Annals AAG* 35 (1945):1–36; Brown, *Historical Geography of the United States* (New York: Harcourt, Brace, 1948), p. 3.

33. Wright's 1966 definition of "human nature in geography" as "the impact upon geographical awareness (perception, cognition, knowledge, belief, study) of human emotions, motives, and behavior," appears to open up this area of investigation more broadly still (*Human Nature in Geography*, Preface, p. vii).

34. It may be that post-World War II American geography's initial concentration on developing links with economics, demography, and social statistics was responsible for this neglect, and that only with the second phase—when geography turned toward the behavioral sciences in its studies of perception and decision-making—could the merits of these pioneering essays be adequately estimated.

35. In *Annals AAG* 51 (1961):241–60; see also Lowenthal, "Is Wilderness 'Paradise Enow'?" *Columbia University Forum* 7.2 (1964):34–40; and his "The American Scene," *Geographical Review* 58 (1968):61–88.

36. Among such geographers are John L. Allen, Martyn J. Bowden, Clarence J. Glacken, R. Leslie Heathcote, G. Malcolm Lewis, Douglas McManis, H. Roy Merrens, and Yi-Fu Tuan. For recent appraisals of and additions to this literature, and analysis of its relations to traditional and modern historical geography, see Hugh C. Prince, "Progress in Historical Geography," in Ronald U. Cooke and James H. Johnson, eds., *Trends in Geography: An Introductory Survey* (Oxford: Pergamon, 1969), pp. 110–22; Prince, "Real, Imagined and Abstract Worlds of the Past," in Christopher Board and others, eds., *Progress in Geography* 3 (London: Edward Arnold, 1971):1–86; and John A. Jakle, "Time, Space, and the Geographic Past: A Prospectus for Historical Geography," *American Historical Review* 76 (1971):1084–1103, as well as the footnotes to essays in the present volume.

37. Ian Burton, Robert W. Kates, and Anne V. T. Kirkby, "Geography," in Albert E. Utton and D. H. Henning, eds., *Interdisciplinary Environmental Approaches* (Costa Mesa, Calif.: Educational Media Press, 1974), pp. 100–26.

38. In *Human Nature in Geography*, p. 83.

39. William A. Koelsch's "College and University Archives as a Resource for the History of American Geography" (paper delivered before the Association of American Geographers, Atlanta, April 17, 1973), elaborates some of the argument set forth in the next few paragraphs.

40. See his "Mysterious Islands: The Wright Papers in the Dartmouth Library," *Dartmouth College Library Bulletin* 9 (1968):44.

41. "Geographers and Archives: A Suggestion," *The Professional Geographer* 16.6 (1964):25–27.

42. In "Mysterious Islands," p. 48.

43. See five articles by Clifford K. Shipton, "The Harvard University Archives," *College and Research Libraries* 3 (1941):50–56; "The Harvard University Archives: Goal and Function," *Harvard Library Bulletin* 1 (1947):101–8; "The Collec-

tions of the Harvard University Archives," ibid., 176–84; "College Archives and Academic Research," *American Archivist* 27 (1964):395–400; and "The Harvard University Archives in 1938 and 1969," *Harvard Library Bulletin* 18 (1970):205–11.

44. On the history and problems of American university archives, see Ernst Posner's "The College and University Archives in the United States," in his *Archives and the Public Interest: Selected Essays by Ernst Posner*, ed. Kenneth Munden (Washington: Public Affairs Press, 1967), pp. 148–58. Several useful references are abstracted in Helen L. Chatfield, "College and University Archives: A Bibliographic Review," *American Archivist* 28 (1965):101–8. In 1973 the Committee on College and University Archives of the Society of American Archivists issued a brief bibliography on academic archives.

45. See "Report of the Committee on College and University Archives," *American Archivist* 13 (1950):62–64; Dwight H. Wilson, "Archives in Colleges and Universities: Some Comments on Data Collected by the Society's Committee on College and University Archives," ibid. 13 (1950):343–50; Philip P. Mason, "College and University Archives: 1962," ibid. 26 (1963):161–65; Robert M. Warner, "The Status of College and University Archives," ibid. 31 (1968):234–37; and Society of American Archivists, College and University Archives Committee, *College and University Archives in the United States and Canada* (Ann Arbor, Mich., 1966, 1972).

46. The use of fugitive student-generated material requires a good deal of low-yield searching. The Library of Congress classification scheme indicates what might be held, even if the material more often than not is either not held or not catalogued; see U.S., Library of Congress, Subject Catalog Division, *Classification: Class L, Education*, 3rd ed. (Washington: G.P.O., 1951), pp. 174–75. George E. Peterson's excellent bibliographical essay in his *The New England College in the Age of the University* (Amherst, Mass.: Amherst College Press, 1964) gives a good indication of the primary materials held by the six small New England colleges he has studied, and might serve also as a model of the general guide. See also the Shipton essays, particularly "The Collections of the Harvard University Archives," and Maynard J. Brichford's "The Illiarch," *Illinois Libraries* 52 (1970):182–204.

47. Henry Davidson Sheldon, *The History and Pedagogy of American Student Societies* (New York: Appleton, 1901) (also published under the title *Student Life and Customs*). Calvin B. T. Lee, *The Campus Scene, 1900–1970* (New York: David McKay, 1970), covers twentieth-century American student life very superficially, lacks footnotes, and has an indifferent bibliography. The behavioral approach to the history of student life suggested by the following works is germane to academic geosophy: Louis Feuer, *The Conflict of Generations: The Character and Significance of Student Movements* (New York: Basic Books, 1969); Oscar and Mary Handlin, *The American College and American Culture: Socialization as a Function of Higher Education* (New York: McGraw-Hill, 1970), and *Facing Life: Youth and the Family in American History* (Boston: Little, Brown, 1971); and several essays in Lawrence Stone, ed., *The University in Society*, 2 vols. (Princeton: Princeton University Press, 1974).

William A. Koelsch

48. In "The Neglect of Students as a Historical Tradition," in Lawrence E. Dennis and J. E. Kauffman, eds., *The College and the Student* (Washington: American Council on Education, 1966), pp. 47–58.
49. "Paideocentric" is adopted from Werner Jaeger, *Paideia: The Ideals of Greek Culture*, 3 vols. (New York: Oxford University Press, 1939–44). Jaeger defines *paideia* as "the shaping of the Greek character," and in his study attempts to "explain the interaction between the historical process by which their character was formed and the intellectual process by which they constructed their ideal of human personality" (vol. 1, Preface, p. vii). There are large implications for geosophy in this approach.
50. In "The History of Geography: A Point of View," pp. 200–201. There is an interesting and unexplained difference in the degree of autonomy Wright assigns to the perceiver in 1925 and in 1946.
51. In "The Neglect of Students," p. 53.
52. See esp. Martyn J. Bowden, "The Perception of the Western Interior of the United States, 1800–1870: A Problem in Historical Geosophy," *Proceedings of the Association of American Geographers* 1 (1969):16–21; and Bowden, "The Great American Desert and the American Frontier, 1800–1882: Popular Images of the Plains," in Tamara K. Hareven, ed., *Anonymous Americans: Explorations in Nineteenth-Century Social History* (Englewood Cliffs, N.J.: Prentice-Hall, 1971), pp. 48–79. A number of dissertations in this area are in progress or have recently been completed at Clark.
53. See Robert W. Kates's excellent brief guide to, and appraisal of, the literature, in his "Human Perception of the Environment," *International Social Science Journal* 22 (1970): 648–59.
54. See "The Activity of Being an Historian," in T. D. Williams, ed., *Historical Studies* 1 (London, 1958):1–19; reprinted in Oakeshott, *Rationalism in Politics and Other Essays* (New York: Basic Books, 1962), pp. 137–67.
55. W. Koelsch, "The Enlargement of a World: Harvard Students and Geographical Experience, 1840–1861," Ph.D. diss., Department of History, University of Chicago, 1966, apparently the only non-biographical dissertation in history of geography since Wright's to be accepted by an American university's department of history. See Warren F. Kuehl, comp., *Dissertations in History*, 2 vols. (Lexington: University of Kentucky Press, 1965–72), which covers dissertations through 1970. Because of limitations of space, documentation for the following statements must be assumed in the original dissertation, which contains a 35-page bibliography and footnotes too numerous to repeat here.
56. In "Time, Space, and the Geographic Past," p. 1103.
57. One of the best recollections of these is Francis Parkman's "Exploring the Magalloway," *Harper's New Monthly Magazine* 29 (1864):735–41, reprinted in Barbara Gutmann Rosenkrantz and William A. Koelsch, *American Habitat: A Historical Perspective* (New York: Macmillan, 1973), pp. 324–39.
58. "In the Woods," *Harvard Magazine*, 5.6–7 (1859):236–53.
59. In "The Neglect of Students," p. 53.
60. The shift in emphasis between 1957 and 1965 from the advocacy of deliberate,

purposeful instruction to the position that "education is the life of the young as they move toward maturity" in the reports of the Committee on the Role of Education in American History (see note 28 above) grew in part out of the early chapters of my Harvard study; personal communication, Richard J. Storr (who drafted both documents) to William A. Koelsch, May 22, 1965.

4

The Place of the Past
in the American Landscape

DAVID LOWENTHAL

AMERICANS: A PEOPLE neglectful of the past, impatient of the present, engrossed only in the future. We easily recognize the portrait. How true a likeness is it? How uniquely American? What are its origins and consequences?

Many new nations, dismissing previous views of the past, manufacture new ones to suit their sovereign status. Today's ex-colonial Asians and Africans energetically evoke old histories or forge fresh ones to provide self-respect with substance and duration. Earlier European nationalists likewise looked backward through a vernacular prism to exalt prior folk traditions. French revolutionaries appealed to classical precedents. Newly independent Americans, however, gloried in their felt lack of history. Seeing Europeans burdened by the past, they rejoiced in their own supposed freedom from its shackles. When they became aware of a need for a history of their own, they set about rediscovering the American past with diligent zeal. But they continued to suppose America to be newly born, Americans to be uniquely untrammeled by the past, and the visi-

For their encouragement and criticism I am grateful to Ruth Miller Elson, Valerie Pearl, and Hugh C. Prince.

89

ble marks of history to be less a solace for lost glories than a hindrance to new endeavors. These assumptions dominated the American mind for a century or more and became part of the enduring national ethos.

This essay will sketch American attitudes toward the past during the first century of the Republic, not as a historical narrative but as a continuing dialogue between revolutionary and traditionalistic ideals. I shall try to account for the initial rejection of history, to discuss the problems this rejection raised, to show what other aspects of the American heritage were emphasized instead, and to explore the implications for the American mind and the American environment of what John K. Wright, in reflecting on American geographical thought, has termed "the law of the disparagement of the past."[1]

The views described herein are representative not in any statistical sense, but in reflecting the passions and prejudices of leaders generally recognized as speaking for their fellow countrymen at large. The ideas and feelings set forth by these statesmen and men of letters prevailed in the schoolroom, the press, and the pulpit, and profoundly influenced American judgments about the place of the past in the landscape.

THE PAST REJECTED

The first decades of nationhood gave rise to a comprehensive antihistorical mystique that has had lasting consequences for both the American landscape and the American personality. A new land unburdened by history, a new people unhampered by their forebears: these were not only aspirations but recognized facts of life, contrasting especially with European obeisance to the past. These feelings were rooted in perceptions of the landscape itself. Compared with Europe, America seemed a land scarcely lived in; American landscapes conveyed little sense of historical depth. Recent in time and transient in quality, man's works seemed puny and trivial in the enveloping wilderness. To be sure, untold generations of Indians had inhabited America, but their relics were few and ephemeral, their impact on the environment not always easy for European settlers to distinguish from that of natural processes.

The paucity of human history in the landscape had saddened, even appalled, early Colonial settlers and travelers accustomed to the relic features of the Old World. The passage of time, however, habituated American eyes to their *tabula rasa*. And with the Revolution came a new spirit: newness was not only tolerated but positively worshiped, and the lack of historical remains became a matter for self-congratulation. Opposition to the past, explicit and emphatic, underlies much of nineteenth-century environmental and architectural practice. The paucity of the visible past and the lack of local historical associations, as George Perkins Marsh explained fifty years after the Revolution, had made Americans heedless of tradition. "Neither the places, the monuments, nor the forms, which in the eye of the European are sacred," were similarly venerated by Americans.[2] Other needs—political, religious, philosophical, psychological—intensified the antihistorical bias and made Americans feel that their country's unique destiny demanded disengagement from the heritage of human history. And certain prevalent presumptions about the nature of history validated these prejudices.

The political motif is the clearest. In breaking imperial bonds, American nationalists were convinced that they were discarding not only the mother country but its age-old traditions, notably reverence for outworn forms and customs. Continuous freedom of choice legitimized the American rebellion. According to Thomas Jefferson, no one should be bound by anything established in the past. Each generation was a "distinct nation" that should as a matter of course erase preceding institutions and select its own. Americans widely concurred with Jefferson's view that "the dead have no rights. They are nothing; and nothing cannot own something. . . . Our Creator made the earth for the use of the living and not of the dead. . . . One generation of men cannot foreclose or burden its use to another." And since half of each adult generation would be dead in eighteen years and eight months, the legal code, too, should expire every nineteen years.[3] Indeed, the basic rationale of English common law, with precedents for judicial decision rooted in the historical past, was anathematized by American revolutionaries. The age of reason, they felt, would supersede the age of history.[4]

Just as the American nation shrugged off the impress of the past, so did individual Americans. A radically new ideal personality emerged, "an individual emancipated from history, happily bereft of ancestry, untouched and undefiled by the usual inheritances of family and race; an individual standing alone, self-reliant and self-propelling," in R. W. B. Lewis's words. Time and memory had corrupted Europeans; but Americans were pristine, like Adam before the Fall, and Adamic potentialities were theirs so long as they remained innocent. "The national and hence the individual conscience was clear just because it was unsullied by the past—America . . . had no past, but only a present and a future."[5] Such was the basic faith born of the American Revolution and nurtured for almost a century by the leading lights of American culture and politics.

This faith had profound implications for religion, too: it buttressed the reformist stance against the doctrine of man's innate sinfulness. While orthodox Christian history intoned the inherited legacy of human corruption, Transcendentalism acclaimed American innocence. Since orthodoxy and autocracy presented so bleak and tainted a view of human history, it is little wonder that many Americans preferred to dispense with it altogether. Not only what happened in history but the past itself was seen as evil.

The new emphasis on individual self-fulfillment, what Quentin Anderson has called the "imperial self," entailed the rejection not only of history but of contemporary institutional and environmental ties. Both society and nature were to be cast off; the American must go forward unfettered, ultimately responsible to and for himself alone. "The height of culture, the highest behavior," as Emerson put it, "consists in the identification of the Ego with the universe." As Anderson notes, Emerson explicitly dismisses "that filiation of memory, custom and expectation, articulate and tacit, which binds a human generation in a humanly qualified place."[6]

To renounce the past meant especially to reject parental influence. The generation gap was a cherished freedom. "I have lived some thirty years on this planet," Thoreau asserted, "and I have yet to hear the first syllable of valuable or even earnest advice from my seniors."[7] The democratic urge, observed Tocqueville, makes men forget their ancestors and lets them "imagine that their whole destiny is in their own hands." In America "the tie that united one generation to another is relaxed or broken; every man there loses all traces of the ideas of his forefathers or takes no heed of them."[8] This was an apt reflection on the social geography that post-Revolutionary Americans created.

Two theories justified American contempt for the past: a cyclical view of history widely current during the Enlightenment, and an exceptionalism that excluded America from the framework of world history. According to the cyclical view as propounded by Hume, countries, like individuals, were born and passed through youth to maturity and old age. John Quincy Adams reminded his fellow Americans that "there is never a rising without a setting sun. . . . Let us remember that we shall fall . . . into the decline and infirmities of old age."[9] Adams himself often forgot. But in any event, America's early stage in this life cycle explained her indifference toward the past. "It belongs to the character of youthful and vigorous nations," in Marsh's phrase, "to concern themselves with the present and the future rather than with the past, and it is not until the sun of their greatness . . . is beginning to decline . . . that a spirit of antiquarian research is excited."[10]

Not surprisingly, American future glories assumed a chauvinist character. "It is for other nations to boast of what they have been," asserted the patriot James K. Paulding; "the history of their youthful exploits . . . only renders decrepitude more conspicuous. Ours is the more animating sentiment of hope, looking forward with prophetic eye."[11] Cadwallader D. Colden, a New York canal builder, made the point vivid: "Did we live amidst ruins and . . . scenes indicating present decay . . . we might be as little inclined as others, to look forward. But we delight in the promised sunshine of the future, and leave to those who are conscious that they have passed their grand climacteric to console themselves with the splendors of the past."[12]

A more radical thesis located America, newly created by rational and blameless men, wholly outside history. Having rejected Europe, Americans had no human past. This view of America was not theirs alone; it was the point of John Locke's apothegm that "in the beginning, all the world was America."[13] The theme still echoed more than a century later: as Noah Webster put it in 1825, because Americans had been created afresh, not by way of the whole sorry race of mankind, "American glory begins at the dawn."[14] Since they viewed the present not as a historical culmination but as a new creation, Americans not only

93

discounted the past but separated themselves from it. History was of little value, for all its lessons were negative. "We have no interest in scenes of antiquity," explained that ardent exponent of Manifest Destiny, John Louis O'Sullivan, "only as lessons of avoidance of nearly all their examples."[15]

The notion that rational man could escape the errors of the past was not uniquely American; it was a major theme in Enlightenment thought and infused the French Revolution, like the American. But Americans, unlike Europeans, could dwell almost wholly in the present. "We have no occasion to roam for information into the obscure world of antiquity," explained Thomas Paine. "The real volume, not of history but of facts, is directly before us, unmutilated by the errors of tradition."[16] The equation of truth with the observable present, of falsehood with the past, was both a metaphysical belief and a moral stance. History's use, as Emerson expressed it, was "to give value to the present hour. I find that whatever is old is corrupt, and the past turns to snakes. The reverence for the deeds of our ancestors is a treacherous sentiment. . . . Give me insight into today, and you may have the antique and future worlds."[17] One consequence of this widespread view, wrote Henry James in 1905, was that the only moment of importance left to Americans was "the present, pure and simple, squaring itself between an absent future and an absent past as solidly as it can."[18]

Post-Revolutionary Americans eliminated history not only from their minds but from their surroundings as well. Jefferson's "sovereignty of the present generation" applied no less to law than to landscape. Inherited land and houses epitomized the tyranny of forebears and the burden of the past. Material transience was often recommended; houses were considered "heaps of bricks and stones" man builds "for himself to die in, and for his posterity to be miserable in. . . . We shall live to see the day," envisages the reformer in Hawthorne's *House of the Seven Gables*, "when no man shall build his house for posterity."[19] The glory of America, thought one observer, was that it was all periodically pulled down.[20] Emerson criticized a Massachusetts state survey for recommending stone houses, on the ground that stone buildings lasted too long. "Our roads are always changing their direction, . . . our people are not stationary";

and so houses must be built that could easily be moved or abandoned.[21] The invention of the balloon frame in the 1830s made possible the prefabrication of housing units that could be dismantled and shifted from place to place in accordance with the needs of a restless and nomadic people.[22] Life and art mirrored each other in celebrating material evanescence. Periodic purification was Holgrave's explicit program.

> Our public edifices—our capitols, state-houses, court-houses, city-hall, and churches—ought [not] to be built of such permanent materials as stone or brick. It were better that they should crumble to ruin once in twenty years, or thereabouts, as a hint to the people to examine into and reform the institutions which they symbolize.[23]

Mistrust of antiquity reached its apogee with Thoreau, who wanted all relics of the past destroyed. America must disown the pattern of England, "an old gentleman who is travelling with a great deal of baggage, trumpery which has accumulated from long housekeeping, which he has not the courage to burn." In *Walden*, Thoreau expounded a social philosophy of "purifying destruction."[24]

Neglect of the past often implied considerable concern with the future. "Instead of moralising over magnificence in a process of decay," wrote the English globe-trotter Laurence Oliphant, the traveler in America must "watch resources in a process of development."[25] Not all Americans professed to share this interest; Emerson, it will be recalled,[26] rejected both the past and the future for the present world, and Henry James felt reduced to a present sandwiched between "an absent future and an absent past." But as James himself agreed, future prospects obsessed Americans in general: it was to make up for their rejected past that they had to invent "a magnificent compensatory future."[27] Separation from history evinced American commitment to what was yet to come. "Is it not better," asked St. John de Crèvecoeur, an eighteenth-century French visitor, "to occupy one's thinking with bright futures and new speculations . . . than to wander through the uncertain and questionable paths of antiquity, only to contemplate tottering ruins, demolished buildings, or the effects of devastating revolutions?"[28]

The disorder Americans saw in their primeval and newly cleared landscapes was another impetus to futurism; American scenery fired the imagination not with its appearance but with its potentialities. "Return in ten years and you will not recognize . . . this district, which today you probably find wild and savage," a New York State settler assured Crèvecoeur. "Our humble log houses will be replaced by fine dwellings. Our fields will be fenced in, and the stumps will have disappeared."[29] It was not always easy to recognize the immanent from the existing landscape. An English traveler in 1827 recounted that a mile outside Rochester, New York,

> we lost sight of every trace of human dwelling, or of human interference with nature in any shape. . . . We came to a spot where three or four men were employed in clearing out a street, as they declared, though any thing more unlike a street could not well be conceived. Nevertheless, the ground had been chalked out by the surveyors' stakes, and some speculators . . . found it necessary to open a street through the woods, to afford a line of communication with the rest of the village.[30]

A German visitor in the 1830s observed that "the Americans *love* their country, not, indeed, *as it is*, but *as it will be*. They do not love the land of their fathers; but are sincerely attached to that which their children are destined to inherit. They live in the future and make their country as they go on."[31] The uncultivated scene brought to mind what would happen rather than what had happened; the wilderness was admired not for itself, but for what could be done with it. The *tabula rasa* should spur Americans to greatness, as the oft-repeated lines implied:

> Though we boast no ancient towers,
> Where ivied streamers twine;
> The laurel lives upon our shores;
> The laurel, boy, is thine.[32]

Attachment to the future provided both a rationale and a substitute for the rejected past. But in derogating the present too, the emphasis on the future produced a cultural landscape that inspired little enduring devotion or interest. Americans often deferred environmental preferences, putting up with temporary makeshifts, building and farming like an army on the move. Thus they invested little that they did with enough care to survive as recognized heritages.

COPING WITH AMBIVALENCE

Opposing the "party of Hope," as Emerson called those who looked forward, was a "party of Memory," who yearned for a storied past.[33] Many Americans adopted both perspectives at one time or another. For all their patriotism, even those who rejected history often felt regret. Few entirely escaped the pull of the past. But because they felt its power, they were all the more determined to resist it. As spokesmen for the present and the future, they could not afford the corruption of nostalgia.

Given the aesthetic taste of the time, theirs was no easy task. To the romantic mind, historical associations were a prime factor in landscape and architecture as well as in painting and poetry. In America, as in Europe, Mme de Staël's *Corinne* expressed the conventional point of view: "The most beautiful landscapes of the world, if they evoke no memory, if they bear the mark of no notable event, are destitute of interest compared to historic lands."[34] Delineation of the past was a major focus of the fine arts. "What are the most esteemed paintings?" asked an American schoolbook of 1806. The correct answer was, "Those representing historical events."[35]

The raw, unfinished look of American landscapes frequently dismayed sensitive Americans home from visits to Europe. To them the uprooting of nature seemed harsh and ugly, the works of man brash and inadequate. Motley concluded that the absence of a "pictured, illuminated Past" left America with "a naked and impoverished appearance."[36] This was no mere bow toward romantic antiquity. It was typical of a thousand complaints that because America was all new it was too empty to live in, that it had "the beauty of a face without an expression, [because] . . . it wants the associations of tradition which are the soul and interest of scenery."[37] European historical depth fulfilled needs that American emptiness could never assuage.

The vital quality of the enduring past enchants the Hawthorne hero who sees, in an English country estate, "the life of each successive dweller . . . eked out with the lives of all who had hitherto lived there. 'The presence of the past' was a rare and successful contrivance for giving length, fulness, body, substance to this thin and frail matter of human life."[38] No new land would serve, noted N. P. Willis, for "the labor and the taste of successive generations can alone create such an Eden."[39]

Continuity and associations were salient themes to Americans enamored of European ruins. Piranesi's etchings of the ruins of Rome were popular throughout the United States. Longfellow rhapsodized over the ruined Alhambra as "wonderful in its fallen greatness"; the Colosseum enraptured Mrs. Hawthorne because it looked "hoary with the years that have passed." She disdained the Renaissance palazzi of Florence because their "ever-enduring newness" made them impossible to imagine as ruins: "They can never decay, and never appear old. . . . They always seem to be finished today, and not to belong to the past."[40]

Not all nostalgic yearnings were deeply felt. The sight of ruins often aroused entirely conventional sentiments, as when the historian Bancroft pretended to "intimately . . . commune with antiquity" and to hear "the small feeble voice, that comes from remote ages," or when Motley made fun of his own reactions to the storied Rhine.[41] To the European eye, ruins integrated past with present; to the American, ruins were literary and visual props, picturesque devices that evoked standard enthusiasms. The truly historical character of the Old World attracted only the rare American. Few shared James Russell Lowell's realization, expressed in 1851, that authentic, life-enhacing tradition required not simply a random collection of relics and ruins but also a comprehensive set of landscapes and townscapes in their past and present totality.[42] Indeed, historical awareness made some Americans "feel so foreign in their own country and century," as Stephen Spender observes of a later generation, "that they start treating history as though it were geography, themselves as though they could step out of the present into the past of their choice."[43]

Yet admiration for the past, however limited in scope, posed serious problems for many. Even propagandists for frontier and freedom sometimes relapsed. Jefferson, who advocated the sovereignty of the present generation, nonetheless adored the Maison Carré at Nîmes and designed Monticello in a classical mode. Thomas Cole, fresh from romanticizing the wilderness, could not bear the absence of traditional associations. Having renounced the Rhine, Cole recreated it on the wild shores of the Hudson, where he painted in temples, towers, and domes.[44] James Fenimore Cooper refused to romance over ruins, and celebrated wilderness virtues in his *Leatherstocking Tales*. But book sales made him wealthy enough to buy back, gothicize, and castellate his family home and become a country squire in Cooperstown, New York.[45] Hawthorne, who wished "the whole past might be swept away" and the burdensome Parthenon "burnt into lime," found it difficult to write in an unhistorical milieu, for "romance and poetry, like ivy, lichens, and wall-flowers, need Ruin to make them grow." Hawthorne exemplified the dilemma of sensitive Americans; his New England stories dwell on just those "shadows, antiquities, and gloomy and picturesque wrongs" that he elsewhere despises in favor of America's "common-place prosperity, in broad and simple daylight."[46]

The ambivalence points up both the charm of the past and its corruption. As American consul at Liverpool, Hawthorne viewed with scorn and pity his fellow countrymen who came to establish links with the past. He condemned "this diseased American appetite for English soil," yet sympathized with the impulse behind it. "I should like," he admitted, "to find a gravestone in one of those old churchyards, with my own name on it." The hero of *Doctor Grimshawe's Secret* renounces the rich past for the freer, if thinner, atmosphere of America's "poor tents of a day, inns of a night."[47] Even for Longfellow, European historical charms gave way to the duties of the American present. Nostalgia for the past, as he expressed it in *Hyperion*, was like "falling in love with one's own grandmother."[48]

Americans considered attachment to historical (that is, European) landscapes not merely wrong or foolish but immoral, unmanly, and unpatriotic. The theme of Old World evil *versus* New World innocence has many aspects; old European buildings, ruined or not, often symbolized the oppression, decadence, and tyranny the American founding fathers had supposedly thrown off. Nineteenth-century American worthies repeatedly advised young men to shun European corruptions and seductions. "Of all the errors which can possibly be committed in the education of youth, that of sending them to Europe is the most fatal," warned Jefferson.[49] "Please don't get expatriated," Longfellow enjoined a friend, for "life is not all cathedrals or ruined castles, and other theatrical properties in the Old World."[50] Mark Twain was more favorably impressed with Italy's depots and turnpikes than with its "vast museum of magnificence and misery," and he rebuked tourists for admiring ruins and castles. American schoolbooks regularly described Italy, architecture and people alike, as a vast ruin.[51] The faded frescoes of Rome sickened Hawthorne, and the durability of dirty buildings dating from Etruscan times made him feel that "all towns should be made capable of purification by fire . . . else they become the hereditary haunt of vermin and noisomeness."[52]

Not even the warmest admirers of European ruins wanted them in the American landscape. "It was quite pardonable in Horace Walpole and Sir Walter Scott to build gingerbread houses in imitation of robber barons and Bluebeard chieftains," a reviewer stated in 1846, "but there can be nothing more grotesque, more absurd, or more affected," than for an ordinary American, "who knows no more of the middle ages than they do of him, to erect for his family residence a gimcrack of a Gothic castle."[53]

Even prosaic, living European landscapes sometimes exhibited too strong a spirit of the past to suit American ways. Hawthorne found the English village unworthy of his countrymen.

> Rather than the monotony of sluggish ages, loitering on a village green, toiling in hereditary fields, listening to the parson's drone lengthened through centuries in the gray Norman church, let us welcome whatever change may come—change of place, social customs, political institutions, modes of worship—trusting that, if all present things shall vanish, they will but make room for better systems, and for a higher type of man to clothe his life in them, and to fling them off in turn.[54]

The American builder Andrew Jackson Downing found

> something touching and beautiful in the associations that grow up in . . . those old manor-houses and country halls of England, where, age after age, the descendants of one family have lived, and loved, and suffered, and died . . . sheltered by the same trees and guarded by the same walls. . . . But it is only an idyl, or only a delusion to us. It belongs to the past. . . . It is no more to be reanimated in the republic of the new world than the simple faith in the Virgin, which built the mighty cathedrals of the middle ages. It could only be reanimated at the sacrifice of the happiness of millions of free citizens.[55]

No American felt the pull of the past more acutely than Henry James. London and Paris had filled him with "nostalgic poison"; his strictures on the paucity of historical associations in America continued throughout his life. The charms and perils of historical atmosphere are most sharply etched in James's last novel, *The Sense of the Past*, whose young hero finds the American past "deplorably lacking intensity." He goes to take over a house in London, left him by an English cousin appreciative of his sense of the past—an old house full of "items of duration and evidence, all smoothed with service and charged with accumulated messages." The very air of London strikes him as marvelously permeated with antiquity: it was "signally not the light of freshness . . . in which the first children of nature might have begun to take notice"— emphatically not a New World aura. On the contrary, "ages, generations, inventions, corruptions had produced it, and it seemed, wherever it rested, to have filtered through the bed of history." The whole milieu comes alive for him with the stamp of "a conscious past, recognising no less than recognised." But the threat of this charmed past hovers about him from the start. To abandon oneself to the past is to succumb to evil. Through the medium of family portraits in his London house the hero travels back through time and becomes a captive of the previous century. He is conscious all the while of his existence in both eras, yet cannot definitively establish his identity in either. History too vividly evoked becomes an abode of nightmare, imprisoning will and repudiating morality. From this suffocating past James's hero barely manages to liberate himself and return to America.[56]

SUBSTITUTES FOR HISTORY

Americans who thus turned their backs on human history renounced not only romantic nostalgia but also a useful adjunct to national identity. Some warned that neglect of the past might vitiate American patriotism. Others, however, found surrogates for historical heritage among such elements as nature, American Indians, and classical prototypes.

NATURE

To many Americans the grandeur of their natural landscapes more than compensated for the lack of historical associations. American nature worship in the early decades of the Republic surpassed the Wordsworthian variety in solemnity and in its awareness of the truly wild. It was spurred on by the famous Buffon-Jefferson controversy over the relative size and potency of Old and New World fauna and flora. It combined a utilitarian zeal in transforming the wilderness with a romantic affirmation of nature's spirituality.[57] What is pertinent here is that Americans consciously substituted nature for history and infused it with historical attributes. Cole and other painters viewed the trunks of dead trees as organic ruins; to travelers on the Hudson, the features of primeval nature seemed analogues of European architectural relics. The aesthetic metaphor was later transferred to the mountain West; "the very idea of the Gothic style of architecture," mused Ferdinand V. Hayden at Yellowstone, might well have "been caught from such carvings of Nature."[58]

Nature served Americans as an ideal type of tradition, older than the human past, untainted with human follies and crimes, and uniquely American in its scenic grandeur. By the early nineteenth century many considered wilderness scenery morally superior to history's stage sets. With Fenno Hoffman, they preferred a "hoary oak" to a "mouldering column" and contrasted Europe's "temples which Roman robbers have reared" and "towers in which feudal oppression has fortified itself" unfavorably with America's "deep forests which the eye of God has alone pervaded."[59]

The notion of American nature as better, older, and purer than European history, as displayed in its monuments, was exemplified by Frederick Jackson Turner's 1884 essay, "Architecture through Oppression." Unlike Europeans, Americans needed no "artificial" palaces and cathedrals—symbols of Old World aristocratic oppression—for "in America we have giant cathedrals, whose spires are moss-clad pines, whose frescos are painted on the sky and mountain wall, and whose music surges through the leafy aisles in the deep toned bass of cataracts."[60] The language betrays the lingering need to humanize nature and to praise scenery in terms evocative of human structures and history. But ultimately nature in America demonstrated that God built better than men.

The difference between historical and natural scenic ideals is exemplified in statements by Thomas Cole, founder of the Hudson River School, America's first self-conscious wilderness aesthetic, and by William Cullen Bryant. Cole defended American scenery against "those who through ignorance or prejudice strive to maintain . . . that it is rude without picturesqueness, and monotonous without sublimity—that being destitute of those vestiges of antiquity, whose associations so strongly affect the mind, it may not be compared with European scenery." But Cole himself was prey to the Old World's blandishments and had not yet defined the virtues of the New. Before his first trip back to Europe in 1829, he decided to visit Niagara Falls for "a 'last, lingering look' at our wild scenery. I shall endeavour to impress its features so strongly on my mind that, in the midst of the fine scenery of other countries, their grand and beautiful peculiarities shall not be erased."[61]

A year later, in an album of landscape scenes by Cole and others, Bryant enumerates some of those "grand and beautiful peculiarities."

> One of the most striking is the absence of those tamings and softenings of cultivation, continued for ages, which, while they change the general face of the landscape, at the same time break up the unity of its effect. . . . Foreigners who have visited our country, particularly in the mountainous parts, have spoken of a far-spread wildness, a look as if the new world was fresher from the hand of him who made it, . . . of something which . . . suggested the idea of unity and immensity, and abstracting the mind from the associations of human agency, carried it up to the idea of a mightier power, and to the great mystery of the origin of things.[62]

The historical landscapes of Europe had such a multiplicity of features that they tended to be diffuse and heterogeneous. By contrast, American natural landscapes were unified, integrated, and coherent. And they suggested a higher order of creativity.

In deifying nature, Americans rejected the proximate for the more remote past, viewing antiquity as eternity rather than as change. They dismissed history to embrace prehistory; the primeval quality of American nature was invoked again and again. The immensity of the Blue

Ridge mountains induced Jefferson to speculate on the eons required to form them.[63] The excavation of a mastodon in Ohio evoked national enthusiasm as evidence of American zoological antiquity. Thoreau downgraded the merely old, by contrast with the truly ancient: the historical past was degenerate, whereas primitive nature was strong, savage, pure, and free.[64] Americans frequently compared the emotional impact of the wilderness with that of ruins. The Florentine archives gave Richard Henry Wilde, a Georgia lawyer and littérateur, the same sense of his "own insignificance and the enduring solitude of the ages" that he had felt while on American wilderness bivouacs.[65] Florida's Lake Worth struck Henry James as older than the Nile in that the American landscape seemed *previous* to any other, "with the impression of History all yet to be made."[66]

INDIANS

American Indians were "prehistoric" for nineteenth-century Americans in much the same way as was nature itself. Once Indians ceased to pose an immediate threat, Americans happily cited the antiquity and nonhistorical character of Indian occupance to highlight the archaic uniqueness of the unchronicled American past. The first archaeological study of the Indian mound builders exemplified this theme. Thanks to E. G. Squier's and E. H. Davis's magnificent *Ancient Monuments of the Mississippi Valley* (1848), a reviewer noted, Americans no longer need suffer

> the reproach [of] the excessive modernness and newness of our country . . . described over and over again by foreign and native journals, as being bare of old associations as though it had been made by a journeyman potterer day before yesterday. . . . We find we have here, what no other nation on the known globe can claim: a perfect union of the past and present; the vigor of a nation just born walking over the hallowed ashes of a race whose history is too early for a record, and surrounded by the living forms of a people hovering between the two.[67]

When not seen as primeval, Indians were identified with the Greeks and Romans. Eighteenth-century American writers and painters regularly portrayed Indians in tunics and togas and with classical visages. In the nineteenth century, James Fenimore Cooper's Indians were eagle-eyed, hawk-nosed, of "Grecian" proportions. With such antiquity close at hand, why bother with the Old World past? Far better for Americans to study their Indians than to read books about the Greeks. A few months among the Hurons, declared the Indian missionary J. F. Lafitau, taught him more about the Trojan War than all the works of classical scholarship.[68]

CLASSICAL PROTOTYPES

Americans' admiration for classical forms and Greek and Roman heroes might seem to belie their disdain for history. But they revered first Rome and then Greece not in historical but in ideal terms, as prototypes for their own virtues. Few American classical buildings, for example, were literal copies of Roman or Greek forms. Rather, classical inspiration was fluid and free: scholarship and accuracy were of little consequence, materials were used regardless of stylistic appropriateness, and eclecticism flourished—all styles were mixed. It was because they viewed the past unhistorically, as revealing only constant and universal principles of human nature, that American minds could, in Commager's phrase, "move with ease from Greece and Rome to China or Peru."[69]

British travelers professed outrage that Americans made everything—privy and prison, theater and church, custom house and state capitol—look like a Greek temple. Americans saw nothing wrong with this. Just because the Greeks had not used the temple style in domestic architecture did not mean that Americans should desist. To them the classical form denoted high culture, proof that they were properly taming and domesticating the wilderness. They were less concerned with the iconographic implications of Greek temples than with stamping "civilization" on their piece of wilderness with a standard temple facade and precut columns.[70]

Builders' manuals make it clear that reverence for antiquity as such played no part in American period taste, even when the appearance of age was desired. "Oak . . . will grow dark with age if left unvarnished . . . ; when dark and old it is most valued in Europe," noted one popular expert. "But what is the use of waiting for oak to grow dark when we can produce the same effect and better furniture with walnut?"[71] Not until the end of the nineteenth century did American antiquarians begin to worry about period correctness and faithfulness to original models.

RETURNING TO THE PAST

As the nineteenth century wore on, Americans increasingly commemorated and informed themselves about the life and times of the Founding Fathers. State, county, and village historical societies produced and preserved voluminous collections of documents. Thousands of town histories, guidebooks, atlases, and gazetteers detailed the antecedents and fortunes of local families. Some of these were little more than genealogies and panegyric sketches. But others made accessible an enormous amount of detailed historical information, bringing to life countless scenes from the past.[72]

Antiquarian zeal of this type was seldom, however, an expression of nostalgia. Not until Americans became generally dissatisfied with the present did they begin to long for the past as such, to revere history for its own sake, and to fantasize a Colonial or Revolutionary golden age. There was no overnight *volte-face* from faith in progress to a passion for the past. The generation before Emerson and Thoreau counted many exemplars of nostalgia, whereas some who scoff at antiques and antiquities may still be found. But the balance began to shift about the time of the Revolutionary centennial. Up to then most Americans were modernists: they viewed the past as an antiquated era which they felt fortunate to have left behind. By the 1880s and 1890s a new note was being heard; the past was in some respects better than the present. "The party of Memory" for the first time began to outvote "the party of Hope."

Several events played a role in this shift. One was the Civil War and its aftermath, four years of carnage and a decade of frustrating Reconstruction. Albums memorializing the Northern and Southern dead and depicting the battlefield were *de rigueur* in every decent home. But they also reminded many of the earlier Revolutionary struggle, more hopeful, less sanguinary, and imbued with the attractive ambience of ancient myth. Old America *à la* Currier and Ives won favor against both the present and Civil War scenes. Thus postwar disillusion inspired nostalgia for the supposedly simpler, happier scenes of the past.[73]

A second event was the Centennial itself. A hundred years is an occasion in the life of any nation, inclining celebrants to self-conscious awareness of their own role in history. The Philadelphia exhibition made few formal references to history; the future still attracted more interest than the past.[74] Yet the Centennial was an appropriate moment to assess America's achievements, and the process was conducive to nostalgia. Few American historians surveying that eventful century did not adjudge the earlier decades more fruitful, less riven by dissension, altogether more admirable than the later ones. In the beginning, all was progress: the painless acquisition of great Western territories, the settlement of the trans-Allegheny frontier, the clearing and cultivation of the wilderness, the universal growth of towns and culture and prosperity. But from about the mid-century American destiny appeared to take a more somber turn. Territorial conquests were made at the cost of external enmities, sectional passions were exacerbated by slavery and the gathering storm of Civil War, and scarcely less stormy antagonisms were engendered by expanding industrial complexes. Initially virtuous, high-minded, individualistic, America seemed to have become corrupt, acquisitive, imperialistic. No wonder that some looked back with nostalgic regret at the vanished America of their forebears. This was the view underlying the Ipswich Historical Society's plea for preserving the old Whipple House as "a link that binds us to the remote Past and to a solemn and earnest manner of living, quite in contrast with much in our modern life."[75]

Besides these events, two parallel processes disillusioned Americans with the present and led them to seek refuge in the past. One was industrialization; the other was immigration from Eastern and Southern Europe. Anti-urban sentiment, though by no means solely American, has been a potent theme in American thought. It came into sharp conflict with reality during the last decades of the nineteenth century, when Americans first realized that the agrarian image of the good life, purveyed since Jefferson, was remote from the way of life led by most. And industrialization made urban living conditions manifestly more noisome and odious than before. The growth of the cities and the decline of rural America arrayed present-day evils against past virtues.[76]

Closely linked with the cities were the immigrants who flocked into them. Cultural differences and sheer numbers distinguished the late nineteenth-century newcomers from previous immigrants. Earlier settlers from Britain and Germany had been more easily assimilated. The Irish in the 1840s and 1850s alarmed many Yankees on account of their Catholicism, their dearth of education, their supposed clannishness, and their lack of rural attachment. Yet at least they were numerically within bounds and spoke English, so that assimilation was not out of the question. The millions of immigrants from Southern and Eastern Europe were formidably unlike older Americans in religion, language, family patterns, diet, expectations in life—all seemingly uncouth and unassimilable. And the cities of the Eastern seaboard and the Middle West soon took on their exotic flavor.[77]

Many older, or antecedent, Americans retreated into a history they considered uniquely their own. They viewed the Colonial past as an exclusive WASP heritage and, in the words of Wendell D. Garrett, spoke of that "vanished era" as "pure American, without a drop of admixture of the blood of recent immigration."[78] The past came to be seen as an escape from the horrid present—a present dominated by "aliens" in America. This stance reversed attitudes not only toward the past in general, but toward the British heritage, which was no longer disparaged but adulated. Anglomania spread outward from its Boston hearth, where it gathered strength as an anti-Irish talisman. Early America came to be viewed as a branch of the British nation, decently Protestant, well-behaved, and charmingly quaint. The Revolution had become an unimportant if not embarrassing interlude, a brief disruption of the closest of bonds. During the 1880s and 1890s nearly all the Sons, Daughters, Dames, and other commemorative genealogical societies originated, with Anglo-Saxon origins a *sine qua non* of admittance.

In focusing especially on the tangible past, however, the new nostalgists resembled their American predecessors. As early preservationists had sought to inculcate patriotism by setting aside the homes of important American heroes, so at the turn of the century some devotees of the old conceived historic buildings as a device for Americanizing immigrants. Most, however, saw the old less as a pot for melting in than as a personal refuge; and they began to surround themselves with what they fancied to be the landscapes, houses, rooms, and furnishings of their ancestors. Household décor emulated colonial models. The collecting of antiques became a passion that soon outran the resources of the past.[79]

*   *   *

Men in one epoch may resolutely set their faces against the past; men of the next may venerate that previous era and deplore their predecessors' heedless neglect. The ebb and flow of historical self-awareness, of anachronistic recognition, of concern with heritage are themselves historically causal. We are inescapably the creatures of the past we have come through, including its own attitudes toward previous pasts.

In breaking old bonds and making new ones, nations rewrite their history, forgetting much, denying more, and replacing past perspectives with new national images and explanations. Jeffersonians denied the past altogether: they saw history as an enemy and distinguished themselves from Europeans in seeking to be free from any past. "Probably no other civilised nation has at any period . . . so completely thrown off its allegiance to the past as the American," stated a national journal in 1842. "The whole essay of our national life and legislation has been a prolonged protest against the dominion of antiquity in any form whatsoever."[80]

This view was characteristic of the time. It has survived as a stereotype into the present but now reflects only half of the truth. "The international image of America is one of organized impatience," notes a modern commentator. "Away with the old, the obsolete and merely picturesque!" But in fact he regards the American past as "marvelously and extravagantly preserved."[81] According to a recent British cross-country traveler, "the West behaves like a pioneer country which knows it is present at its own birth"; restoring the Front Street saloon in Dodge City, Kansas, "is as if William Rufus had already begun to preserve the site of the Battle of Hastings."[82]

To keep up with the demand for memorabilia from the past, we have constantly brought "antiquity" closer and closer to our own time—at first antiques had to be at least a hundred years old, later the limit was fifty years, today anything even twenty years old is a cherished artifact, and nostalgia is for last week. Americans have expanded their sense of the past by incorporating within it things that have scarcely ceased to breathe.

Since the first Centennial, Americans have more and more turned back to the past. Disenchantment with the present, nostalgia for romanticized childhoods and wildernesses, fear of Armageddon, revulsion against the pace of change—these are some of the forces underlying that return. But the past so eagerly sought is frequently missing, having perished of neglect, of inanition, or of willful destruction in the name of progress. Where we can no longer preserve or restore, we reconstruct or invent the vanished past. Many of our venerated objects, buildings, and landscapes are newly coined or borrowed to meet the public demand for heritage. "Antiquing" has become a national pastime. Preservation and restoration are activities as virtuous as the ecological movement and, indeed, are often confused with it—nostalgia as human ecology.[83]

The comments of British passengers on the last trip of the famed *Brighton Belle*, in May of 1972, stress the difference between English and American historical needs and styles.

> It's the end of a tradition. We shouldn't throw away our traditions like that. Soon we won't have any left. And where will it go. The trains will probably go to America. . . . I suppose they'll run her back and forth across London Bloody Bridge in Arizona. . . . You Yanks buy everything. Well, you need tradition over there, don't you?[84]

The very manner in which Americans now cherish the tangible past betrays antihistorical habits of thought. Much architectural preservation is avowedly antiquarian; the valued past is merely museumized, not integrated with the present; ancestral virtues and defects are portentously evaluated.[85] These patterns all reflect continued dependence on the present and disengagement from the past. Disregard for history is manifest in American environmental action, too. The passage of seventy years has not outdated Henry James's judgment of the American scene as bleak and empty, thin and transient. It is not only the present-day landscape that looks temporary and unfinished, but also those memorabilia whose paucity James deplored. For many Americans the past is still only a foreign body, alien and intrusive in the great national landscape of today and a positive impediment to realizing the greater creations of tomorrow.

NOTES

1. John K. Wright, "On Medievalism and Watersheds in the History of American Geography," in *Human Nature in Geography* (Cambridge: Harvard University Press, 1966), pp. 161, 166.
2. George P. Marsh, *The Goths in New-England* (Middlebury, Vt.: J. Cobb, 1843), p. 33. See David Lowenthal, *George Perkins Marsh, Versatile Vermonter* (New York: Columbia University Press, 1958), pp. 59, 101, 141.
3. Jefferson to John W. Eppes, June 24, 1813; Jefferson to Samuel Kercheval, July 12, 1816; Jefferson to Thomas Earle, Sept. 24, 1823; in *The Writings of Thomas Jefferson*, Albert Ellery Bergh, ed., 20 vols. (Washington: Thomas Jefferson Memorial Association, 1907), 13:270–71, 15:42–43, 15:470.
4. Daniel J. Boorstin, *The Lost World of Thomas Jefferson* (Boston: Beacon Press, 1960), pp. 206–10; Roscoe Pound, *The Formative Period of American Law* (Boston: Little Brown, 1938), pp. 7–8, 144–45. American opposition to historical precedent was encouraged by Jeremy Bentham, who urged Americans "to shut our ports against the Common Law, as we would against the plague" (quoted in Daniel J. Boorstin, *The Americans: The National Experience* [New York: Random House, Vintage Books, 1967], p. 36).
5. R. W. B. Lewis, *The American Adam: Innocence, Tragedy, and Tradition in the Nineteenth Century* (Chicago: University of Chicago Press, Phoenix Books, 1955), pp. 5, 7; see also pp. 54–76; and Wright, "What's 'American' about American Geography," in his *Human Nature in Geography*, p. 131.
6. Emerson, *The Natural History of Intellect and Other Papers* (1893), *in The Complete Works of Ralph Waldo Emerson*, Century ed., 12 vols. (Boston and New York: Houghton Mifflin, 1912), 12:62; Quentin Anderson, *The Imperial Self: An Essay in American Literary and Cultural History* (New York: Alfred A. Knopf, 1971), pp. 228–29.
7. Henry David Thoreau, *Walden and Other Writings* (1854) (New York: Random House, Modern Library, 1937), p. 8. See also C. Vann Woodward, "The Future of the Past," *American Historical Review* 75 (1970):711–26.
8. Alexis de Tocqueville, *Democracy in America* (1835), trans. Henry Reeve, 2 vols. (New York: Alfred A. Knopf, Vintage Books, 1945), 2:104–6.
9. "The Former, Present and Future Prospects of America," *Columbian* 1 (January 1887):83–86, quoted in David D. Van Tassell, *Recording America's Past: An Interpretation of the Development of Historical Studies in America 1607–1884* (Chicago: University of Chicago Press, 1960), p. 45. See also Stow Per-

sons, "Progress and the Organic Cycle in Eighteenth-Century America," *American Quarterly* 6 (1954):147–63.

10. Marsh, *The Goths in New-England*, p. 7.

11. "The American Naval Chronicle," *Analectic Magazine* 6 (1815):249, quoted in J. Mishell George, "James Kirke Paulding, a Literary Nationalist," M.A. thesis, Columbia University, 1941, p. 96.

12. *Memoir, at the Celebration of the Completion of the New York Canals* (New York: Corporation of New York, 1825), pp. 77–78.

13. Quoted in Lewis, *American Adam*, p. 42. See also Boorstin, *Lost World of Jefferson*, p. 169.

14. Quoted in Lewis, *American Adam*, p. 5.

15. Quoted in Henry Steele Commager, *The Search for a Usable Past and Other Essays in Historiography* (New York: Alfred A. Knopf, 1967), p. 8.

16. *The Rights of Man* (1791–92), in *The Complete Writings of Thomas Paine*, Philip S. Foner, ed., 2 vols. (New York: Citadel Press, 1945), 1:376.

17. "Works and Days," in *Society and Solitude* (1870), in *Complete Works*, 7:177; "The American Scholar" (1837), in *The Portable Emerson* (New York: Viking Press, 1946), p. 43.

18. James, *The American Scene* (1907) (Bloomington: Indiana University Press, 1968), p. 161.

19. Nathaniel Hawthorne, *The House of the Seven Gables* (1852) (New York: Washington Square Press, 1940), pp. 296, 298, 207. See also Anderson, *The Imperial Self*, p. 33.

20. George Wharton, quoted in Perry Miller, *The Life of the Mind in America from the Revolution to the Civil War* (New York: Harcourt, Brace and World, 1965), p. 303.

21. Emerson, "Agriculture of Massachusetts," in his *Natural History of Intellect*, pp. 360–61. See also John A. Kouwenhoven, *Made in America: The Arts in Modern American Civilization* (New York: Doubleday, 1948), p. 49.

22. Kouwenhoven, *Made in America*, pp. 49–59; Boorstin, *The Americans*, pp. 148–52; Walker Field, "A Re-examination into the Invention of the Balloon Frame," *Journal of the American Society of Architectural Historians* 2 (1942):3–29.

23. Hawthorne, *House of the Seven Gables*, p. 207. This image, like Hawthorne's later "Earth's Holocaust," a fable of a vast prairie bonfire of all the world's "wornout trumpery," may have come from William Bartram's description of an American Indian "busking" ceremony: "they collect all their worn-out cloaths and other despicable things, sweep and cleanse their houses, squares, and the whole town, of their filth, which with all the remaining grain and other old provisions, they cast together into one common heap, and consume it with fire" (Bartram, *Travels through North and South Carolina . . .* [1791], Mark Van Doren, ed. [New York: Dover Publications, n.d.], p. 399; see also "Earth's Holocaust" [1844], in *Complete Works of Nathaniel Hawthorne*, Riverside ed., 13 vols. [London: Kegan, Paul, Trench, 1883], 2:430).

24. *Walden*, pp. 60–61.

25. Laurence Oliphant, *Minnesota and the Far West* (Edinburgh and London: William Blackwood & Sons, 1855), p. 1.

26. "American Scholar," p. 43.
27. *The American Scene*, pp. 160–61.
28. Michel-Guillaume St. Jean [J. Hector St. John] de Crèvecoeur, *Journey into Northern Pennsylvania and the State of New York* (1801), trans. Clarissa S. Bostelmann (Ann Arbor: University of Michigan Press, 1964), p. 456.
29. Ibid., p. 493.
30. Basil Hall, *Travels in North America, in the Years 1827 and 1828*, 3 vols. (Edinburgh: Cadell, 1830), 1:163–64.
31. Francis J. Grund, *The Americans in Their Moral, Social, and Political Relations*, 2 vols. (London: Longman, 1837), 2:263–64. See David Lowenthal, "The American Scene," *Geographical Review* 58 (1968):61–88.
32. Joseph Bartlett Burleigh, *The Thinker, a Moral Reader . . . designed to arouse the minds of youth, and to inculcate pure and noble principles*. Part 1 (1855), p. 122; quoted in Ruth Miller Elson, *Guardians of Tradition: American Schoolbooks of the Nineteenth Century* (Lincoln: University of Nebraska Press, 1964), p. 36.
33. "Historic Notes of Life and Letters in New England" (*Atlantic Monthly*, 1883), in *The Portable Emerson*, p. 514; Lewis, *American Adam*, pp. 7–8.
34. Germaine Necker de Staël, *Corinne, ou l'Italie* (1807), 2 vols. (Paris: Treuttel et Wurtz, 1836), 1:322.
35. Charles Peirce, *The Arts and Sciences Abridged . . .* (1806), quoted in Elson, *Guardians of Tradition*, p. 233. On the paucity of subject matter suitable for American painters, see Neil Harris, *The Artist in American Society: The Formative Years, 1790–1860* (New York: George Braziller, 1966), pp. 15, 84–86.
36. [John Lothrop Motley], "Polity of the Puritans," *North American Review* 69 (1849):493–94. See also Cushing Strout, *The American Image of the Old World* (New York: Harper and Row, 1963), pp. 74–85; and David Levin, *History as Romantic Art: Bancroft, Prescott, Motley, and Parkman* (Stanford, Calif.: Stanford University Press, 1959), pp. 7–9.
37. "On Poetry in Its Relation to Our Age and Country," *Prose* 1:24, quoted in William Cullen Bryant II, "Poetry and Painting: A Love Affair of Long Ago," *American Quarterly* 22 (1970):875.
38. *Doctor Grimshawe's Secret: A Romance* (1882), in *Complete Works*, 13:229.
39. *Pencillings by the Way; the Complete Works of Nathaniel Parker Willis* (1848), quoted in Strout, *American Image*, p. 84.
40. Henry Wadsworth Longfellow, *Outre-Mer and Driftwood* (1835), in *Complete Poetical and Prose Works*, Riverside ed., 11 vols. (London: Geo. Rutledge & Sons, 1886–93), 1:227; Sophia Hawthorne, *Notes on England and Italy* (New York: Putnam, 1870), pp. 407–8. Equally genuine were Henry Ward Beecher's tears on beholding Kenilworth Castle, for "I had never in my life seen an *old* building. I had never seen a ruin" (*Star Papers; or, Experiences of Art and Nature* [New York, 1855], p. 57, quoted in Harris, *Artist in American Society*, p. 129). On Piranesi in America, see Howard Mumford Jones, *O Strange New World; American Culture: The Formative Years* (New York: Viking Press, 1964), p. 236.
41. George Bancroft to Andrews Norton, Jan. 9, 1819, Bancroft Papers, Massachu-

setts Historical Society, quoted in Levin, *History as Romantic Art*, p. 7; Motley to his parents, Aug. 12, 1832, in *The Correspondence of John Lothrop Motley*, George W. Curtis, ed., 2 vols. (New York: Harper & Bros., 1889), 1:24–26.

42. "A Few Bits of Roman Mosaic" (1854), *Literary Essays*, in *Lowell's Prose Works* (Boston: Houghton Mifflin, 1913), 1:211–13. See also Lewis, *American Adam*, pp. 189–91.

43. Stephen Spender, *Love-Hate Relations: A Study of Anglo-American Sensibilities* (London: Hamish Hamilton, 1974), p. 121.

44. Elliot S. Vesell, "Introduction," in Louis Legrand Noble, *The Life and Works of Thomas Cole* (1853), Elliott S. Vesell, ed. (Cambridge: Harvard University Press, 1964), p. xxiii; Roderick Nash, *Wilderness and the American Mind* (New Haven: Yale University Press, 1967), pp. 78–82.

45. James Fenimore Cooper, *Notions of the Americans, Picked Up by a Travelling Bachelor*, 2 vols. (London: Henry Colburn, 1828); *Gleanings in Europe, by an American*, 2 vols. (Philadelphia: Carey, Lea & Blanchard, 1837). See also Van Wyck Brooks, *The World of Washington Irving* (Philadelphia: Blakiston, 1945), pp. 421–25.

46. Hawthorne, Sept. 29, 1855, March 27, 1856, *English Notebooks*, Randall Steward, ed. (New York: Modern Language Association of America, 1941), pp. 243, 294; *The Marble Faun: or, the Romance of Monte Beni* (1859), in *Works of Nathaniel Hawthorne*, Centenary ed. (Columbus: Ohio State University Press, 1962–72), 11:3, Preface. See also Commager, *Search for a Usable Past*, pp. 5–6; Kouwenhoven, *Made in America*, pp. 151–68.

47. "Consular Experiences," in *Our Old Home: A Series of English Sketches* (1862), in *Works*, 5:20; Hawthorne, cited in James T. Fields, *Yesterdays with Authors* (1882), p. 74, quoted in Randall Stewart, "Introduction," *English Notebooks*, p. xxxviii; *Doctor Grimshawe's Secret*, 13:230.

48. Longfellow, *Hyperion* (1839), in *Complete Works*, 2:139.

49. To Maury Walker, Aug. 19, 1795, in *The Papers of Thomas Jefferson*, J. P. Boyd, ed. (Princeton: Princeton University Press), 8:409.

50. To Louise Chandler Moulton, quoted in Edward Wagenknecht, *Henry Wadsworth Longfellow* (New York: Oxford University Press, 1966), p. 135.

51. Mark Twain, *The Innocents Abroad* (1869) (New York: New American Library, 1966), pp. 182–85; Elson, *Guardians of Tradition*, p. 150. Some still condemn antiquity viewing abroad as immoral and un-American. A typical tirade against tours of chateaus and other remains of "an idiotic class system . . . cobwebs, cobblestones, mustiness and decay" urges that we "inspect today's–not yesterday's, not ruined, not medieval–farms and shops" (R. L. Duffus, "Still 'The Innocents Abroad,'" *New York Times Magazine*, Aug. 2, 1959, pp. 14, 26).

52. *The French and Italian Notebooks*, III, Norman Holmes Pearson, ed. (Ph.D. diss., Yale University, 1941), pp. 603–4, quoted in Strout, *American Image*, pp. 91–92.

53. Review of work of W. H. Ranlett (collectively published as *The American Architect*), in *The New York Mirror*, Oct. 17, 1846, quoted in Talbot Hamlin, *Greek Revival Architecture in America* (1944) (New York: Dover Publications, 1964), p. 325.

54. Hawthorne, "Leamington Spa," in *Our Old Home*, p. 60.

55. A. J. Downing, *The Architecture of Country Houses* (1850) (New York: Dover Publications, 1969), pp. 268–69.

56. James, *The Reverberator, and Other Tales* (1888), in *Novels and Tales*, New York ed., 26 vols. (London: Macmillan, 1908), 13:195; *The Sense of the Past* (New York: Charles Scribner's Sons, 1917), quotations on pp. 33, 66, and 65.

57. See John K. Wright, "Notes on Measuring and Counting in Early American Geography," in his *Human Nature in Geography*, pp. 235–37; Perry Miller, *Errand into the Wilderness* (Cambridge: Harvard University Press, 1956), pp. 211–12; Percy G. Adams, *Travelers and Travel Liars 1660–1800* (Berkeley and Los Angeles: University of California Press, 1962), pp. 182–85; Lowenthal, "American Scene," pp. 62–65.

58. Quoted in William Cullen Bryant, ed., *Picturesque America; or, The Land We Live In*, 2 vols. (New York: D. Appleton, 1872), 1:300. See also Paul Shepard, "Dead Cities in the American West," *Landscape* 6.2 (1956–57):25–28; Wallace Stegner, *Beyond the Hundredth Meridian: John Wesley Powell and the Second Opening of the West* (Boston: Houghton Mifflin, 1954), pp. 170–73; David Lowenthal, "Recreation Habits and Values: Implications for Landscape Quality," in *Challenge for Survival: Land, Air, and Water for Man in Megalopolis*, Pierre Dansereau, ed. (New York: Columbia University Press, 1970), pp. 103–17. For Cole and the Hudson, see Paul Shepard, *Man in the Landscape: A Historic View of the Esthetics of Nature* (New York: Alfred A. Knopf, 1967), pp. 185–86.

59. [Charles Fenno Hoffman], *A Winter in the West*, 2 vols. (New York: Harper & Bros., 1835), 1:195–96.

60. In *University Press* 15 (June 21, 1884):12, quoted in William Coleman, "Science and Symbol in the Turner Hypothesis," *American Historical Review* 62 (1966):46.

61. "Essay on American Scenery," *American Monthly Magazine*, n.s. 7 (1836):4, quoted in William Cullen Bryant II, "Poetry and Painting," p. 875; Cole to Robert Gilmor, April 26, 1829, in Noble, *Thomas Cole*, p. 72.

62. *The American Landscape* (1830), p. 510, cited in Bryant, "Poetry and Painting," pp. 864–65.

63. Jefferson, *Notes on the State of Virginia* (1787), William Peden, ed. (Chapel Hill: University of North Carolina Press, 1955), pp. 18–19.

64. Thoreau, *A Week on the Concord and Merrimack Rivers* (1849) (New York: New American Library, 1961), pp. 55–56.

65. Wilde (1835), in William R. Taylor, *Cavalier and Yankee: The Old South and American National Character* (New York: Braziller, 1961), p. 27.

66. *American Scene*, p. 462. See also Donald Emerson, "Henry James: A Sentimental Tourist and Restless Analyst," *Transactions of the Wisconsin Academy of Sciences* 52 (1963):17–24.

67. "The Western Mound Builders," *Literary World* 3 (1848):767–68, quoted in William Stanton, *The Leopard's Spots: Scientific Attitudes toward Race in America, 1815–59* (Chicago: University of Chicago Press, 1960), p. 85.

68. Joseph François Lafitau, *Moeurs des sauvages ameriquains, comparées aux moeurs*

des premiers temps, 2 vols. (Paris, 1724), cited in Henri Baudet, *Paradise on Earth: Some Thoughts on European Images of Non-European Man*, trans. Elizabeth Wentholt (New Haven: Yale University Press, 1965), pp. 45, 50. See also Percy G. Adams, *Travelers and Travel Liars*, p. 187.

69. Henry Steele Commager, "The Past as an Extension of the Present," *Proceedings of the American Antiquarian Society*, vol. 79, pt. 1 (1969), p. 20. See also Hamlin, *Greek Revival Architecture*, pp. 330–35; E. P. Richardson, *Painting in America: The Story of 450 Years* (New York: Crowell, 1956), pp. 86–89, 93.

70. New York correspondent of *Architectural Magazine* (London, December 1834), quoted in Alan Gowans, *Images of American Living: Four Centuries of Architecture and Furniture as Cultural Expression* (Philadelphia and New York: J. B. Lippincott, 1964), p. 270; John Buchman, "Owego Architecture: Greek Revival in a Pioneer Town," *Journal of the Society of Architectural Historians* 25 (1966):215–21.

71. Samuel Sloane, *Homestead Architecture* (Philadelphia, 1867), pp. 311ff., quoted in Gowans, *Images of American Living*, p. 338.

72. Van Tassell, *Recording America's Past*, pp. 95–110.

73. Merle Curti, *The Roots of American Loyalty* (New York: Columbia University Press, 1946), p. 191; Gowans, *Images of American Living*, p. 352; Russell Lynes, *The Tastemakers* (New York: Grossett & Dunlap, 1954), pp. 67–70.

74. John Brinckerhoff Jackson, *American Space: The Centennial Years, 1865–1876* (New York: W. W. Norton, 1972), pp. 104–5.

75. Thomas F. Waters, in *Ipswich Historical Society Publication* 6, p. 8, quoted in Charles B. Hosmer, Jr., *Presence of the Past: A History of the Preservation Movement in the United States before Williamsburg* (New York: Putnam, 1965), p. 113. For the general malaise, see Elson, *Guardians of Tradition*, pp. 27–28; Henry F. May, *The End of American Innocence* (New York: Alfred A. Knopf, 1959), pp. 44–45.

76. Strout, *American Image*, pp. 135–38; Samuel P. Hays, *The Response to Industrialism, 1885–1914* (Chicago: University of Chicago Press, 1957).

77. John Higham, *Strangers on the Land: Patterns of American Nativism, 1860–1925* (New Brunswick: Rutgers University Press, 1955). For a typical plea to return to rural Anglo-Saxon virtues in the face of immigration, industrialism, and Roman Catholicism, see Joseph Strong, *Our Country* (1886), Jurgen Herbst, ed. (Cambridge: Harvard University Press, 1963).

78. Wendell D. Garrett, "The Required Past: The Impulse to Collect American Antiques, 1890–1917," MS, 1965.

79. Hosmer, *Presence of the Past*, pp. 138, 299; Curti, *Roots of American Loyalty*, pp. 134, 191–94; Van Tassell, *Recording America's Past*, p. 102.

80. *Democratic Review* (1842), quoted in Lewis, *American Adam*, p. 159.

81. Patrick O'Donovan, "The Practical Idealists," in *The United States* (New York: Time, Inc., Life World Library, 1965).

82. T. H. White, *America at Last: The American Journal of T. H. White* (New York: Putnam, 1965), p. 112.

83. David Lowenthal, "Past Time, Present Place: Landscape and Memory," *Geographical Review* 65 (1975):1–36.

84. Quoted in Alvin Shuster, "Last Trip for Famed British Train," *New York Times*, May 2, 1972, p. 4.
85. David Lowenthal, "The American Way of History," *Columbia University Forum* 9.3 (1966):27–32.

5

The Great American
Desert in the American Mind:
The Historiography of a
Geographical Notion

MARTYN J. BOWDEN

"The Seven Banes of Geography" surely must include erroneous or misleading *idées fixes*. . . . An *idée fixe* is an idea (whether true or false,
helpful or misleading) that has "set" like concrete and is no longer
amenable to change in the light of factual evidence or rational thought.

John K. Wright[1]

THE HISTORY OF GEOGRAPHICAL THOUGHT is studded with *idées fixes*, true
and false. One of these is the recent academic notion that for fifty years
(1820–70) the American public believed that a Great American Desert
existed east of the Rockies. The same fixed idea of this earlier view was
held by many better-educated Americans in the 1880s and 1890s. The
fixed idea is false because the desert belief was far from universally held

---

My colleagues William Koelsch, James Wood, and Douglas Johnson have improved
this paper by their critical comments. Thanks are due also to Saul Cohen, who facilitated my research in the summer of 1972 by arranging a National Science Foundation
Department Development Grant, and to James Wood, who proved a conscientious
and critical research assistant.

in America in the mid-nineteenth century. It is doubtful whether the primary-school educated in most regions of the United States ever held a desert image of the lands beyond the Missouri River. Not even among the well-educated in New England, among whom the desert belief was strongest, did the view persist for longer than forty years that a vast desert existed east of the Rockies.[2]

Yet the conviction that for a half-century (1820–70) the American people believed in such a Great American Desert took hold of the American academic mind after 1931. This conviction is consistent with scholars' collateral appraisals of the Plains as a region of environmental stress in which desert conditions are in many sections approximated and periodically reached. This recent concept of the Plains as semi-arid desert plains (1931—) succeeded two other desert notions: first, that the Great American Desert concept was an accurate appraisal of a true desert (the arid plains, 1880–1905); second, that the Great American Desert was an erroneous popular concept (the subhumid prairie-plains, 1905–31). To these may be added a recent (1947—) minority interpretation of the Plains as a stable grassland ecosystem in long-term equilibrium occupied by adaptable folk who held no fixed views about the existence of a nineteenth-century Plains desert.

The objectives of this essay are to reconstruct the dominant images of the nineteenth-century Plains environment as conveyed in the writings of historians and geographers after 1880; to compare these with collateral images of the Great American Desert; and to account for the changes in the imagery of both the nineteenth-century Plains and the Great American Desert. Why did changes in the imagery of the Plains and Desert occur? Why did they occur when they did in the early 1900s and in the early 1930s? Why has the desert notion hung on so tenaciously over the last forty years? It is contended here that these image changes reflect the variable Plains climate of the past century and the views and preconceptions of prominent historians, notably Turner, Webb, and Malin.

THE NATIONAL AND ROMANTIC HISTORIANS
AND THE NEGLECTED PLAINS

In the late nineteenth century, when the notion of the existence of a desert east of the Rockies was dropping out of school geography texts, history-writing in America was dominated by literary romantics and by national historians.[3] None of the prominent writers of either school was concerned with the American West, much less with conceptions of the Plains environment whether as garden or as desert. James Schouler, Henry Adams, James F. Rhodes, Justin Winsor, and later Woodrow Wilson and Edward Channing wrote voluminous histories of the American nation dealing largely with the national political and military record, as George Bancroft had done.[4] The one exception was J. B. McMaster, "the first national historian to appreciate the importance of the West and give it a significant part in the history of the U.S.," in the estimate of W. T. Hutchinson.[5] McMaster portrayed the Plains as "that magnificent stretch of rolling prairie which lies between Missouri and Iowa on the east and the Rocky Mountains on the west," and deplored the adoption, by certain politicians in the Oregon debates of the 1820s, of Stephen Long's concept of the "desert region."[6] He disapproved of map makers' practice of labeling the Plains in the Canadian River area "the Great American Desert" (1853).[7] "Some desert," he wrote, "was encountered in the Plains by Colorado gold-seekers" (presumably at the Cimarron),[8] but nowhere did he imply that an unfavorable view of the region was held by the populace or that the Plains environment inhibited agricultural settlement.

McMaster's views of the Plains were akin to Turner's, contemporaneous with Paxson's, and stated after the widespread circulation of Turner's early frontier essays. His views can thus be associated with the early Turnerians, whose images of the Plains I shall analyze farther on. The neglect of the West by the national historians was paralleled by that of the great romantic historians—Parkman, Motley, and Prescott.[9] In the years before Turner began to dominate American history, it was left to romantic writers of lesser literary and historical merit, such as Randall Parrish, to produce the early histories of the Plains and views of the Plains environment of the past.

ROMANTIC PLAINS HISTORIANS

CONQUEST OF A REAL AND COGNIZED DESERT

To romantic historians the desert environment of the Plains was a fact. The desert had been conquered or its effects mitigated by the invasion of the Anglo-Saxon settler, whom they generally idealized. Col. Henry Inman's *Old Santa Fe Trail* crossed "apparently interminable sand dunes and barren stretches" as well as the territory of the Comanche Indians, who were likened to the Arabs of the Desert.[10] His image of the Plains is strongly colored by descriptions of the Cimarron and Arkansas rivers whose "surrounding prairies are naturally arid and sterile and [produce] but little vegetation." While Inman's main concern was with the past, he could not resist adding that "now under a competent system of irrigation, the whole aspect of the landscape [Arkansas river] has changed. . . . [It] has all the luxuriance of the garden."[11]

Authors of a promotional bent admitted that observers with inexperienced eyes were "grievously disappointed at the arid aspect of the plains" and at the "thin and grey . . . grass," but attributed this reaction in part to a misconception.[12] To these promoter-historians the desert was being conquered by farmers who increased soil fertility simply by turning the sod.[13]

The once-popular novelist and transport historian Frank H. Spearman treated "the Great American Desert" as a mid-century problem overcome during the 1880s. This desert image nevertheless remained, as he believed, "obstinately fixed in the minds of thousands of otherwise intelligent people, *who have not kept pace with the developments* of the past quarter century" (*italics mine*). While admitting that "the first wave of civilization was driven back" in the mid-1870s Spearman contended that after "many reverses and failures . . . a permanent foothold [had] been established in the desert by the sturdy pioneers." The farmer, he said, had been aided by the fact that "there is no known limit to the richness and depth of this *desert* soil" (*italics mine*), and by the fact that the plowed sod "absorbs rain instead of shedding it like a rubber coat." Thus "the climate retains its atmospheric moisture better, and the rainfall becomes more regular, less falling at a time, but falling oftener."[14]

Clearly, the real desert was different from environments farther east and had demanded unusual adjustments but in time had yielded to the frontiersman. Spearman wrote just as the wave of Plains settlers peaked, before the droughts of the late 1880s and early 1890s. Between 1888 and 1893 the boomers on whom he had relied for "scientific information" further exaggerated the positive attributes of the environment to counteract the reports of droughts and of other hazards that were filtering eastward. The proportion of promotional pamphlets stressing the inexhaustibility of the soil, the possibilities of irrigation, and the similarities of the eastern and western parts of Kansas and Nebraska increased markedly between 1887 and 1892, as did the proportion of reports of rain following the plow to 1890. An increased proportion of the pamphlets—approximately half—mentioned the Great American Desert, applauding earlier settlers who had gone "forth to subdue the refractory powers of nature, to convert a desert into a garden."[15] The most exaggerated reports of this era were sources for romantic Plains historians published between 1895 and 1907.

A historian at the University of Kansas, Frank W. Blackmar, writing eighteen years after Spearman, concluded that there was a "real desert, apart from the myth which existed in the minds of geographers and philosophers," but that the region's "desert conditions are gradually disappearing through the efforts of the man who digs and toils and subdues nature."[16] After the turn of the century other Western scholars, Hiram M. Chittenden for one, echoed this position. In Chittenden's *American Fur Trade of the Far West* (1902) descriptions of barren and difficult areas of the western interior preface a lengthy characterization of its three environmental belts. Of these the least favored was the belt west of the 101st meridian, which included, as he wrote, many "desolate tracts [that] present the hopeless side of the Western country and constitute in the aggregate the Great American Desert." To Chittenden

FIGURE 1

HISTORIOGRAPHIC INTERPRETATIONS (1880–1974) OF THE GREAT
AMERICAN DESERT CONCEPT & THE PLAINS ENVIRONMENT (1820–70)

Historians' Conceptions 1880–1974 of Plains Environment 1820–70

Historians' Assessment 1880–1974 of Accuracy of Plains People's Desert Concept of the Plains 1820–70

Time	1880	90	1900	10	20	30	40	50	60	70	80	

Arid Plains — ROMANTIC PLAINS HISTORIANS — Accurate

Desert Rim (Webb, 1957)

Semiarid Desert Plains — LATER TURNERIANS (Webb, 1931, Billington, Riegel) — Slightly Inaccurate

Grassland Ecosystem (Malin, 1944)

(Paxson, Branch)
EARLY TURNERIANS (Turner, McMaster)

Subhumid Prairie-Plains — Very Inaccurate

	1880	90	1900	10	20	30	40	50	60	70	80
National View of Trans-Missouri Lands	Garden			Frontier			Problem Region Needing Government Aid				
Major Depressions		←				←					
Plains Rainfall	W	SD	M	W	DSs M	M	SD	M	SDs M	W	M

D = drought; W = wet; M = average; s = Southern plains; S = severe.

"the early geographers were not wrong in placing such a desert on their maps. . . . Their error lay rather in its location and in their failure to note the many important exceptions."[17]

This phase of Plains historiography ends with Randall Parrish's *The Great Plains.* Parrish closes a section entitled "The Conquest of the Great American Desert" with the words: "The hour and the men had come; the Great American Desert was a thing of the past."[18] To Parrish the Desert existed as the westernmost of "three distinct belts," each 150 miles wide, occupying the lands between the Rockies and the Missouri. Having conquered the rolling prairie and then the level plain, Parrish's Anglo-Saxon heroes were faced with an environmental challenge in the last belt: the arid desert with fertile valleys. Badlands, canyons, and drifting sands characterized this belt to the exclusion of other surfaces. Soils were poorest here and "streaked with alkali." Trees were replaced by cactus, Spanish bayonet, and sagebrush, and rainfall decreased steadily westwards.[19] Nevertheless, Parrish assures us, this formidable environment was conquered by man and God: "The labor and skill of civilized man, the gradual increase of rainfall, and the development of irrigation have all combined to work a modern miracle, redeeming the arid waste. The desert has become transformed into a garden."[20]

Why did these nineteenth-century historians posit the existence of an authentic desert east of the Rockies? It was a consequence of exclusive reliance on secondary and promotional sources, and an unquestioned acceptance of myths disseminated by the national gazetteers.[21] After 1865 promoters were increasingly exercised to show that Americans at mid-century had widely believed that a desert existed east of the Rockies, that this desert concept was erroneous, and that pioneers had shown it to be erroneous. On the other hand, reports of droughts, grasshoppers, and environmental deficiencies in the mid-1870s and in the late 1880s and early 1890s made it seem that there was truth in the desert concept: conditions in the Plains in the early 1890s were desert-like. And so the promoters gradually turned from extolling the Plains pioneers for failing to be deterred by the erroneous belief in a desert, to extolling them for their tenacity in settling a true desert.[22] To the promoters a grassland incorrectly conceived by American pioneers as a desert became, with time, a desert correctly conceived by American pioneers as a desert (see Fig. 1).

Martyn J. Bowden

In the late 1880s and 1890s, self-glorifying pioneer reminiscences and state and county histories written for local consumption portrayed settlers confronting and overcoming the real desert, aided by physical changes, unsuspected environmental attributes, and a Beneficent Creator.[23] These histories, together with the works of gazetteers and promoters, were the sources most readily accessible to Inman, Parrish, and other romantic Plains historians who wrote for a national audience in the 1890s and the early years of this century. It was they who authenticated the desert as history and made it a contemporary truth.

EARLY TURNERIANS

RICH PRAIRIE-PLAINS AND THE DESERT MYTH OF THE EXPLORERS

With the opening of the twentieth century the trans-Allegheny West became central to the professional concerns of American history, and scholarly historians for the first time began to address themselves to the history of the Plains, although usually as a postscript to the Midwest.[24] From the beginning, their interpretation of the Plains environment was significantly different from that of their nonacademic predecessors. Compared with accounts published before 1907 and after 1931, those published between these years rarely dwelt on the physical environmental problems and deficiencies of the Plains. And on those occasions when the Plains environment was described, it was generally assessed as rich prairie-plains with subhumid plains in the Far West, rather than as a real desert.[25]

With the physical environment minimized as a factor in Plains history or viewed favorably in most accounts, there was little need to claim that a desert conception of the region had existed in the public mind between 1820 and 1870. Most historians of this period saw it as an erroneous and short-lived notion restricted to explorers and some politicians or as a widely held notion that had well-nigh disappeared by 1850.[26] Of the many factors that lie behind this reinterpretation of the Plains desert by historians in the first thirty years of this century, two loom as particularly significant. One was the acceptance of Turner's view of the Plains environment implicit in his theory of the frontier—a theory that had become widely accepted by historians and the people at large between 1907 and the Great Depression of the 1930s. The other was the favorable climatic conditions prevailing in the Plains region during this same period and the resultant fading of the region's problems from national attention.

Turner is best known for two hypotheses, frontier and sectional. The frontier hypothesis brought him national renown and, in Hofstadter's phrase, "the attention of his peers for four generations."[27] It is primarily a location theory[28] in which space is differentiated into three zones: an uncivilized wilderness, a broad, partly civilized frontier, and a fully civilized core. The physical environment is a significant but only secondary distorting factor. Thus the distinctiveness of an area in socio-economic and political terms stems largely from its relative position within these spatial zones.[29] Compared with lands east of the Missouri, the Great Plains were farther from Eastern markets, and were reached by the frontier fifty years later.[30] In Turner's view the social and political problems of the Plains in the 1890s resulted from three locational factors: the region's size and remoteness, its closed space situation unique on the American frontier,[31] and westward overexpansion on the part of migrants who brought Midwestern farming practices into cyclically arid lands.[32]

In sum, if a distinctive Plains pioneer with unique problems emerged, this was largely a consequence either of his location in American space or of his inexperience on the American frontier. Scattered references in Turner's works suggest that if he had applied the frontier theory to the Great Plains he would have emphasized the physical environment as a constraining factor (in this case aridity) more than he did in the sections to the east.[33] But neither he nor his students produced a synthesis of Plains history, and in their application of the frontier thesis, its implicit locational determinism was emphasized more than the physical environment.[34]

Turner spent the greater part of his academic life supporting and popularizing the sectional hypothesis, with much less success than he achieved with the frontier hypothesis.[35] The sectional hypothesis rested on an environmental theory in which physical factors combined to produce sections (large regions) whose conflicts, as Billington states, "underlay much of the political decision-making of the nineteenth century."[36] In retrospect it is surprising to realize that these environmental contrasts between sections are largely physiographic.[37] While many historians found the sectional hypothesis appealing, they were justifiably skeptical about accepting physiography (or even the physical environment) as the major determinant of sectional differences.[38] Most simply avoided the question of the ultimate cause of sectional differences.

Furthermore, the physiographic differences between certain sections were slight: the Great Plains, for example, differ from the Central Lowlands physiographically in their increasing elevation westward. The boundary between the regions is rarely sharp, and the geomorphic differences are so slight that physiographers since Powell have debated whether or not the Great Plains constitutes a landform division distinct from the Central Lowlands.[39] Implicit in Turner's strong emphasis upon physiography is the notion that in Kansas, Nebraska, and the Dakotas his idealized frontiersmen confronted a wilderness no worse than that encountered at other sectional boundaries.[40] Turner did show that aridity increased westward with elevation and that this increase periodically produced arid plains east of the Rockies.[41] Yet his characterization of Kansas, Nebraska, and the Dakotas as "prairie states"[42] suggests that the arid plains were not extensive. Furthermore, when he did write about the Plains climate, he portrayed it as somewhat wetter than it is, on average. On the whole, Turner's view of the Plains, conveying little about the climate and nothing about the soil, was vague and optimistic about both rainfall and vegetation.[43]

Between 1907 and 1930 the Turnerian interpretation of American history became standard in American colleges and in American historiography.[44] The resulting adoption of Turner's frontier and sectional hypotheses ensured that location became the critical behavioral factor and that physiography would be of secondary importance, to be stressed by only a few of Turner's disciples. Accordingly, the physical environment was of limited importance in historical explanation and description during the decades 1910–30.

The minimization of the physical environment's importance in Turnerian interpretation and Turner's overassessment of Plains rainfall influenced many writings about the Plains between 1907 and 1930.

Frederic L. Paxson and John Widtsoe, for example, attribute the crop failures of the 1890s to the farmers, not to the disastrous droughts;[45] and those who wrote of the range cattle industry of the 1860s and 1870s saw the industry as an economic response, in a richly endowed region, to distance from the market, more than as a response to an agriculturally unfavorable environment.[46] These writers minimized the significance of the physical environment. Most writers of the time simply overlooked it.[47]

Like the romantic Plains historians (1890–1907), the later Turnerians (1931–) viewed the unique physical environment of the trans-Missouri lands as significant for, and challenging to, the pioneer settler. To these historians, both romantics and later Turnerians, the desert concept of the Plains was proof of popular realization of the region's singular character; accordingly the desert was heavily stressed in their interpretations. By contrast, the early Turnerians (1907–30) sometimes assessed the Plains environment as wetter than it was, and their settlers, like Turner's, tended to mirror the promoters' images of the Plains as a rich prairie.[48] These pioneers, according to the early Turnerians, looked west as Dick Garland had done from Wisconsin in 1868 and from Iowa in 1880 and saw wheat and corn lands at least as rich as those at home, easier to clear, and cheaper.[49] The desert concept had no place in these views and received at most a passing reference. Turner himself only once mentioned a Great American Desert in the Plains in his published writings.[50]

PAXSON AND BRANCH

TURNERIANS AND THE PLAINS ENVIRONMENT

Frederic L. Paxson was a student of McMaster, and like his teacher he was influenced by Turner. He was a prolific writer on the frontier and the Plains, and his *The Last American Frontier* commended him as Turner's successor at the University of Wisconsin in 1910. Although sometimes considered a Turnerian, Paxson had certain "qualifications and reservations about the frontier thesis," and between 1910 and 1930 he differed from Turner in asserting that the American people conceived of the Plains as desert at various times in the nineteenth century. Yet he grew less and less confident that the desert conception of the Plains had served as a barrier to settlement. This changing view of the desert parallels Paxson's increasing support of Turner's frontier hypothesis between 1907 and 1926,[51] and his growing tendency to assess the Plains climate of the nineteenth century as favorable to agriculture in the way Turner conceived the climate.[52]

Like Turner, too, Paxson seldom referred to the Plains environment and appears to have accepted John Wesley Powell's physiographic province beyond the Missouri. He noted open plains between the Arkansas and Platte rivers and higher plains rising gradually westward to the Rockies. Soils were "doubtful," and rainfall became "more scanty as the slopes approach the Rockies." Still, the "semi-arid plains," divided by a "rainfall line" (seemingly near the 100th meridian) from the "easy farming country" to the east, were capable of growing staple grains—and had done so by 1890. His Plains country as presented in his writings after 1915 was no more difficult than Turner's.

To the early Paxson the Great American Desert became "a reality in frontier life in 1819." He felt that "a general confidence in the desert characteristics of the semi-arid plains" persisted until 1873.[53] The belief in the desert and in its corollary, the government-created Indian barrier —together with lack of easy highways westward—were, he maintained, responsible for the halt of the frontier at the Missouri for a half-century.[54] By the 1920s, however, Paxson had become skeptical of the grip of the desert concept on the mind of the populace. According to the later Paxson, the Santa Fe trade quickly revealed the desert as a myth, and travel through and across the Plains country on the Oregon Trail dispelled the notion of barrenness. By 1924 Paxson believed that a short-lived tradition of the desert had died before 1850.[55]

E. Douglas Branch's Westward: The Romance of the American Frontier confirms the early Turnerian view of the desert concept. The Great American Desert was a Government explorers' legend, ignored by or unknown to fur traders, Missourians, and frontiersmen—a legend that "never did any great harm," he concluded.[56] Branch's book is the last in this second phase in Plains historiography. His interpretation is dominated by Turner's romantic, idealized frontier. Compared with the accounts of the later Plains historians, Branch's Plains physical environment was characterized simply, conceived favorably, and thought by the settlers to be more like the Midwest in its rainfall and vegetation than it actually was.[57]

Why did so favorable a view of the Plains go unchallenged for so long? I suggest that social and economic conditions in the nation, together with the Plains climate between 1910 and 1930, contributed to the survival of the frontier thesis and associated assumptions, implicit and explicit, about the rainfall of the Plains in the nineteenth century. The frontier thesis became a national myth after one crisis in American values in the 1890s, and survived approximately thirty years, until the next crisis of the 1930s brought on by the Great Depression. In the Plains region, disastrous droughts such as had focused national attention on the worst extremes of the Plains climate in the 1890s did not command the nation's attention again until the Dust Bowl years of the 1930s (see Fig. 1).

Throughout the nineteenth century the West had been viewed largely as the Garden of the World, where, in Billington's words, "bountiful nature washed all newcomers of evil and transmuted them into models of republican virtue, all endowed with a lofty morality that matched their physical strength. This agrarian myth was basic to the nation's folklore."[58] Yet by the 1890s the growth of industry and of large cities, the rise of immigration, and a national depression—at its deepest when Turner delivered his frontier essay in 1893—inspired well-educated Americans to serious doubts about the agrarian ideal. "Every dispatch from the western plains heightened their doubts," continues Billington, "for there the agrarian depression of the 1880s and 1890s shattered legends of frontier affluence."[59] A succession of dry years catalyzed the Populist movement. By the mid-1890s the myth of the Garden was no longer tenable.

Turner's genius, in 1893, was to "put into definite shape a good deal of thought that [had] been floating around rather loosely," as Theodore Roosevelt stated in a letter to Turner—to rewrite the Garden myth into an historical hypothesis that placed the entire past in new perspective, and to reaffirm American faith in rural values.[60] Turner, according to Billington, "told historians that American democracy was a home-grown product of the West. This was a comfortable theory, Jeffersonian rather than Marxist in its implications, offering a safe explanation of the conflict between eastern capitalism and western Populism, between the trusts and the people, between management and labor."[61]

The frontier thesis began to gain national support as economic conditions improved, as rainfall increased on the Plains, and as the Populist star waned in the western Plains. For thirty years it was, as Hofstadter called it, "the characteristic American view of the American past,"[62] unquestioned even by Turner's fellow historians. Nothing in the economic and social conditions in the nation encouraged a reappraisal of the thesis. And nothing in the Plains climate prompted a questioning of the Turnerians' assumptions about either the past climate or popular conceptions of it; for after 1900 the Plains were as well watered and stable climatically as Western historians of the period 1900–1930 conceived them to have been in the middle of the nineteenth century.[63]

A national depression coinciding with a decade of drought in the Plains in the 1890s had contributed to the destruction of the Garden, with its easily conquered yet very real desert, and cleared the way for the Turnerian restatement of the myth as the frontier thesis. Similar circumstances—the Great Depression and the droughts of the 1930s—undermined faith in the remote and indistinct desert of the Turnerian frontier[64] and swept in as a replacement Walter Prescott Webb's thesis of a distinctive arid-land civilization born beyond the 98th meridian in a real and permanent Great American Desert. Thus the Plains environment had a considerable role in both the rise and the fall of the frontier thesis as a national myth. Conversely, nearly universal acceptance of the frontier thesis did much to ensure that between 1905 and 1930 the Plains environment was forgotten by the American people and assessed too favorably by American historians.

LATER TURNERIANS

SEMI-ARID PLAINS, DESERT RIM, AND PEOPLE'S DESERT

Walter Prescott Webb's *The Great Plains* (1931) revolutionized the imagery of the nineteenth-century Plains environment and re-established the Great American Desert as a dominant element in Plains settlement history. In Webb's thesis, the lands beyond the 98th meridian were sufficiently arid to create an institutional break unlike anything encountered before or since on the American frontier, and in the pioneers' encounter with this arid and deficient environment a new and distinctive civilization was born.[65]

This thesis required him to establish that the environment of the Plains region differed markedly from that of regions farther east. This he did by depicting the general coincidence of its distinctive vegetation zones, physiography, prehistoric culture, and climate, and demonstrating that within this region catastrophe was endemic.[66] The Dust Bowl gave strong support to his thesis and convinced many that the Plains were far drier than the lands east of the 98th meridian.[67] Historians praised Webb's new interpretation. Social scientists lauded it as explaining a baffling problem—the American farmer's inability to effect a stable adjustment to the short-grass plains.[68] Government agencies used it to support the growing Dust Bowl mythology, their conservation policies, and their corresponding versions of Plains environmental history.[69] During the drought years of the 1930s, people were disposed to accept a thesis about which they might have been skeptical in the (wetter) 1920s, when the entire Plains received sufficient rainfall for agriculture.

Webb's thesis required that the settlers were aware both that the lands beyond the 98th meridian were arid and that the settlers, as agriculturalists, could not take Eastern institutions west of this line. To Webb, proof of the people's perception of this institutional fault line lay in two responses: (1) the long halt of the frontier at the edge of the region, (2) the surge into the region that was made possible by four technological fixes—the revolver, barbed wire, the steel windmill, and the railroad. The proof that the people perceived the fault was furnished by their fifty-year image of the trans-Missouri West as the Great American Desert.[70]

Webb found the proof in Ralph C. Morris's paper of 1926, "The Notion of a Great American Desert East of the Rockies,"[71] which brought the desert notion to historians' attention after twenty years in which the Great American Desert had hardly been mentioned. Morris cites many writers who believed in the existence of a Great American Desert in the nineteenth century, but fails to mention the many writers who did not conceive the Plains as a desert. Furthermore, he leaves the impression that the desert idea was widespread among the American people through the mid-nineteenth century. The fifty-year desert posited by Morris was asserted explicitly by Webb without further research.

The desert idea was significant for one hundred years, according to Webb, but for at most thirty years, according to Paxson (in the 1920s). Many early Turnerians felt that the desert idea had disappeared among the populace by 1850, but to Webb the decade 1850–60 was the high point of its acceptance. He maintained that the idea was strong in the popular mind until the 1870s—long enough to stop the waves of the frontier but not to stem the tidal surge of population after the Civil War. By contrast, Branch had contended that the desert had little effect on the frontier, and that what little effect it did have was an indirect result of the creation of the Indian frontier.[72]

In 1931 Webb felt that the notion of the desert had held up the frontier, and later he contended that a periodic desert, correctly perceived as a desert by explorers and prospective settlers, had caused the fifty-year halt of the frontier at the Missouri (1820–70). In the 1950s he went farther, to maintain that a desert existed in the Plains sections of what he called the Desert States (Colorado, Wyoming, Montana, New Mexico) and at times in the Plains sections of what he called the Desert Rim States (see Fig. 1).[73]

Webb's environmentalist interpretation of Plains history in 1931 and his later view of the western Plains as true desert were not fully acceptable to many Western historians.[74] Yet all the later Turnerians seemingly adopted uncritically Webb's image of the Plains environment, and, to a large extent, they and most geographers accepted his interpretation of the desert tradition. Leroy Hafen and Carl Rister, for example, divide the United States into "two quite different sections" at the 20-inch rainfall line or the 98th meridian, and Billington has a "line of Semiaridity" west of which less than 20 inches of rain fall each year (not enough for ordinary farming). West of this boundary is a static, stable region: to Hafen and Rister "the first distinctive geographic unit of Western America encountered by Anglo-Americans," to Billington "the giant physiographic province known as the Great Plains . . . the first of the unfamiliar regions that made pioneering difficult."[75]

The Great Plains was viewed from an Eastern outsider's position as a deficient region. The terms "waterless," "treeless," "semiarid" appear continually. Billington adds "parched earth," "endless vistas," "cloudless heavens." This portrayed a region much more hostile to the pioneer than the Turnerians before Webb had ever conceived it. Physical environment rather than location was now seen to present the major obstacle to the struggling pioneers and to have halted the westward spread of Turner's agricultural zones at a dry-farming stage.[76] It was the dry environment of the 1930s that the settlers were thought to have faced between 1865 and 1895.

The hazards that Webb used so effectively to prove the region's distinctiveness were often overstressed by later Turnerians. In one account it was drought, hot winds, clouds of grasshoppers, sandstorms, northers or black blizzards, rodents, and prairie dogs; in another it was spring floods and torrents, searing waves of heat, "drought that withered grass, cracked the parched soil, and burned young crops to a crisp," "blasts from hell," "milewide clouds of grasshoppers," and prairie fires.[77] Fred A. Shannon's attack on Webb at the Skytop Conference in 1940 pinpointed for historians some of Webb's omissions and errors of physical fact. Yet Webb's emphases and physical generalizations continued to be copied, often without comprehension.[78] Climatologists had mapped and measured rainfall variability in the Plains,[79] but historians treated the climate as unvarying from year to year, and the fertile soils were rarely if ever mentioned. In sum, the later Turnerians wrote more about the physical environment than did the early Turnerians, and they believed the climate to be drier.

Historians' acceptance of Webb's unfavorable image of the Plains environment facilitated their adoption of his interpretation of the desert myth. As Robert E. Riegel wrote, "west of the Mississippi lay millions of acres of wild land which everyone felt sure would never be desired for white settlement. . . . They were viewed not only as extremely dry, but as practically sterile. Until after the Civil War the great majority of American citizens were satisfied that the plains of the Far West comprised the 'Great American Desert.' "[80] Billington notes that "by 1825 every literate American believed the region west of the 95th meridian to be a great, unusable desert." Indeed, "until after the Civil War the impression persisted that the farming frontier could never invade that in-hospitable region." Billington termed it a "psychological barrier."[81]

Historians in the 1940s and 1950s had no doubt that the desert idea was held by the populace for the fifty years 1820–70. The remarkable contrast in interpretation between the early and the later Turnerians is largely attributable to Webb, who became the recognized authority on the desert concept.[82] Geographers, though for their part less willing to accept Webb's interpretation of the physical geography of the Plains, nonetheless showed themselves uncritical of Webb's desert myth.[83] With but one major exception, both historians and geographers have followed Webb's 1931 reinterpretation of the desert concept seemingly without questioning his evidence.[84]

MALIN'S GRASSLANDS AS ECOSYSTEM

The exception is James C. Malin. His books *Winter Wheat in the Golden Belt of Kansas* and *The Grassland of North America*[85] stress the need for historians to understand the complex interrelations of the Plains environment as presented in the scientific literature. These books attempted to make historians aware of folk experimentation and resource-fulness, which Malin viewed as a major factor in Plains agricultural history. His historian contemporaries, he felt, looked at the Plains as non-Plainsmen. Like the settlers, these non-Plainsmen in their histories found the Plains deficient in rainfall (subhumid), inferior in vegetation (treeless), and inadequate for humid-land agriculture. Malin's *Grassland*, by contrast, revealed the Plains as a rich and agriculturally productive grassland ecosystem. Native grasses were the vegetation best adapted to the region, and the soils were more versatile and productive than forest soils.[86] No other historian has understood the Plains environment so well as Malin. He knew the variability of annual rainfall in the Plains and its non-cyclical pattern through time. He was aware that the drought of the 1930s was uncommonly severe. Malin thus ran no danger of projecting the short-term dry conditions of the 1930s back to the mid-nineteenth century and postulating a long-term desert, as Webb had done.

Malin's faith in nineteenth-century folk knowledge also made it inconceivable to him that the "myth of the Great American Desert was held universally," as Webb and others had contended. "At no time," Malin wrote, "were either the literature or the maps in general agreement on the existence of a great desert or of its extent. . . . Pioneers, eager to occupy the land, were optimistic about the possibilities of the country . . . , [and] those favorable to the aggressive westward expansion were sure and determined that all that was necessary to make the grassland blossom like the rose was to let in the population." Malin saw the desert myth as restricted generally to those who opposed the rapid settlement and development of the trans-Mississippi West.[87]

Yet Malin's views have until recently carried little weight among historians and have failed to reach the wider audience enjoyed by Webb. Among the causes, perhaps, were Malin's contentious nature, his lack of students, his decision to publish his own works, and their difficult format.[88] Moreover, Malin published mainly during a period of good rainfall, when yields and prices were high and national attention was not on the Plains. His writings alienated many of his natural allies—the geographical historians whom he attacked for their poor understanding of environmental processes in the Plains. In any case, Malin made few converts; and when drought in the Plains in the 1950s raised the specter of a second Dust Bowl Webb reinforced the old deficiency view by characterizing the Great Plains as a "permanent and periodic" desert.[89]

The fifteen years of prosperity in the Plains since 1959 might be expected to have favored the spread of Malin's more accurate views of the Plains environment, but good rains and supported prices ensure that the region has enjoyed no visibility in the nation. Some environmental historians, however, have used Webb's dry plains and desert as the classic example of Western agricultural man's disastrous interference with nature.[90]

In the unlikely event that national attention is focused on the Plains during wet and prosperous years in the 1970s and 1980s, the recent *idée fixe* about the Great American Desert in the nineteenth century may be replaced by another view (akin to that of Malin?). Conversely, in the likely event that the Dust Bowl returns—and places the Plains in the national attention—within the next twenty years, Webb's desert *idée fixe* will set unalterably in the academic mind like reinforced concrete.[91]

Martyn J. Bowden

EFFECTS OF THE ENVIRONMENT ON IDEAS

What is remarkable about these shifts in the historiography of the desert is that they were neither prefaced by a critical scholarly appraisal of previous notions nor undermined by new evidence. Rather, they reflect the fluctuating environmental conditions of the Plains in the twentieth century, the governmental and popular concern for a problem region, and the emphases of a few prominent historians within the Turnerian tradition—Paxson, Webb, Billington, and Turner himself.

The reliance of historians on promotional and biased sources produced the desert notion of 1880 to 1907. The stature of Turner, the power of the frontier hypothesis, and an extended period without serious drought in the Plains favored the desert notion of 1907 to 1931. And the timely and brilliant writing of Webb in *The Great Plains*, in conjunction with droughts in the 1930s and 1950s, has done much to perpetuate the most recent concept of the desert since 1931.

In the 1920s and 1930s geographers, fearful of the label "environmental determinist," were engaged in what John K. Wright in his unpublished papers called "bathwaterism": throwing out the baby (in this case environmental factors) with the bathwater (the environment as the determining factor in human behavior). In two essays in 1925 Wright warned geographers not to avoid the study of the effects of the environment on ideas. "The different characters that geographical ideas have assumed in different times," he wrote, "have been conditioned partly by environmental and partly by human factors."[92] The idea of the Great American Desert has been influenced by both factors.

NOTES

1. In *Human Nature in Geography* (Cambridge: Harvard University Press, 1966), p. 291.
2. Martyn J. Bowden, "The Perception of the Western Interior of the United States, 1800–1870: A Problem in Historical Geosophy," *Proceedings, Association of American Geographers* 1 (1969):16–21, and idem, "The Great American Desert and the American Frontier, 1800–1882: Popular Images of the Plains

138

and Phases in the Westward Movement," in T. K. Hareven, ed., *Anonymous Americans: Exploration in Nineteenth Century Social History* (Englewood Cliffs, N.J.: Prentice-Hall, 1971), pp. 48–79.

3. Richard Hofstadter, *The Progressive Historians: Turner, Beard, Parrington* (New York: Alfred A. Knopf, 1968), pp. 3–43.

4. Henry Adams, *History of the United States*, 9 vols. (New York: Charles Scribner's Sons, 1889–91); George Bancroft, *History of the United States of America*, 6 vols. (New York: D. Appleton, 1883–85); Edward Channing, A *History of the United States*, 6 vols. (New York: Macmillan, 1905–25); James F. Rhodes, *History of the United States from the Compromise of 1850* (New York: Macmillan, 1893–1919); James Schouler, *History of the United States of America under the Constitution*, 7 vols. (New York: Dodd, Mead, 1880–1913); Woodrow Wilson, A *History of the American People*, 5 vols. (New York: Harper & Bros., 1902); Justin Winsor, ed., *Narrative and Critical History of America*, 8 vols. (Boston: Houghton, Mifflin, 1884–89). For biographical studies of these historians, see William T. Hutchinson, ed., *The Marcus W. Jernegan Essays in American Historiography* (New York: Russell & Russell, 1937). The neglect of the West is specifically noted in the essay on Channing by Ralph R. Fahrney (p. 300), and that on Rhodes by Raymond C. Miller (p. 175).

5. "John Bach McMaster," in Hutchinson, ed., *American Historiography*, p. 138. See also Eric F. Goldman, *John Bach McMaster: American Historian* (New York: Octagon Books, 1971), pp. 79, 100, 133–34.

6. John B. McMaster, A *History of the People of the United States from the Revolution to the Civil War*, vol. 5, 1821–30 (New York: Appleton, 1900), pp. 27, 480–81.

7. Ibid., vol. 8, 1850–61 (New York: Appleton, 1913), p. 363.

8. Ibid., p. 400; Ray A. Billington, *Frederick Jackson Turner: Historian, Scholar, Teacher* (New York: Oxford University Press, 1973), p. 284.

9. David Levin, *History as Romantic Art: Bancroft, Prescott, Motley, and Parkman* (Stanford: Stanford University Press, 1959).

10. Henry Inman, *The Old Santa Fe Trail: The Story of a Great Highway* (New York: Macmillan, 1898), pp. 281, 320.

11. Ibid., p. 253.

12. In A. A. Hayes, Jr., *New Colorado and the Santa Fe Trail* (New York: Harper Bros., 1880), pp. 31, 37.

13. See Bradley Baltensperger, "Plain Folk and Plains Promoters: Pre-Migration and Post-Settlement Images of the Central Great Plains," Ph.D. diss., Clark University, 1974, chap. 2.

14. In "The Great American Desert," *Harper's New Monthly Magazine* 77 (June–November 1888):244.

15. Baltensperger, "Plain Folk and Plains Promoters," chap. 4.

16. In "The Mastery of the Desert," *North American Review*, no. 182 (1906), pp. 684, 686.

17. In *The American Fur Trade of the Far West* (New York: Francis P. Harper, 1902), 2:751–55.

18. *The Great Plains: The Romance of Western American Exploration, Warfare, and Settlement, 1527–1870* (Chicago: A. C. McClurg, 1907), p. 382.
19. Ibid., pp. 18–27, 381. The belts are taken from Chittenden's *American Fur Trade* without attribution, but Parrish exaggerated their salient characteristics.
20. Ibid., p. 28.
21. See, e.g., the authorities cited by Parrish in his "Note of Acknowledgements" (ibid., p. ix). Included are gazetteers such as Albert D. Richardson (*Beyond the Mississippi*) and Samuel Bowles (*Across the Continent*) and promotional histories such as John N. Holloway's *History of Kansas* and Leverett W. Spring's *Kansas*.
22. See Baltensperger, "Plain Folk and Plains Promoters," chap. 4.
23. Parrish, *Great Plains*, in his "Note of Acknowledgements" cites *Transactions* of the Nebraska and Kansas historical societies and several state histories.
24. Walter P. Webb's *The Great Plains* (Boston: Ginn, 1931), was the first major monograph on the region, although specialized studies had been made of the Plains range cattle industry. The neglect of the region "so far as synthesis goes especially" was noted in letters by Frederick Jackson Turner in 1927 and 1929 (Billington, *Frederick Jackson Turner*, pp. 456–57, 559). The work that had previously come closest to a Plains synthesis was Frederic L. Paxson's *The Last American Frontier* (New York: Macmillan, 1910).
25. Compare the physical environments of Paxson, *Last American Frontier*, pp. 11–12, 373, and Frederick Jackson Turner, *The Rise of the New West, 1819–1829* (New York: Harper & Bros., 1906), p. 111, with that of Ray A. Billington, *The Far Western Frontier, 1830–1860* (New York: Harper, 1956), pp. 30–34, 101–3, 262. Studies making little or no mention of the physical environment are Roy Gittinger, *The Formation of the State of Oklahoma* (1803–1906) (Berkeley: University of California Press, 1917); Cardinal Goodwin, *The Trans-Mississippi West, 1803–1853* (New York: Appleton, 1922); Emerson Hough, *The Passing of the Frontier: A Chronicle of the Old West* (New Haven: Yale University Press, 1918); and W. J. Ghent, *The Early Far West: A Narrative Outline, 1540–1850* (New York: Longmans, Green, 1931).
26. McMaster, *History of the People of the United States*, 5:480–81, and Hough, *Passing of the Frontier*, gave credence to the explorers' and politicians' desert; E. Douglas Branch, *Westward: The Romance of the American Frontier* (New York: Appleton, 1930), pp. 308, 452, 471, and Gittinger, *Formation of Oklahoma*, p. 216, believed that the desert theory was widely accepted by the people before 1850.
27. In *Progressive Historians*, p. 164. See also Billington, *Frederick Jackson Turner*, pp. 444–45.
28. This follows from Turner's adoption of a unilinear evolutionary succession model and from its application in space. In its ideal form Turner's frontier theory is identical with the theories of J. H. von Thünen and E. W. Burgess. Rings of socio-economic activities in a recognized sequence spread outward from a core. All three theories are locational (hence geographic but not environmental) deterministic theories in that behavior is predicted by position in space, not by the

physical environment. That Turner's frontier thesis is locational rather than environmental is recognized by Hofstadter, who felicitously describes it as "the grand spatial metaphor that . . . dominated the first phase of his work" (*Progressive Historians*, pp. 51, 95, 100–101, 152–53, 163; quoted on p. 100).

29. The idea of unilinear succession was common in nineteenth-century thought. Friedrich List, Achille Loria, and others placed the idea in social, economic, and political contexts that influenced Turner. See Ray A. Billington, *The Genesis of the Frontier Thesis* (San Marino, Calif.: The Huntington Library, 1971), pp. 34–37, 136–43; and J. L. M. Gulley, "The Turnerian Frontier: A Study in the Migration of Ideas," *Tijdschrift voor Economische en Sociale Geografie* 50 1959):65–66.

30. Turner, *The Frontier in American History* (New York: Holt, Rinehart and Winston, 1962), pp. 238–39: "The Populist is the American farmer who has kept in advance of the economic and social transformations that have overtaken those who remained behind." See also Turner, *Rise of the New West*, pp. 218, 234–35.

31. *Frontier in American History*, pp. 146–48, 219–20, 239, 257–58. "Failures in one area can no longer be made good by taking up land on the American frontier" (p. 219).

32. Turner, *The Early Writings of Frederick Jackson Turner*, ed. Fulmer Mood (Madison: University of Wisconsin Press, 1938), p. 288.

33. See Turner, *Frontier in American History*, pp. 219, 239, 257; idem, *Rise of the New West*, p. 111.

34. When Turner writes about the wilderness and how the environment of the frontier affects man's behavior, it does not matter whether the soils are podzols or chernozems or whether the climate is maritime or continental. What matters is that the environment at that point in space and time is unconquered by civilized man. Turner's exaggeration of the uniformity of the frontier experiences and his consequent neglect of natural differences were remarked by George W. Pierson, "The Frontier and the Frontiersmen of Turner's Essays," *Pennsylvania Magazine of History and Biography* 64 (1940):478.

35. Billington, *Frederick Jackson Turner*, 217, 228–32, 370, 398, 416–17, 465–71; Hofstadter, *Progressive Historians*, pp. 94–95; Turner, *Early Writings*, pp. 275–90.

36. In *Frederick Jackson Turner*, p. 444.

37. Turner had already stressed the significance of physiographic differences before publication of John Wesley Powell's *The Physiography of the United States* (New York: American Book Company, 1896), which greatly impressed him and which he recommended widely. Turner, *Early Writings*, pp. 74–75, 237, 277–80, 283, 287; W. R. Jacobs, ed., *The Historical World of F. J. Turner* (New Haven: Yale University Press, 1968), p. 203; Billington, *Frederick Jackson Turner*, pp. 200, 209, 213–17, 372, 453–54.

38. See Billington, *Frederick Jackson Turner*, pp. 228–32, 370–75.

39. Differences among early physiographers are illustrated in W. L. G. Joerg, "The Subdivision of North America into Natural Regions: A Preliminary Enquiry,"

Annals of the Association of American Geographers (hereafter *Annals AAG*) 4 (1914):55–83; and G. Malcolm Lewis, "Changing Emphases in the Description of the Natural Environment of the American Great Plains Area," *Transactions, Institute of British Geographers* 30 (1962):75–90. Cf. also Nevin M. Fenneman, "Physiographic Divisions of the United States," *Annals AAG* 18 (1928): 261–353; and Edwin H. Hammond, "Analysis of Properties in Land Form Geography: An Application to Broad-Scale Land Form Mapping," *Annals AAG* 54 (1964):11–19 and map supplement.

40. In Turner's writings published before his death there is no suggestion, such as that found in Parrish, *Great Plains*, and Webb, *Great Plains*, that the environmental encounter in the Plains produced a new type of civilized man. The idea of sharp environmental contrast does not appear in Turner's posthumously published *The United States, 1830–1850: The Nation and Its Sections* (New York: Henry Holt, 1935), which might fairly be taken as indicating the ideas shared with his graduate students in the Harvard period. Turner and his contemporaries saw a greater environmental challenge at the tree/tall grass border than at the tall grass/short grass border (see Branch, *Westward: Romance of the American Frontier*, p. 403, and note 49 below).

41. Turner, *Frontier in American History*, pp. 244–49; Turner, *Early Writings*, p. 288.

42. Turner, *Frontier in American History*, pp. 236–38; Turner, *United States, 1830–1850*, p. 254.

43. Turner's vagueness and imprecision, particularly in the definition of terms, was occasioned in part by the popular nature of the readership for many of his essays (Billington, *Frederick Jackson Turner*, pp. 194–99, 282–83, 447–49). The same vagueness affected Plains writers—e.g., Edward E. Dale, *The Range Cattle Industry* (Norman: University of Oklahoma Press, 1930), who sees the greater part of the lands beyond the Mississippi as treeless prairie (pp. 33–34, 135–36), and John Widtsoe, *Dry Farming* (New York: Macmillan, 1911), who characterizes the lands "east of the Rocky Mountains [as] the subhumid district which receives from 20 to 30 inches of rainfall annually" (pp. 24, 36). For Turner's neglect of the physical environment, apart from physiography, see Gene M. Gressley, "The Turner Thesis—A Problem in Historiography," *Agricultural History* 32 (1958):237, and Pierson, "The Frontier and the Frontiersmen."

44. For dating Turner's conquest of historians, see Billington, *Genesis of the Frontier Thesis*, pp. 3–4, and *Frederick Jackson Turner*, pp. 283–85, 444–45; and Hofstadter, *Progressive Historians*, p. 99. For the national acclaim accorded Turner, see Billington, *Turner*, pp. 193, 285, 446–48; Gressley, "The Turner Thesis," pp. 230–31, 247–49.

45. Paxson, *The New Nation* (Boston: Houghton Mifflin, 1915), p. 179, wrote of the "poor quality of the settlers, . . . a less capable class of farmers, . . . less likely to succeed than that of any previous frontier." Widtsoe, *Dry Farming*, pp. 358–59, and 399–400, contended that in good years farmers brought into a subhumid region "the humid agriculture." The "failures . . . [of the 1890s] were due to improper methods of soil culture," and a "lack of proper agricultural in-

formation and practice." The idea of farmers' taking their humid agricultural practices too far west into a subhumid region is found clearly in Turner, *Early Writings*, p. 288.

46. Dale, *Cattle Range Industry*, p. xiii, sees the cattle fringe as an early stage in the Turnerian succession and "always present at the western edge of an advancing agricultural frontier." See also Hough, *Passing of the Frontier*, pp. 41, 54.

47. Examples are Goodwin, *Trans-Mississippi West*, Gittinger, *Formation of Oklahoma*, and Ghent, *Early Far West*.

48. See note 49 below. The boomers' images and the Midwestern settlers' adoption of these images are considered in Baltensperger, "Plain Folk and Plains Promoters," and Martyn J. Bowden, "Desert Wheat Belt, Plains Corn Belt: Environmental Cognition and Behavior of Settlers in the Plains Margin, 1850–1899," in B. Blouet and M. Lawson, eds., *Images of the Plains* (Lincoln: University of Nebraska Press, in press).

49. Hamlin Garland's *The Westward March of American Settlement* (Chicago: American Library Association, 1927), states his father's motives and visions (pp. 23–24) and implies, as do others, that the environmental change from forest to prairie for the settler was more traumatic than the shift from tall to short grass lands. Garland's emphasis in 1927 on the speed and facility of displacement of cowboy by successful settler on the Plains frontier is a marked change from his "realist" position in *A Son of the Middle Border* (New York: Macmillan, 1917). Garland, a Wisconsinite and a year older than Turner, interpreted the West to Easterners just as Turner did (Hofstadter, *Progressive Historians*, pp. 48–50; Billington, *Frederick Jackson Turner*, p. 446). Unlike Turner's family, Garland's family moved to the Plains from Wisconsin and Iowa, and this encounter with the Plains may account for Garland's realism. Garland's mellowing between 1917 and 1927, however, parallels the change in historiography effected largely by Turner and his students.

50. Turner, *The Rise of the New West*, pp. 124, 127; see also note 26 above.

51. On the basis of two quotations in Paxson's work, Gressley, "The Turner Thesis," makes a point that he feels "has often been overlooked when discussing Paxson's work. He can definitely be considered a part of the frontier school." The fact that he is not an obvious Turnerian makes him a good control case for measuring Turner's influence in this period.

52. This reconstruction of Paxson's Plains environment is drawn from a few scattered sentences in his major works, notably *The Last American Frontier*, pp. 11–12, 373; *The New Nation*, pp. 149–50, 179–80; *Recent History of the United States*, 1763–1893 (Boston: Houghton Mifflin, 1921), pp. 62, 156, 161–62, 164, 168. In 1924 Paxson recognized that within the "easy farming country," the lands west of the Missouri were "less attractive than the well-watered farm lands of Indiana, Illinois, or Wisconsin" (*Recent History*, p. 423).

53. Frederic L. Paxson, "The Pacific Railroads and the Disappearance of the Frontier in America," *Annual Report of the American Historical Association for the Year 1907* (Washington: Government Printing Office, 1908), pp. 108, 111. That the people believed in the Plains desert at least until the 1860s was made

explicit by Paxson in 1910 in *Last American Frontier*, pp. 12–13, 86–87, 324. He notes in one passage, however, that by 1857 the fiction of the Great American Desert had been destroyed by overland traffic (p. 52).

54. Paxson, *Last American Frontier*, pp. 12–13, 21–23, 30–32, 68, 85; idem, *Recent History*, pp. 156, 161.

55. Frederic L. Paxson, *History of the American Frontier* (Boston: Houghton Mifflin, 1924), pp. 326, 329, 332, 340 for the Santa Fe and Oregon Trails, and pp. 340, 423–24, 431 for the desert tradition.

56. Branch, *Westward: Romance of the American Frontier*, p. 308. The name Great American Desert appears in only two other places in Branch's text: in paraphrasing Josiah Gregg's account of the Cimarron area on the Santa Fe Trail (pp. 348–49), and when writing of the Colorado railroad promoters' difficulty in attracting settlers to eastern Colorado—which might be thought of as the semipermanent home of the Great American Desert (p. 557). To Branch the Great American Desert was in Utah and Nevada (p. 548). Most of his contemporaries shared this view—e.g., J. Russell Smith, *North America* (New York: Harcourt, Brace, 1925), pp. 485–506.

57. Branch's debt to what Henry Nash Smith calls Turner's "poetic vision" is obvious throughout this literary classic, but clearest in the preface and the bibliographic note (*Westward*, pp. vii, 599). Branch's concept is more elaborate than most in this period, and at times suggestive of Webb and later Turnerians.

58. *Genesis of the Frontier Thesis*, pp. 72–75. See also Henry Nash Smith, *Virgin Land: The American West as Symbol and Myth* (1950; New York: Vintage Books, 1957); Rush Welter, "The Frontier West as Image of American Society, 1776–1860," *Pacific Northwest Quarterly* 52 (1961):1–6.

59. *Genesis of the Frontier Thesis*, p. 74. See also Billington, *Frederick Jackson Turner*, p. 282.

60. Roosevelt to Turner, Feb. 10, 1894, in Billington, *Genesis of the Frontier Thesis*, p. 82; see also pp. 75, 83.

61. Billington, *Turner*, p. 282.

62. Hofstadter, *Progressive Historians*, p. 54. See also Billington, *Turner*, p. 444.

63. The one rather dry year in the 34-year normal to near-normal precipitation period after 1895 was 1910. See Merlin P. Lawson and others, *Nebraska Droughts: A Study of Their Past Chronological and Spatial Extent*, Occasional Papers no. 1, Department of Geography, University of Nebraska (Lincoln, 1971), pp. 4–8; Earl E. Lackey, "Annual-Variability Rainfall Maps of the Great Plains," *Geographical Review* 27 (1937):665–70.

64. Hofstadter, *Progressive Historians*, pp. 90–93; Billington, *Turner*, pp. 418–420, 449–50.

65. Webb, *The Great Plains*, Preface and pp. 7–10, 140–41, 453; idem, *The Great Frontier* (Boston: Houghton Mifflin, 1952), pp. 239–41.

66. Webb, *Great Plains*, pp. 3–7, 10–26, 47–52; James C. Malin, *The Grassland of North America: Prolegomena to Its History* (Lawrence, Kans.: By the author, 1947), p. 259.

67. See Richard H. Dillon, "Stephen Long's Great American Desert," *Proceedings, American Philosophical Society* 111 (1967):107–8.

68. Selection of the book by the Social Science Research Council for reappraisal was a measure of its "outstanding significance." The bases for selection are indicated on pp. vii–ix and 3–5. See Fred A. Shannon, "An Appraisal of Walter Prescott Webb's The Great Plains: A Study in Institutions and Environment," *Critiques of Research in the Social Sciences: III* (Social Science Research Council, 1940), pp. 3–111. See also Malin, *Grassland of North America*, p. 260.

69. Malin, *Grassland*, pp. 131–48.

70. Webb, *Great Plains*, pp. 140–41, 152–60, 167–179, 270–72, 295–317, 337–48; Webb, *Great Frontier*, pp. 241–79.

71. In *Mississippi Valley Historical Review* 13 (1926):190–200. Webb does not cite Morris, but he does cite Ernest S. Osgood, *The Day of the Cattleman* (Minneapolis: University of Minnesota Press, 1929), which gives prominence to Morris's essay.

72. Webb, *Great Plains*, pp. 152–53, 159, 225. See notes 26 and 55 above and Branch, *Westward: The Romance of the American Frontier*, pp. 308, 471.

73. Walter Prescott Webb, "The American West as Perpetual Mirage," *Harper's Magazine* 214 (1957):25–31; idem, "The West and the Desert," in his *An Honest Preface and Other Essays* (Boston: Houghton Mifflin, 1959), pp. 175–93 (reprinted from *Montana, The Magazine of Western History*, Winter, 1958).

74. Shannon, "Appraisal of Webb's The Great Plains," p. 10. LeRoy R. Hafen and Carl Coke Rister, *Western America* (New York: Prentice-Hall, 1941), cites Webb's *The Great Plains* only once.

75. Hafen and Rister, *Western America*, pp. viii–ix, 628; Ray A. Billington, *Westward Expansion: A History of the American Frontier*, 2nd ed. (New York: Macmillan, 1960), pp. 406–8.

76. Billington, *Westward Expansion*, p. 413, Hafen and Rister, *Western America*, pp. viii, 425, 604, 627–28, 643.

77. Hafen and Rister, pp. ix, 427–29, 643, 647; Billington, *Westward Expansion*, pp. 711–13. Billington assures us that "these intolerable conditions did not endure always" (p. 713).

78. Shannon, "Appraisal of Webb's The Great Plains," pp. 12–31; Bruce Nelson, *Land of the Dacotahs* (Minneapolis: University of Minnesota Press, 1946), pp. 11–12, 147–52, 216; Ina Faye Woestemeyer, ed., *The Westward Movement* (New York: Appleton-Century, 1939), pp. 289–96; Billington, *Westward Expansion*, pp. 406–8. Billington's account of the "Natural Setting" of the Plains is sophomoric. By his account the rainfall in the Plains is life-giving moisture soaked up by easterly winds in the High Plains. Some 30–46 inches of it is evaporated during the growing season alone. West of the line of Semiaridity, however, less than 20 inches falls each year (pp. 407–8). It is no wonder that in such a chaotic environment he finds "vegetation that struggled for existence." Billington's account draws on an equally erroneous interpretation of evaporation in Webb, *Great Plains*, pp. 20–21, the errors of which were pointed out in 1939 by Shannon, "Appraisal," pp. 27–28.

79. Richard J. Russell, "Dry Climates of the United States, II, Frequency of Dry and Desert Years," *University of California Publications in Geography* 5 (1932): 245–74; Lackey, "Annual-Variability Rainfall Maps of the Great Plains"; C.

Warren Thornthwaite, *Atlas of Climatic Types in the United States, 1900–1939*, U.S. Department of Agriculture Miscellaneous Publications no. 421 (1941).

80. In *America Moves West*, 3rd ed. (New York: Holt, 1956), p. 304.

81. In *Westward Expansion*, pp. 413, 453, 470.

82. This point was made specifically by Hafen and Rister, in *Western America*: "For a dependable narrative on the evolution of the Great Plains desert concept, consult W. P. Webb, *The Great Plains*" (p. 300); and "the Great Plains desert concept is well presented in Ralph C. Morris, 'The Notion of a Great American Desert East of the Rockies'" (p. 301).

83. The Morris-Webb position is supported in Walter M. Kollmorgen, "Some Geographic Misconceptions of the Climate of Nebraska and the Great Plains" (Ph. D. diss., University of Nebraska, 1933), esp. pp. 15–30, 45–59, and 62–76). See also his Presidential address, "The Woodsman's Assaults on the Domain of the Cattleman," *Annals AAG* 59 (1969):215–18. In the preface to the only historical geography of the United States yet completed, Ralph H. Brown cites the Great American Desert idea as the classic example of the effectiveness of belief, as against actual knowledge, in modifying the course of settlement. In the first sentence of his three-chapter consideration of the Plains he refers to Webb's book and supports both his two-civilizations idea and his technological-environmental interpretation of Plains history; see *Historical Geography of the United States* (New York: Harcourt, Brace, 1948), pp. iii–iv, 369–425. More recently G. Malcolm Lewis has been the strongest supporter of the Morris-Webb view in his "Regional Ideas and Reality in the Cis-Rocky Mountain West," *Transactions, Institute of British Geographers* 38 (1966):136–38, and his "Changing Emphases in the Descriptions of the Natural Environment of the American Great Plains Area," ibid., 30 (1962):77–79. Among other geographers who accept the myth are Thomas F. Saarinen, *Perception of the Drought Hazard on the Great Plains*, University of Chicago, Research Papers in Geography no. 106 (1966), p. 14; E. Cotton Mather, "The American Great Plains," *Annals AAG* 62 (1972):237–39, 245–46. The tribute to Webb at the Association of American Geographers' meetings in Dallas, 1959 (see *Annals* 50 [1960]:85–97), is a measure of Webb's influence on geographers who study the American West.

84. See, e.g., Robert G. Athearn, *High Country Empire* (New York: McGraw-Hill, 1960), pp. 19–26, 54–60, 63–65; idem, *Forts of the Upper Missouri* (Englewood Cliffs, N.J.: Prentice-Hall, 1967), pp. 52–54, and 62–63; W. Eugene Hollon, *The Great American Desert: Then and Now* (New York: Oxford University Press, 1966), pp. 64–66, 131; John A. Hawgood, *America's Western Frontiers* (New York: Alfred A. Knopf, 1967), pp. 90, 310–12, 340, 353–57; Dillon, "Stephen Long's Great American Desert," pp. 93–95, 104–7; Robert N. Manley, *Centennial History of the University of Nebraska* (Lincoln: University of Nebraska Press, 1969), p. 3. Three geography textbooks and four maps from a 28-year period constitute Webb's evidence that the desert idea spread to the people in 1820 and remained in the mind of the populace for at least 40 years (Webb, *Great Plains*, pp. 152–60).

85. Malin, *Grassland of North America*, pp. 1–81, 120–55, 221–27, 250–51, 323–

30; *Winter Wheat in the Golden Belt of Kansas* (Lawrence: University of Kansas Press, 1944).

86. Malin, *Grassland* (rev. ed., 1956), pp. 153–55, 442.

87. Ibid., pp. 442–43. This heretical position, presented first in 1952 and published in *Scientific Monthly*, April 1953, differs from the more orthodox view revealed in 1947 (ibid., pp. 173–76). Believers in the desert concept were mainly the well-educated, esp. on the Eastern Seaboard and a dwindling minority after 1850 (Bowden, "The Great American Desert," pp. 58–68).

88. Robert G. Bell, "James C. Malin and the Grasslands of North America," *Agricultural History* 46 (1972):414–24, and "James C. Malin: A Study in American Historiography" (Ph.D. diss., University of California, Los Angeles, 1968). See also papers at Western Historical Association meeting, New Haven, Fall 1972, by Gould Coleman, "History in Recent America: The Life of James C. Malin," and by Robert W. Johannsen, "James C. Malin: An Appreciation."

89. See note 73 above.

90. E.g., John Opie's paper "Faustian Man and Frontier Expansionism," presented at Annual Meeting, American Historical Association, New York, December 1971.

91. John R. Borchert's A.A.G. Presidential address predicts "The Dust Bowl in the 1970s" (*Annals AAG* 61 [1971]:1–22). There is much evidence to refute Borchert's thesis of rhythmic droughts in the Plains and to conclude that droughts occur randomly "except for a small rhythmic component of slightly more than two years." See Merlin P. Lawson, "The Climate of the Great American Desert," Ph.D. diss., Clark University, 1973, chap 5. But if severe droughts in the Plains show no cyclical pattern, they are recurrent. Dust-bowl conditions may recur in the 1970s as the suitcase-farming frontier expands in response to grain shortages and high prices. A series of Dust Bowls like that of the 1930s will occur again soon and receive extensive coverage in the news media. And Webb's desert view of the Plains will be affirmed in the academic and popular minds. For the prospects of a man-induced Dust Bowl, see Leslie Hewes, *The Suitcase Farming Frontier* (Lincoln: University of Nebraska Press, 1974), pp. 161–86.

92. Wright, *Human Nature in Geography*, p. 20. Reprinted with revision from "A Plea for the History of Geography," *Isis* 8 (1926):477–91. The essay that explicitly encourages geographers to study the effects of the environment on geographical ideas is "The History of Geography: A Point of View," *Annals AAG* 15 (1925):192–201.

6

The Rise and Decline

of "Sequent Occupance":

A Chapter in the History

of American Geography

MARVIN W. MIKESELL

Among the most valuable of the lessons to be learned from the history of science are those concerning the ways in which science has hitherto reflected human nature and will doubtless always continue to reflect it.

John K. Wright[1]

HISTORIANS OF SCIENCE usually display confidence in their findings; for the new in their inquiries inevitably seems superior to the old, and the progress they detect can usually be explained by successful experimentation. That the "riddle of the universe" will always frustrate science does not discourage the expectation that each new effort may result in a significant discovery: all that is needed is the right combination of intellect, design, and tools.

This image of relentless movement toward wisdom is no doubt held also by most geographers, even though the "new" of their enterprise is not always more virtuous or more powerful than the "old." Nor are the changing currents of geographical thought always manifestations of progress. In addition to the refinements that are the hallmarks of a cumulative literature, the writings of geographers reveal also sporadic excite-

149

ments that can be explained only by the fickleness of human nature. We embrace new ideas, use them for a while, then cast them aside. And the ideas thus abandoned may never have been disproved by objective standards; they may simply have been discarded because they were no longer fashionable. If one looks back, the landscape of American geography may seem littered with the detritus of abandoned tasks. But this impression is misleading, since our landscape is more accurately described as a scene composed of both relics and novelties.

The discussion that follows provides an account of the fate of a particular geographical concept. Since there are few precedents for this kind of inquiry, my effort, like Wright's "bibliobiography,"[2] is experimental. I have selected sequent occupance for the reason that this concept attracted considerable attention in its time and because the period of its use can be delimited with reasonable precision. The term "sequent occupance" was introduced by Derwent Whittlesey in 1929;[3] and although it is still used occasionally by American geographers,[4] it had virtually disappeared from our literature by the end of the 1950s. During this period of approximately thirty years, sequent occupance evolved from novelty to relic without ever being subjected to critical review.

INTRODUCTION OF THE CONCEPT

"Human occupance of area, like other biotic phenomena, carries within itself the seed of its own transformation."[5] Whittlesey offered both a model and a case study to support this seminal declaration. The case study dealt with an area in New England where four stages of occupance, each expressive of internal evolution, could be identified. First was an Indian stage, characterized by hunting and collecting in a forest. Next came a farming stage, during which gentle slopes were plowed and steep slopes were grazed. In the present stage the area was covered with second-growth forest, and occupance was limited to occasional grazing. On the basis of this progression, a fourth stage, when the forest would be cut periodically by nonresident owners, was hypothesized.

Whittlesey described each of these stages or "generations of human occupance" as being "linked to its forebear and to its offspring," and their progression impressed him as being a consequence of internal forces analogous to the multiplication and destruction of living cells. Stage 1 was upset by technological innovations. As destruction of the forest commenced, stage 2, farming, began. Farming, in turn, succumbed to decreasing yields, initiating a contemporary era of secondary forest.

But the model seemingly validated by this study was imperfect. As its author admitted, "the present era of idle land and renascent forest" was seen to represent "not a distinct mode of human occupance but a transitional period in which vestiges of the farming epoch linger on in the casual grazing of the margins, and in which an earnest of the epoch to come is offered by constantly meliorating tree growth." Moreover, although alterations evolving from the inherent character of a particular mode of occupance "follow a normal pattern and at length usher in a new and consequent mode," external forces are "likely to interfere with the normal course, altering either its direction or rate, or both." Hence normal sequences might be rare, perhaps only ideal.

Whittlesey's caution about "normal sequences" might have checked the adoption of his model if geographers had not been conditioned by exposure to the Davisian conception of an ideal erosion cycle to believe that external or disruptive forces could be incorporated into schemes of internal evolution; and Whittlesey may have endorsed this notion in a later study of Ellsworth, Maine, when he referred to "chorological rejuvenation" produced by tourism.[6] In any case, the qualifications Whittlesey suggested at the end of his 1929 essay proved to be less important than his notion of an ideal sequence and the promise of prediction it offered.

The erosion cycle had already encouraged a generation of American geographers to think in such terms, and it seemed reasonable to suppose that these ideas could be transferred from the brown to the black lines on topographic maps.[7] Moreover, historical investigations designed to produce generalizations of an evolutionist character had already been conducted by several geographers, and these studies seemed to offer an alternative to environmentalism.[8] Yet, ironically, sequent occupance could also be welcomed as a way of avoiding the more emphatic historicism that was evident in the conception of geography as a discipline devoted to narrative study of the processes that transform natural landscapes into cultural landscapes. By presenting stages or cross-sections rather than a more complete account of the development of landscapes, geographers could subordinate the chronological to the chorological and thus avoid the commitment to detailed historical and even prehistorical investigation that Sauer had recommended.[9]

The adopters of sequent occupance may also have been encouraged by a desire to decorate their discipline with neologisms. "Occupance" was already well established in the American geographical literature, and the response to Whittlesey's phrase seems to have been generally favorable, although geographers sensitive to the authority of their dictionaries occasionally rendered it as "sequence of occupancy." In any case, contributors to the *Annals* offered these endorsements:

> It should soothe the ear, slip easily into the mind, and, if possible define itself or almost define itself. Such a word is Mr. Whittlesey's "occupance."[10]

> We should ask, before a new word is offered, "Will this word by its fitness and its sound win friends?" Some terms are pleasant to the ear; I like Whittlesey's phrase "sequent occupance" and Trewartha's "confluence site." They have a pleasant sound and the advantage of meaning what their derivations suggest. These are two qualities that a new word ought to have; it should have an agreeable sound and it should define itself.[11]

APPLICATIONS

Was sequent occupance a new concept or merely a new term? Most of the ideas in Whittlesey's essay were already familiar to American geographers. Preston James recalls that the procedures and objectives later identified with sequent occupance were discussed during the annual spring field conferences held in the Midwest in the 1920s.[12] Nevertheless, several features of Whittlesey's presentation suggest more than a new label for a familiar enterprise. The assumptions that landscape evolution could be described in terms of diagnostic stages, that the progression of these stages could be predicted, and that variations from predicted or normal sequences would result from exogenous forces added up to a new generalization about landscape evolution and not merely to a reiteration of what had already been verified. Moreover, since these ideas were evident in physiography and plant ecology, sequent occupance is probably best described as an analogue model—an attempt to transfer concepts from natural science to human geography. In short, sequent occupance was a heuristic device, and as such could endure only if it inspired work comparable in rationale to Whittlesey's New England study.

Such work seems to have been initiated almost immediately, for within two years Dodge presented a study of sequent occupance on an Illinois prairie, and Thomas published a paper on sequent occupance in a section of St. Louis.[13] These studies seemed to confirm the idea that the interplay of landscape-building forces could be examined effectively by means of a series of temporal cross-sections. Dodge described three stages: pioneer settlement along a tributary of the Illinois River, first expansion into the prairie, and completion of the settlement of the prairie. Thomas found five stages: pioneer, farmer, village, mining, and manufacturing.

Moreover, Thomas drew profiles representing typical landscape features during each of these stages and thus initiated a method of illustration that soon became a characteristic feature of sequent occupance studies. The use of this illustrative technique also implied belief that sequent occupance studies might be likened to the use of single frames from a motion picture to capture the essence of landscape evolution. This additional idea—that the stages, or cross-sections, could be regarded as portraits—was endorsed by Whittlesey's later assertion that "stage of occupance" should refer to "an epoch during which the human occupance of an area remains constant in its fundamental aspects."[14]

The several ideas implicit in the introduction and early application of sequent occupance soon enjoyed currency among geographers. During the "Conference of Regions," which highlighted the 1935 meeting of the Association of American Geographers, Robert Hall declared that "more and more emphasis must be directed toward cultural succession"; and the Davisian formula—structure-process-stage—was given human-geographical connotation by George Cressey's assertion that cultural landscape "equals the fundament, plus the culture, plus the sequent occupance or succession."[15] In a later conference on cultural geography, Hall recommended that an attempt be made to "layer occupance upon

occupance in much the same manner as the geologist studies stratifica-
tions."[16]

The enthusiasm evident in these remarks was more emphatically expressed in 1934, when James used sequent occupance as one of the
organizing themes in a textbook. His major theme, derived from Siegfried Passarge's concept of *Landschaftsgürtel*, was the division of the
earth into bioclimatic realms. In the textbook the several strategies followed by James in his account of the human geography of these realms
included sequent occupance or "the concept of a succession of cultures
more or less separate in time, and each marking the face of the earth in
accordance with its own mode."[17] Thus he described three stages of occupance for the Mediterranean scrub-forest lands: first, a pioneer stage,
characterized by "scattered or patchy distribution of settlements in the
midst of undeveloped lands"; then a stage of elaboration "when the outline of settlement is filled in and begins to show a closer and closer relationship to the underlying qualities of the land"; finally, a climax stage,
when "adjustment becomes nicer and more detailed" and "each significant change in the character of the soil, the surface, and drainage, or any
other feature of the land is reflected by a change in the way that land is
used."[18]

The most striking evidence of the early popularity of sequent occupance was its use in doctoral dissertations. The first such use seems to
have been at the University of Michigan, where studies by Glendinning,
Kendall, and Davis contain brief sections on the sequential development
of settlement and land use.[19] Later Meyer presented an account of the
"sequent occupance forms and functions" of the Kankakee Marsh of
northern Indiana and Illinois, and Alfred Wright offered a study of
three periods in the evolution of the industrial geography of the middle
Miami Valley of Ohio.[20] Meyer's work was especially important in that
it offered a detailed description of sequent occupance and because the
"silhouettes" illustrating the several stages of his study brought the idea
of "snap-shot historical geography" to effective realization.

Still, the fact that sequent occupance probably attained a climax in
Meyer's work of 1936 did not discourage further application of the ideas
and research strategies embodied in the concept. For example, sixteen
out of sixty-four dissertations completed at the University of Chicago be-

tween 1939 and 1956 reveal explicit or implicit adoption. Six of these studies present the sequential development of settlement and land use as their major theme,[21] and the other ten offer cross-sections for particular dates or descriptions of longer intervals as a contribution to understanding contemporary scenes.[22] The group of six apply sequent occupance as an organizing theme, whereas the other ten adopt the idea of the cross-section as a convenient way to present necessary historical background.

Historical geography had of course been practiced by University of Chicago students since the time of Sauer and Parkins[23] and was presented, largely in terms of an evolutionary view of "human adjustment" to varied environments, in the teaching of Barrows.[24] Moreover, two dissertations completed at Chicago employ terminology ("youth," "adolescence," "maturity," "old age") that belongs to a parallel adventure in geographical ideology.[25] Therefore, many of the Chicago students who adopted frameworks or approaches that can be described as sequent occupance may only have glanced at Whittlesey's essay of 1929 or may have received its message indirectly. The distinction here is not unlike that between the "Turner thesis" and historical interpretations that are merely "Turnerian."[26] In any case, the use of sequent occupance at the University of Chicago developed slowly but persistently after 1939, reached a peak in 1948, and then declined until the final study of this type was presented in 1956. This evidence of rise and decline offers ample opportunity for speculation, but first we need to know more about the rationale and accomplishment of the many geographers who tried to re-create a succession of geographies.

PERSISTENT FEATURES OF DESIGN

Sequent occupance studies may be grouped according to their organization and presentation. Economic or land-use criteria were used most commonly in the determination of stages—that is, subsistence-farming stage, lumbering stage, mining stage, industrial stage, and so on—but few studies displayed consistency in this regard. For example, Ackerman defined five periods in the sequent occupance of a suburban Boston community: aboriginal Indian, colonial subsistence, dairying and manufacturing, rural depopulation, and intensive truck farming and residential property expansion.[27] Similarly, in his study of the High Plains of Michigan, Davis referred to an Indian period, a period of French fur trader and Jesuit missionary activity, a period of British control, and a period of American forest clearing and pioneer agriculture.[28] As the use of ethnic, economic, demographic, and political labels in these studies implies, different stages were defined by different criteria.

Occupance periods, or stages, were usually given ethnic or political labels (for example, Indian, British, American) but were described in terms of land use, settlement, or communication (pioneer farming, urbanization, impact of the railroad). In other words, definitive expressions were coined to fit the character of each stage and little effort was made to coordinate such expressions with those used to describe previous stages. Indeed, the literature of sequent occupance includes many examples of cross-sections that differ so notably in emphasis that the connection among sections is difficult to establish. Since each stage usually introduced a new directing force, the design of sequent occupance studies often did not allow for, or proceed from, a persisting analysis of trends.

On the other hand, at least a few contributions to the sequent occupance literature placed stress on a particular process or landscape feature. Nicholson's treatment of the settlement of southwestern Ontario,[29] where "development could be traced in several stages following changes in the mode of transportation," evokes processes, whereas Dodge's assertion of "the fundamental importance of drainage" in the sequent occupance of an Illinois prairie reflects the primacy of landscape features.[30] A third class of sequent occupance studies, devoted to more specific aspects of occupation, evinced consistency in the definition of stages. Thus, McCune's study of the dominance of different plantation crops in Ceylon produced a statistically defined sequence consisting of a cinnamon period, a coffee period, a tea period, and so on.[31] Faced with a more complex transition in the agricultural history of Southern California, Gregor suggested a subsistence stage, a grain stage, a mixed-crop stage, and a specialized fruit and nut stage.[32]

Effort might expectably have been devoted to the selection of the times to be studied. Yet many studies—especially those employing sequent occupance as historical background—offered information for purely arbitrary intervals. Thus, Pounds presented descriptions of the Ruhr at 1800, 1850, and 1900 "as a prelude to examination of the Ruhr in the mid-twentieth century."[33] Similarly, Sorensen offered descriptive cross-sections of Springfield, Illinois, in 1855 and 1890 as "a background for at least a casual investigation of the genesis of selected patterns in the contemporary city."[34]

RE-EXAMINATIONS

Students of sequent occupance allowed themselves a wide range of options. They could take account of several elements of material or non-material culture or deal with only a particular variable, such as population density, transportation facilities, or land use. A further option concerned the interval of time within which descriptions were supposed to be valid—a year, a decade, a century, or even longer intervals, such as, for example, the Indian, Spanish, and American periods in the history of California. Finally, Whittlesey's concept was extended from a small part of New England to a number of areas in the United States and even to one of the world's major natural realms.

The fact that most of these options were evident soon after the introduction of sequent occupance should have encouraged both a serious re-examination of Whittlesey's initial assumptions and a critical review of the derivative literature. It is surprising that this did not happen, since geographers enjoyed excellent communication in the 1930s. A possible key to this neglect is found in Stanley Dodge's suggestion that sequent occupance might be merely "a useful expedient"; yet he also suggested a three-part definition that would have imposed a measure of discipline on the rapidly expanding literature.

> If "sequent occupance" does not become merely a phrase to cover a vague idea, three things must be involved in its meaning, (1) the idea of sequence, of time, (2) the idea of the thing or things occupying, and (3) that of the thing or things occupied.[35]

This suggestion, published only two years after the appearance of Whittlesey's essay, does not appear to have influenced later studies. Nor was much heed paid to the complaint of Richard Dodge that he could find "no agreement as to ways in which aspects of former occupance, reflected in the cultural features of the landscape, should be classified."[36]

Whittlesey himself made no substantial contribution to the evolving lore of sequent occupance, although his comments after 1929 indicate a retreat from the confidence displayed in his initial essay. Indeed, as already indicated, by 1933 he was ready to assert that the stage of occupance should be defined in reference to a relatively quiet interval: "an epoch during which the human occupance of an area remains constant in its fundamental aspects."[37] The same essentially ahistorical tone appears also in Whittlesey's contribution to the conference on cultural geography during the 1936 meeting of the Association of American Geographers, when he held that "sequent occupance implies that what has existed in the past is our concern only if it has left vestiges and so exists also, in effect, in the present."[38]

This was a far cry from Whittlesey's first contention that studies of sequent occupance would lead to both retrospective and predictive generalizations. Yet even in 1929 he was cautious about "normal sequences" and included disclaimers in his endorsement of biological and physiographical analogies. It is not surprising, therefore, that Whittlesey's most emphatic reassessment of sequent occupance was based on methodological grounds. Indeed, only in this prescriptive context can the question posed in his Presidential address of 1944 be understood: "Is there a solution for the puzzle of writing incontestable geography that also incorporates the chain of events necessary to understand fully the geography of the present day?"[39] Viewed in this light, sequent occupance seemed to offer geographers an opportunity to include both historical and geographical dimensions and yet still practice their craft according to Hartshorne's guidelines for the separation of geography and history.[40] The idea of employing static cross-sections to avoid confusions of historical and geographical objectives—an idea Hartshorne had adopted from Hettner[41]—was congenial to the introspective spirit of American geographers in the 1940s. Such studies were, in Whittlesey's words, "indubitably geographic" and could "be judged with propriety by geographers."[42] Yet the assumption that the primary and logical emphasis of geographical research should be on the present day encouraged a skeptical attitude toward even this restricted or subordinate view of historical geography." As Whittlesey cautioned,

> No series presenting the geography of consecutive earlier periods has yet been prepared for any large area. When done, the series would presumably recreate the geographic landscapes for all the epochs for which records can be found. From studies which have been made, it appears that much of the latter would have no relevance to present-day geography of the area. The sequence of wanted items might be culled from the facts presented, but it would not leap to the reader's eye and mind.[43]

DECLINE

The fact that Whittlesey felt obliged to question the relevance of his concept after a decade and a half of its extensive employment suggests that the future of sequent occupance was in doubt among geographers concerned primarily with the present day. Moreover, the restricted conception of the scope and objective of sequent occupance studies which was implicit in the methodology of Hettner and Hartshorne precluded any substantial use of the concept by geographers who sought support and inspiration from the neighboring fields of history and anthropology. Too grand in its initial form to attract such scholars, sequent occupance became too restricted for their taste after it had been redefined to conform to an ahistorical methodology.

In addition, the assumption that sequent occupance might be a route to a new determinism in geography clearly was not taken seriously. As James indicated,

> There is, of course, nothing inevitable about such a sequence of stages. In some cases areas may stagnate almost indefinitely in the stage of elaboration. In others a region may advance rapidly from a pioneer stage to the development of a number of areas of climax. . . . In still others, which may have reached a climax, events may cause a retrogression.[44]

Studies employing sequent occupance as a convenient device for the presentation of historical background displayed even more skepticism. Thus Pounds claimed "no particular importance" for the dates or periods of his historical surveys, and he did not "altogether refrain from tracing one pattern from that which preceded it."[45] Wheeler's disclaimer is even more emphatic.

> Although these dates are convenient points of reference, it must be emphasized that they do not represent sharp breaks in the sequence of development. Each period has tended to merge gradually with the next, and many of the institutions, attitudes, and cultural features of particular periods have survived in succeeding periods, or even to the present time.[46]

More generally, it is probably safe to assume that sequent occupance entered American geographical lore during a phase of antithesis rather than thesis, when the prospect of historical determinism replacing environmental determinism had little appeal. It began to fade away at the time of a new impetus toward functional and generic theses. When regional geographers began to embrace the several concepts that would turn attention toward economic and urban geography, even the half-hearted historical interest that they took in sequent occupance could be dismissed as antiquarianism.

As for the few geographers who developed an explicit commitment to historical geography, the prospect of writing several past geographies, especially for arbitrarily or vaguely defined periods, held little appeal. To be sure, comprehensive reconstructions had been achieved for particular past periods, notably by Brown,[47] but the sequent occupance approach required nothing less than a succession of such reconstructions. Viewed in Clark's terms as the study of "changing geographies" or the "geography of change,"[48] the "snap-shot" approach of sequent occupance had little utility for historical geography. Even if conceived as merely the geography of a past period of time, historical geography framed by reference to "an epoch when the human occupance of an area remains constant in its fundamental aspects" would permit only implicit consideration of the forces that produce change. Not surprisingly, therefore, sequent occupance receives relatively little attention in surveys of historical geography.[49]

Sequent occupance presented corresponding difficulties to cultural geographers, especially to those associated with Sauer at Berkeley. The emphasis on independent development *in situ* could not be adopted by scholars who had placed major emphasis on migration and diffusion. Several key sequent occupance notions (supercession, stage, uniformity) were in conflict with other notions (transition, overlap, pluralism) that figured prominently in cultural geography. Cultural geographers with an anthropological perspective could dismiss sequent occupance as a form of the discredited notion of "unilinear evolution."[50] And geographers concerned primarily with material culture could not be excited by an approach that offered effects without causes and demanded acceptance of the premise that process is implicit in stage. Indeed, for all its defects, the Turner thesis was probably a more useful approach, for it entailed recognition of the importance of movement. Turner, in his address of 1893, invited his listeners to "stand at Cumberland Gap and watch the procession of civilization, marching single file—the buffalo following the trail to the salt springs, the Indian, the fur-trader and hunter, the cattle-raiser, the pioneer farmer—and the frontier has passed by."[51] In contrast, Whittlesey might be said to have invited his readers to stand on the edge of a small area in New England and watch it transform itself.

Cultural geographers felt also that the sequent occupance focus on relatively static intervals, with its concomitant use of profiles or silhouettes, tended to mask or misrepresent actual sequences. Kniffen's study of transportation development in the lower Mississippi Valley exemplified this criticism effectively, for each of the modes of transport that he described, beginning with pirogues and canoes and ending with airplanes, extended well into the period of its successors.[52] Horses on trails and roads overlapped the use of flats and keelboats, river steamboats and tugboats, and extended even into the era of automobiles on highways. Based on intensity of use, the horseback stage was in large measure also a riverboat stage; the transition from rail to highway dominance was likewise gradual.

Similarly, the effectiveness of Broek's famous study of the Santa Clara Valley is largely attributable to his skill in combining four descriptive cross-sections (the primitive landscape, the landscape of Spanish-Mexican times, the landscape of the early American period, and the present landscape) with three accounts of the social and economic forces that fostered landscape change.[53] Broek's study, in dealing with overlap as well as succession and with turbulent as well as relatively static intervals, presented a more complete picture of landscape evolution than a series of static cross-sections alone could have offered.

Since cross-sections had doubtful merit in historical research, the methodological value of sequent occupance rested on its one testable hypothesis—the dubious assumption that change results largely from internal forces. But sequent occupance studies in fact usually demonstrated the importance of external forces and diffusion. Such studies might have led to descriptive or classificatory generalizations, but even these possibilities were frustrated by shifts of emphasis. Hence it is not an exaggeration to suggest that the fate of sequent occupance was decided when those who adopted it failed to take account of the suggestions made by Stanley Dodge in 1931 and Richard Dodge in 1934. Had their suggestions been accepted or at least kept in mind, it might have been possible to compare similar stages of occupance in different regions or the effects of different processes on landscape evolution. In fact, by accepting any one of a wide range of options in the design of their studies, the adopters of sequent occupance produced a literature that was additive rather than cumulative. James's assertion in 1948 that "explanatory studies in sequent occupance add up to something,"[54] in effect begged two important questions: whether such studies had indeed been explanatory and whether the something they added up to could provide a basis for a comparative study.

As a new style of regional description, sequent occupance did inspire some works appropriate to the humanistic and artistic traditions of geography,[55] and the rare studies focused on a particular process or landscape feature were effective by the standards applied to regional geography.[56] But the formidable historiographic problems that sequent occupance entailed could not be solved by the scholarship most commonly employed. Indeed, as suggested above, sequent occupance reached an early culmination in Meyer's work of 1936, for subsequent studies by American geographers (excepting those by Meyer himself) were not of comparable quality.[57] From its initial status as a model, sequent occupance retrogressed to become merely an organizational device in regional studies. Even in Whittlesey's later work, sequent occupance was only a subordinate theme in a program that led to his proclamation of the *compage* as geography's most compelling challenge.[58]

These comments may provide an adequate explanation for the demise of sequent occupance, although the fact that the concept was not subjected to such criticism while it was in widespread use suggests that the fickleness of human nature, mentioned earlier as a necessary postulate in the history of geography, may have figured prominently in its decline. The enthusiasm shown toward Whittlesey's concept in the 1930s offers an additional illustration of human nature in geography, for it is surely significant that most people readily identify "stages" in their own lives and that attempts to impose such schemes on the history of civilization can be traced into antiquity.

This final generalization is of course merely speculative: although we can hope to detect trends in the published lore of an academic discipline, it is difficult to be confident about subtle currents of influence and rationale. In any case, the issue just raised can be rephrased as a question: Was sequent occupance a predictable or inevitable adventure for American geographers? This question has to be answered affirmatively, if we endorse the premise that most scholars find it difficult to accept purposelessness or disorder. Neither history nor geography can be written indiscriminately; and since time cannot be comprehended as a continuum, the search for order in historical geography must entail sequential arrangement. Therefore, when geographers embraced the idea of historical explanation as an alternative to environmental explanation, sequent occupance had instant appeal. Nor is geography unique in this respect; for concern about causes and effects is a necessary part of any scholarly enterprise, and extension of this concern requires the use of temporal stepping stones. It is not surprising, therefore, that each of the groups devoted to the study of mankind, even economists,[59] has at least flirted with stages, cycles, and inevitable progressions; nor is it surprising that attempts to offer such schemes as an explanation of human destiny —from Hesiod and Varro to Marx and Spengler and on to the "universal historians" of our time—figure prominently in intellectual history.[60] Whittlesey may be placed in this company, for although the scale of his generalizations was less than universal he seems clearly to have believed, if only for a moment, that he had found a key to cultural evolution.

Marvin W. Mikesell

SUMMARY

It is often claimed that the character of current geographical thought exhibits the contrast between the old and the new. Yet no decade in the history of geography has been devoid of this contrast. Moreover, the assertion that the contrast of old and new is or has been a prominent feature of our lore begs a perplexing question, for one is always tempted to ask whether the changing fashions of geography reflect the refinement of a science or simply the fickleness of human nature. The fact that we are often unable to answer this question means that a good case can be made for experimentation in the history of geography.

In 1962 John K. Wright offered one such experiment by treating the career of Ellen Semple's "Influences of Geographic Environment" as a case study in the history of American geography. I have attempted here to examine the career of sequent occupance, which was introduced to American geographers in the 1920s, was widely used in both teaching and research in the 1930s and 1940s, and then faded from our scene in the 1950s. Sequent occupance probably became popular because it was an "analogue model," built in emulation of the erosion cycle and the concepts of succession and climax in plant ecology. Sequent occupance seemed also to promise a historical determinism to replace environmental determinism. But it was Whittlesey's case study, rather than his highly tentative generalizations about landscape evolution, that encouraged the proliferation of sequent occupance studies, and the large literature thus inspired proved to be additive rather than cumulative.

Since sequent occupance was not subjected to serious criticism while it was in widespread use, we can only speculate on the reasons for its eventual decline. Speculations that seem plausible include the influence of ahistorical methodology in the decade after 1939 and the formidable difficulties inherent in the re-creation of a succession of geographies. In addition, few geographers interested in the past viewed with favor a conceptual framework that emphasized local development rather than diffusion and that required acceptance of the Davisian assumption that process is implicit in stage. But since the weaknesses and inherent difficulties of sequent occupance were seldom mentioned, its abandonment in the

1950s may have been prompted by a general but unstated realization that the program, which seemed exciting in the 1930s, had become a routine and redundant exercise a generation later. If so, the life cycle of sequent occupance—from initiation through adoption and application to neglect—may best be explained, in Wright's terms, as a manifestation of "human nature in geography."

NOTES

1. In "Human Nature in Science," *Science* 100 (1944):299–305; reprinted in John K. Wright, *Human Nature in Geography* (Cambridge: Harvard University Press, 1966), p. 54.
2. See Wright, "Miss Semple's 'Influences of Geographic Environment': Notes Toward a Bibliobiography," *Geographical Review* 52 (1962):346–61; reprinted in *Human Nature in Geography*, pp. 188–204.
3. In "Sequent Occupance," *Annals of the Association of American Geographers* (hereafter *Annals AAG*) 19 (1929):162–65.
4. E.g., C. Langdon White, "Sequent Occupance in the Santa Clara Valley, California," *Journal of the Graduate Research Center, Southern Methodist University* 34 (1965):277–99; Gerald H. Krausse, "Historic Galena: A Study of Urban Change and Development in a Midwestern Mining Town," *Bulletin of the Illinois Geographical Society* 13 (1971):3–19; and C. Daniel Dillman, "Occupance Phases of the Lower Rio Grande of Texas and Tamaulipas," *California Geographer* 12 (1971):30–37.
5. Whittlesey, "Sequent Occupance," p. 162.
6. In "The Urbanization of a Farm Village," *Annals AAG* 21 (1931):142–43 (abstract).
7. For an earlier attempt to make this transfer, see John L. Rich, "Cultural Features and the Physiographic Cycle," *Geographical Review* 10 (1920):297–308.
8. E.g., several publications of Preston E. James, which appeared before Whittlesey's essay and might well be regarded as studies of sequent occupance. See esp. "Some Geographic Relations in Trinidad," *Scottish Geographical Magazine* 42 (1926):84–93; "A Geographic Reconnaissance of Trinidad," *Economic Geography* 3 (1927):87–109; and his later evaluation of the predictions made in these studies in "Changes in the Geography of Trinidad," *Scottish Geographical Magazine* 73 (1957):158–66. See also his better known study of "The Blackstone Valley," *Annals AAG* 19 (1929):67–109.
9. Carl O. Sauer, "The Morphology of Landscape," *University of California Publications in Geography* 2 (1925):19–53.
10. J. Russell Smith, "Are We Free to Coin New Terms?" *Annals AAG* 25 (1935):18.
11. R. H. Whitbeck, comment on Preston E. James's "The Terminology of Regional Description," *Annals AAG* 24 (1934):87.

12. Personal communication, June 4, 1973. For the character of these conferences and a list of participants, see James's *All Possible Worlds: A History of Geographical Ideas* (Indianapolis: Bobbs-Merrill, 1972), pp. 411–12.

13. Stanley D. Dodge, "Sequent Occupance on an Illinois Prairie," *Bulletin of the Geographical Society of Philadelphia* 29 (1931):205–9; Lewis F. Thomas, "The Sequence of Areal Occupancy in a Section of St. Louis, Missouri," *Annals AAG* 21 (1931):75–90.

14. Whittlesey, "Coastland and Interior Mountain Valley: A Geographical Study of Two Typical Localities in Northern New England," in John K. Wright, ed., *New England's Prospect* (New York: American Geographical Society, 1933), p. 451n.

15. In "A Conference on Regions," *Annals AAG* 25 (1935):129 and 133.

16. In "Round Table on Problems in Cultural Geography," *Annals AAG* 27 (1937): 168.

17. Preston E. James, *An Outline of Geography* (Boston: Ginn, 1934), p. 33.

18. Ibid., pp. 126–27. This formulation represents an elaboration of ideas first presented by James in his studies of Trinidad.

19. Robert M. Glendinning, "The Lake St. Jean Lowland, Province of Quebec," *Michigan Papers in Geography* 5 (1935):313–41; Henry M. Kendall, "The Central Pyrenean Piedmont of France," ibid., pp. 377–414; Charles M. Davis, "The High Plains of Michigan," ibid., 6 (1936):303–41.

20. Alfred H. Meyer, "The Kankakee 'Marsh' of Northern Indiana and Illinois," ibid. 6 (1936):359–96; Alfred J. Wright, "The Industrial Geography of the Middle Miami Valley, Ohio," ibid., pp. 401–27.

21. James Glasgow, "Muskegon, Michigan: The Evolution of a Lake Port" (1939); Carl F. Carlson, "Aurora, Illinois: A Study in Sequent Land Use" (1940); Wilfred G. Richards, "The Settlement of the Miami Valley of Southwestern Ohio" (1948); James S. Matthews, "Expressions of Urbanism in the Sequent Occupance of Northwestern Ohio" (1949); Ida M. Shrode, "The Sequent Occupance of the Rancho Azusa de Duarte: A Segment of the Upper San Gabriel Valley of California" (1948); and Maurice E. McGaugh, "The Settlement of the Saginaw Basin," *University of Chicago, Department of Geography Research Papers*, no. 16 (1950).

22. Robert L. Wrigley, Jr., "The Occupational Structure of Pocatello, Idaho" (1942); Elizabeth Eiselen, "A Geographic Traverse across South Dakota" (1943); Edward L. Ullman, "Mobile: Industrial Seaport and Trade Center" (1943); Edward B. Espenshade, Jr., "Urban Development at the Upper Rapids of the Mississippi" (1944); Howard J. Nelson, "The Livelihood Structure of Des Moines, Iowa" (1949); Jesse H. Wheeler, Jr., "Land Use in Greenbrier County, West Virginia," *University of Chicago, Department of Geography Research Papers*, no. 15 (1950); Clarence W. Sorensen, "The Internal Structure of the Springfield, Illinois, Urbanized Area," ibid., no. 20 (1951); Richard S. Thoman, "The Changing Occupance Pattern of the Tri-State Area: Missouri, Kansas, Oklahoma," ibid., no. 31 (1953); Sheldon D. Ericksen, "Occupance in the Upper Deschutes Basin, Oregon," ibid., no. 32 (1953); and David E. Christensen, "Rural Occupance in Transition: Lee and Sumter Counties, Georgia," ibid., no. 43 (1956).

23. Carl O. Sauer, *The Geography of the Ozark Highland of Missouri* (Chicago: Geographic Society of Chicago, 1915); Almon E. Parkins, *The Historical Geography of Detroit* (East Lansing: Michigan Historical Commission, 1918).
24. Harlan H. Barrows, *Lectures on the Historical Geography of the United States as Given in 1933*, ed. William A. Koelsch, University of Chicago, Department of Geography Research Papers no. 77 (1962).
25. Herbert L. Minton, "The Evolution of Conway, Arkansas" (1939); and Bernard H. Schockel, "Manufactural Evansville, 1820–1933" (1947). The most emphatic assertion of this kind of organic analogy during the period of our concern appears in Griffith Taylor's "The Seven Ages of Towns," *Economic Geography* 21 (1945):156–60, and Samuel Van Valkenburg's *Elements of Political Geography* (New York: Prentice-Hall, 1944).
26. For discussion of this distinction, see J. L. M. Gulley, "The Turnerian Frontier: A Study in the Migration of Ideas," *Tijdschrift voor Economische en Sociale Geografie* 50 (1959):65–72, 81–91.
27. Edward Ackerman, "Sequent Occupance of a Boston Suburban Community," *Economic Geography* 17 (1941):61–74.
28. See note 19 above.
29. Norman L. Nicholson, "The Establishment of Settlement Patterns in Ausable Watershed, Ontario," *Geographical Bulletin* 1 (1952):1–13.
30. See note 13 above.
31. Shannon McCune, "Sequence of Plantation Agriculture in Ceylon," *Economic Geography* 25 (1949):226–35.
32. Howard F. Gregor, "Agricultural Shifts in the Ventura Lowland of California," *Economic Geography* 29 (1953):340–61.
33. Norman J. G. Pounds, *The Ruhr: A Study in Historical and Economic Geography* (Bloomington: University of Indiana Press, 1952), p. 15.
34. "The Internal Structure of the Springfield, Illinois, Urbanized Area," p. 45.
35. "Sequent Occupance on an Illinois Prairie," p. 205.
36. Richard E. Dodge, "The Interpretation of Sequent Occupance," *Annals AAG* 28 (1938):233.
37. "Coastland and Interior Mountain Valley," p. 451.
38. In "Round Table on Problems in Cultural Geography," *Annals AAG* 27 (1937): 168–70. In his response to Whittlesey's presentation, Stanley Dodge suggested that "sequent occupance might well be limited to those points in the whole history of population growth where significant population changes have taken place."
39. Derwent Whittlesey, "The Horizon of Geography," *Annals AAG* 35 (1945):32.
40. Richard Hartshorne, "The Nature of Geography: A Critical Survey of Current Thought in the Light of the Past," *Annals AAG* 29 (1939), esp. chap. 4, "The Relations of History and Geography." Hartshorne's subsequent discussion of this theme, which includes an endorsement of the study of "differences from place to place changing through time," appeared too late to influence the fate of sequent occupance. See his *Perspective on the Nature of Geography*, Monograph Series, Association of American Geographers, no. 1 (Chicago: Rand McNally, 1959), esp. chap. 8, "Time and Genesis in Geography," p. 103.

41. Alfred Hettner, "Das Wesen und die Methoden der Geographie," *Geographische Zeitschrift* 11 (1905):556.
42. In "The Horizon of Geography," p. 38.
43. Ibid., pp. 31–32.
44. *An Outline of Geography*, p. 127.
45. *The Ruhr*, p. 15.
46. "Land Use in Greenbrier County, West Virginia," p. 48.
47. Ralph H. Brown, *Mirror for Americans: Likeness of the Eastern Seaboard, 1810* (New York: American Geographical Society, 1943).
48. Andrew H. Clark, "Geographical Change: A Theme for Economic History," *Journal of Economic History* 20 (1960):613.
49. See, e.g., Andrew H. Clark, "Historical Geography," in P. E. James and C. F. Jones, eds., *American Geography: Inventory and Prospect* (Syracuse: Syracuse University Press, 1954), pp. 71–105; H. Roy Merrens, "Historical Geography and Early American History," *William and Mary Quarterly* 22 (1965):529–48; and Hugh C. Prince, "Real, Imagined and Abstract Worlds of the Past," *Progress in Geography* 3 (London: Edward Arnold, 1971):1–86.
50. Julian H. Steward, *Theory of Culture Change: The Methodology of Multilinear Evolution* (Urbana: University of Illinois Press, 1955), pp. 11–29.
51. Frederick Jackson Turner, "The Significance of the Frontier in American History," *Annual Report of the American Historical Association for 1893* (Washington, 1894), pp. 199–227; reprinted in *The Frontier in American History* (New York: Henry Holt, 1920, 1947), p. 12. See also Ralph H. Brown's durable *Historical Geography of the United States* (New York: Harcourt, Brace, 1948), which emphasizes the westward movement of the American settlement frontier.
52. See Fred Kniffen, "Geography and the Past," *Journal of Geography* 50 (1951): 126–28.
53. Jan O. M. Broek, *The Santa Clara Valley, California: A Study in Landscape Changes* (Utrecht: Oosthoek, 1932). See also H. C. Darby's "An Historical Geography of England Twenty Years After," *Geographical Journal* 126 (1960): 147–59, in which Broek's design is endorsed as an effective strategy for the presentation of historical geography in a book composed of contributions by several authors. The book anticipated by Darby has since been published: H. C. Darby ed., *A New Historical Geography of England* (Cambridge: Cambridge University Press, 1973).
54. In "Formulating Objectives of Geographic Research," *Annals AAG* 38 (1948): 274.
55. See, e.g., Edward C. Higbee's "The Three Earths of New England," *Geographical Review* 42 (1952):425–38.
56. See, e.g., Glenn T. Trewartha, "A Second Epoch of Destructive Occupance in the Driftless Hill Lands," *Annals AAG* 30 (1940):109–42; and Robert B. Hall, "Tokaido: Road and Region," *Geographical Review* 27 (1937):353–77.
57. Alfred H. Meyer, "Circulation and Settlement Patterns of the Calumet Region of Northwestern Indiana and Northeastern Illinois (The First Stage of Occupance—The Pottawatamie and the Fur Trader)," *Annals AAG* 44 (1954):245–

75; and ". . . (The Second Stage of Occupance—Pioneer Settler and Subsistence Economy)," 46 (1956):312–56.

58. Whittlesey, "Southern Rhodesia: An African Compage," *Annals AAG* 46 (1956):1–97.

59. E.g., W. W. Rostow, *The Stages of Economic Growth* (Cambridge: Cambridge University Press, 1960).

60. For elaboration of this theme, see Arthur O. Lovejoy and George Boas, *Primitivism and Related Ideas in Antiquity* (Baltimore: The Johns Hopkins Press, 1953); and Fritz L. Kramer, "Eduard Hahn and the End of the 'Three Stages of Man,'" *Geographical Review* 57 (1967):73–89.

7

Unearthly Delights:

Cemetery Names and the Map of

the Changing American Afterworld

WILBUR ZELINSKY

Geosophy . . . is the study of geographical knowledge from any or all points of view. . . . It extends far beyond the core area of scientific geographical knowledge or of geographical knowledge as otherwise systematized by geographers. . . . It covers the geographical ideas, both true and false, of all manner of people—not only geographers, but farmers and fishermen, business executives and poets, novelists and painters, Bedouins and Hottentots—and for this reason it necessarily has to do in large degree with subjective conceptions.

John K. Wright[1]

AMERICANS DO NOT ENJOY thinking about death. This dismal truism can be documented by any number of examples, mostly tactics of avoidance. Thus, although funerals and cemeteries represent a robust economic enterprise, hard statistics are difficult to come by, as Jessica Mitford discovered.[2] Cemeteries obviously account for an appreciable fraction of the land surface of the United States, but even the most tentative of percentage figures are unobtainable. Although we can only speculate about the gross number of cemeteries, the total probably falls somewhere between 10,000 and 100,000, depending, in part, on how one defines the term.

This collective national amnesia with respect to a distasteful subject is perhaps best illustrated by the astonishing fact that in virtually none of our planned towns, cities, or suburbs is land set aside for the departed. As William H. Whyte has noted, in discussing our latter-day quasi-utopian urban schemes, "in no new town plan I have seen is there space allotted to a cemetery."[3] Similarly, in few of the many maps and drawings of nineteenth-century American cities that I have recently examined is the cemetery an integral part of the initial plan.[4] When the cemetery did come into being in a plan or in actuality, it was obviously an afterthought.

Even though death is not a favorite topic for the data-gathering organizations of a future-oriented society with scant regard for its past, the dearth of scholarly interest is nonetheless striking. Economists, sociologists, and geographers have all pointedly shunned the theme of mortality,[5] although it is a commonplace that funerary practices offer some of the most profound insights into the social and psychological structure of cultural groups, past and present. There has been some interesting, but hardly exhaustive, work by art historians and archaeologists on American gravestones,[6] and some landscape architects have considered the design of the more elaborate American cemeteries.[7] But among geographers only Darden, Deane, Francaviglia, Jackson, Kniffen, Knight, Pattison, and Price have written on the cemetery as an element in the cultural landscape, and then only in cursory or introductory essays.[8] Even in the economics of land use, where one might logically expect a sharp focus of geographical interest, attention has been minimal.[9]

MATERIALS AND METHODS

I wish to suggest two productive research strategies for the student of American necrogeography concerned with a fuller understanding of the cultural landscape or with changing geosophical notions. The first is the analysis on a local, regional, and national basis of the spatial patterns of our cemeteries, including size, shape, number, site, situation, and internal design.[10] The second—and the one to be pursued here—exploits the information implicit in the names chosen for our cemeteries. My thesis is that these names are quite literally a legend for a map that has never been drawn—that of the American concept of the afterworld—and that this geosophical design has undergone revision over the past century or more in a manner traceable through toponymic evidence.

Even though most Americans to all appearances have contemplated death and the afterlife only reluctantly, intermittently, usually privately, and—at least until quite recently—hazily, their envisaged abodes for the deceased do have real form and measurable attributes, just as is the case for other mental objects. Moreover, these attributes can be charted by considering cemetery names. Just as future archaeologists could reconstruct the objective American scene with some realism if our place names alone were to survive, so we can piece together, however provisionally, the configuration of the ever-changing eternal resting place of our dead from its nomenclature. And, of course, such an exercise might tell us quite a bit about ourselves and our living world.

The central contention of this essay—that cemetery names meaningfully, if blurredly, convey our collective image of an afterworld—is far from being robust. Methodical analysis is patently impossible until we know a great deal more about two neglected topics: the American cemetery in its major social and geographical contexts, and the social psychology of place-naming in the United States. Thus I offer the assumption as a statement of faith and intuition, one that happens to yield interesting results, rather than as a hypothesis subject to rigorous testing at this time.

In working with this theme, I am beset by two troublesome dualities. The nature of the object being named is ambiguous. The cemetery may be classified either as a this-worldly park, a place of solace and comfort intended primarily for the bereaved, or as a metaphor or working model of the afterlife, a sort of vestibule into the land of the departed and a point of attachment between the here and the there, or as both simultaneously. (Obviously, it may also be an expression of reverence toward the body as the vessel or temple of the soul, from which it is temporarily separated.) Toponymic evidence can be cited to support either interpretation. If I have chosen the second alternative in this essay, it is without any intention of slighting the scholarly potential of treating cemeteries and their names as parts of the living landscape.[11]

Another possible dualistic theme is whether a significant distinction exists between the way namers of cemeteries regard these places (and the afterworld which in my thesis the cemetery epitomizes) and the way their clientele regards them. The American situation contrasts sharply with most Old World experience, for in America a small number of persons were obliged to confer names quickly and self-consciously on all manner of things and places.[12] The problem (echoing the Wrightian phraseology quoted in my epigraph) is whether the unsystematized geographical ideas of persons who were, at least for the moment, "business executives and poets," spontaneously and faithfully reflected the geosophy of the population at large. Or did they foist their own biased notions upon the common herd? A reliable answer awaits more factual evidence than is at hand. In the meantime, I venture my hunch that there was genuine convergence, a give-and-take of attitudes. Thus, the careful contrivance of names and the artfully planned physical layout of cemeteries must have colored popular concepts about burial places and the shadowy configuration of an afterworld. But at the same time the name-smiths must have striven diligently to divine the impulses of the popular mind and to chart the channels along which such impulses might be led, just as has been happening with the naming of new automobiles and residential subdivisions. Quite possibly the leaders are leading and being led at the same time.

In the most thoughtful effort to date to categorize American place-names, George R. Stewart has proposed ten classes: descriptive names, association names, possessive names, incident names, commemorative names, commendatory names, coined names, transfer and shift names, folk-etymology names, and mistake names.[13] To this list I suggest adding an eleventh category—projective names, a group abundantly represented among the designations applied to suburbs, subdivisions, cemeteries, and towns platted and promoted by land speculators.[14] Such names are not derived from the history of the locality or the namers, and even if they do happen to describe some aspects of the place in question, such a congruence is accidental as often as not.

The distinctiveness of the projective place-name lies in the fact that it describes either a physical entity which does not yet exist (but may later materialize) or else some fanciful, mentally contrived landscape that can be realized only in the imagination. It is generally intended to elicit a specific emotional response. The critical attribute is image-mongering, whether inspired by greed or by disinterested idealism.

Not all American cemetery names ought to be characterized as projective. More than half of those listed in the sources used in this study are possessive or locational. Possessive names refer to a municipality or other jurisdiction, church group, fraternal organization (usually I.O.O.F. or Masons), to an ethnic group (Colored Cemetery, Serbian National Cemetery, German Lutheran Cemetery, for example), or to a founding family or commercial proprietor. The locational cemetery name is simply taken directly from a hill, stream, lake, neighborhood, or landmark feature at or near the burial place. Although there are many borderline cases, such possessive and locational names have been conscientiously excluded, when considering specific names, so that in this essay we are left for most purposes with a group of projective and commemorative names.

Source materials constitute a major problem for the collector of cemetery names. Only two systematic attempts at comprehensive coverage are available; they are for the years 1957 and 1967,[15] and both are restricted to extant cemeteries with business offices, thus excluding countless family plots, other casually managed rural burial grounds, and abandoned graveyards, most of which are unnamed. A more complete inventory could be compiled by scrutinizing the several thousand large-scale topographic quadrangles published by the United States Geological Survey, but such an exercise would require an inordinate amount of (pleasant!) drudgery and would still be incomplete until that far-off day when the final quadrangle has been issued.

The American Cemetery Association's 1967 directory has approximately ten thousand names as against eight thousand in the 1957 list. Because of the obvious qualitative as well as quantitative superiority of the later compilation, I have devoted most of my attention to it. For earlier cemetery names, the most useful source has proved to be the county and city atlases issued in profusion, with lavish pictorial and verbal as well as cartographic material, especially between the years 1865 and 1895.[16]

From the magnificent collection of the Division of Maps, Library of Congress, I have been able to identify 703 projective and commemorative names from the late Colonial period through 1910.[17] I made no attempt to collect and tabulate material on the internal nomenclature of cemeteries—that is, the designations of lanes, driveways, specific sections, or other features—since only a small percentage of burial places are so elaborately named.

SOME GENERAL OBSERVATIONS

It will not be possible in this essay to pursue the ultimate geographical implications of the source materials that were consulted. Nonetheless, Table 1 provides a statistical footing for what is to follow. The spatial distribution of registered cemeteries as of 1967 was more uneven than that of the living population. An attempt to derive an equation to explain the territorial array of cemeteries at the state level could be quite rewarding. It would have to take into account not only size, density, concentration, and arrangement of population but also longevity of settlement, religious composition, ethnicity, regional culture, terrain, and a variety of economic considerations.

The identity and incidence of three elements of cemetery names are singled out for analysis here: generic terms, the more common specific names, and the referents imbedded in the specific names—that is, the things and qualities invoked by the words and affixes used to denote particular cemeteries. But it may be useful to begin by considering the general character of projective cemetery names, which as a group diverge markedly from every other class of American place-names. Several attributes are readily detected. Not too surprisingly, such names are dignified and solemn but not somber. Whimsy, braggadocio, and horseplay —conspicuous elements in many categories of American place-names— are virtually unknown. Indeed, the only two examples of playfulness to come to light are Mount Ever-Rest and Foreverglades Mausoleum, the latter located near Palm Beach, Florida. The term "death" is never used; nor is there any reference to pain, mourning, grief, or other unpleasant sensation. Shadowland and Silent City are the most lugubrious examples

FIGURE 1

NUMBER OF INHABITANTS AND CEMETERIES, BY STATE, 1967

State	Population in 1,000s	Cemeteries[1]	Population : Cemetery Ratio	State	Population in 1,000s	Cemeteries[1]	Population : Cemetery Ratio
Utah	1,022	132	7,742	Missouri	4,587	205	22,376
New Hampshire	691	88	7,852	Indiana	5,012	220	22,782
Iowa	2,772	340	8,153	Wyoming	319	13	24,538
Vermont	420	43	9,767	Kentucky	3,201	122	26,238
Pennsylvania	11,672	1,030	11,332	Florida	6,035	218	27,683
Connecticut	2,913	248	11,766	Arkansas	1,972	71	27,775
Massachusetts	5,434	414	13,126	Michigan	8,608	303	28,409
Idaho	701	52	13,481	New Mexico	1,002	34	29,471
Ohio	10,448	763	13,693	North Carolina	5,059	165	30,661
Montana	699	49	14,265	Texas	10,857	336	32,312
Illinois	10,887	760	14,325	Virginia	4,541	140	32,436
Maine	982	64	15,344	South Carolina	2,638	78	33,821
Oregon	1,981	124	15,976	Washington	3,208	93	34,495
South Dakota	668	41	16,292	Tennessee	3,936	112	35,143
Rhode Island	901	53	17,000	Maryland	3,680	104	35,385
Wisconsin	4,194	246	17,049	Georgia	4,490	120	37,417
New York	18,023	1,024	17,601	Oklahoma	2,516	67	37,552
Colorado	2,012	110	18,291	Alaska	271	7	38,714
California	18,990	1,014	18,738	Arizona	1,637	42	38,976
North Dakota	632	33	19,152	Alabama	3,533	86	41,081
New Jersey	6,981	362	19,285	Mississippi	2,344	57	41,123
Delaware	524	27	19,407	District of Columbia	808	19	42,526
West Virginia	1,807	91	19,857	Louisiana	3,663	75	48,840
Minnesota	3,625	176	20,597	Nevada	438	8	54,750
Nebraska	1,443	66	21,864	Total	197,863	10,147	19,499
Kansas	2,281	102	22,363				

[1] Cemeteries registered in American Cemetery Association, *International Cemetery Directory* (Columbus, Ohio, 1967).

I can find, and the word "burial," as part of the generic "burial park" and "burial garden," is the only allusion to interment. So far does euphemism prevail that—as with undertakers' establishments—the uninitiated would have trouble divining the real function of many a burial place, especially the more recent, given no clue but its name. Although the naming process is rarely documented,[18] the namers have obviously pondered carefully the emotional impact and image-building potential of their word choice. In so doing, they severely restricted their environmental frame of reference and forswore many terms frequently applied to other works of man or to natural features.

The result is a euphonious, rather stylized evocation of an idealized habitat for the deceased and the mourners who visit them—and, from a commercial point of view, one likely to melt the sales resistance of the potential purchaser. In essence many of the more elegant projective names are brief prose-poems (mini-*haiku?*), as a few examples should suffice to demonstrate: Green Bower Wildwood Cemetery, Skylawn Memorial Gardens, Green Sanctuary, Lawn Heaven Burial Estates, Ocean View—the Cemetery Beautiful, Chapel of the Chimes, Hills of Eternity, Pleasant Walk Cemetery, Wanderer's Rest, Serenity Gardens, Valhalla Chapel of Memories.

GENERIC TERMS

The prevalence of the term "cemetery" has been so strong among burial grounds bearing explicitly generic terms—96.6 per cent before 1914, and 82.4 per cent as of 1967—that it might appear at first that little could be learned about the American concept of the afterworld from the choice of such terms (see Table 2).[19] As often happens, however, it is the minority that speaks most clearly. The number of generic terms has expanded considerably.[20] Thus, the posthumous landscape is more explicitly depicted, and we begin to see it as a grassy, retrospective parkland. Until a half-century ago, only blunt, drab terms such as *cemetery, burial ground, potters field,* and *graveyard* were in use, with Memorial Cemetery appearing only around the turn of the century, and then in California. Today at least thirty-one generic terms are current, and new terms may still be emerging.[21] The recent coinages continue to have a euphemistic flavor. Thus, Memorial Estates or Gardens of Memory hardly reeks of mortality or suggests the croak of the raven. There is increasing emphasis on memories—pleasurable, one presumes—and on the

TABLE 2

GENERIC TERMS IN NAMES OF AMERICAN CEMETERIES[1]

	Pre-1914[2]		1957[3]		1967[4]	
	No.	%	No.	%	No.	%
Cemetery	679	96.6	6,789	84.7	8,323	82.4
Memorial (Memory) Park	2		671	8.4	857	8.5
Memory (Memorial) Gardens	—		239	2.9	486	4.8
Memorial Cemetery	5	0.7	64	0.8	75	0.7
Memorial Park Cemetery	—		53	0.7	57	0.6
Mausoleum	—		34	0.4	55	0.5
Burial Park (Cemetery)	—		5	0.1	39	.04
Burial (Burying) Ground	13	1.8	34	0.4	34	0.3
Gardens of Memory	—		23	0.3	33	0.3
Crematorium	—		14	0.2	26	0.3
Gardens	—		12	0.2	25	0.2
Chapel	—		6	0.1	14	0.1
(Memorial) (Lawn) (Cemetery)	—		9	0.1	12	0.1
Cemetery Park	—		5	0.1	11	0.1
Park	—		11	0.1	11	0.1
Memorial Estates	—		4		9	
Abbey	—		3		4	
Lawn	—		6		4	
Memorial Chapel	—		3		4	
(Memorial) Shrine	—		2		4	
Burial Gardens	—		1		3	
Churchyard	—		6		3	
Memorial Garden Cemetery	—		5		3	
Sanctuary	—		—		2	
Burial Estates	—		3		1	
Abbey Mausoleum	—		1		1	
Columbarium	—		3		1	
Field	—		—		1	
Plot	—		—		1	
Potters Field	3		1		1	
Graveyard	1		1		—	
Total	703		7,998		10,100	

[1] Excluding those lacking explicit generic terms.
[2] Compiled by author from county and city atlases.
[3] American Cemetery Association, *International Cemetery Directory*, 1957.
[4] American Cemetery Association, *International Cemetery Directory*, 1967.

park-like and edenic nature of the modern burial place. Both trends are merged in the two items that have enjoyed a dramatic increase in popularity in recent years: Memorial (or Memory) Park and Memory (or Memorial) Gardens.[22] There is also a sharp swing toward the use of compound terms such as Memorial Lawn or Lawn Cemetery and a heavy reliance on certain specific and quasi-generic terms that are being rapidly transformed into full-fledged generics—as, for example, *lawn, park, abbey, chapel,* and *rest-haven.* All in all, the terminology of late twentieth-century American cemeteries seems to be in a state of rapid flux; in a few more years this changing vocabulary may provide less equivocal clues to evolving American landscape tastes.

SPECIFIC NAMES

All the specific projective and commemorative names that were recorded ten times or more in 1967 are listed in Table 3. As with the stock of generic terms, so too with specific names: a broadening of vocabulary is discernible. The 75 items noted in Table 3 accounted for 42.4 per cent of all those recorded for the nineteenth-century group but only slightly more than one-third of the names of registered cemeteries in 1967. The increased incidence of saints' names may be explained in part by the growth of Roman Catholic and Eastern Orthodox populations; yet many of these names are associated also with Protestant cemeteries. Certain nonhagiographic biblical and theological terms such as Calvary, Holy Cross, Sacred Heart, Mount Olivet, Holy Sepulchre, Trinity, Zion, Mount Sinai, Resurrection, and Mount Lebanon transcend denominational lines, and some secular names, such as Mount Hope and Graceland, likewise have a distinct bouquet of the spiritual. Oddly enough, the most frequent of the pagan allusions is Valhalla. Only one secular personage, Abraham Lincoln, appears in Table 3—but in the view of many historians, our sixteenth president underwent the process of canonization almost immediately after his assassination.[23]

Three further aspects of Table 3 call for comment before we can take an inventory of the environmental references in the secular specific names. First, there have been some remarkably abrupt changes in nam-

TABLE 3

	Number of Occurrences			Number of Occurrences	
	Pre-1914[1]	1967[2]		Pre-1914[1]	1967[2]
St. Mary	15	236	Graceland	2	31
(Mount) Calvary	16	189	Maple Grove	7	31
St. Joseph	11	155	Riverview	4	29
Evergreen	17	136	St. James	1	26
Greenwood	13	109	Holy Sepulchre	2	25
St. John	10	107	Mount Carmel	1	25
Sunset	—	107	Mount Pleasant	9	24
Woodlawn	8	99	St. Francis	—	24
Fairview	7	96	Fairmount	1	23
Riverside	11	93	Lakeside	1	23
St. Patrick	6	81	Woodland	11	22
Oak Hill	7	77	Lincoln	1	21
Highland	—	69	West Lawn	—	20
(Mount) Hope	11	69	Arlington	—	18
Oakwood	9	67	Maple Hill	2	18
Hillcrest	—	65	St. Ann	—	18
St. Peter	1	63	Cedar Hill	2	17
Union	11	61	Oakdale	—	17
Greenlawn	4	56	Chapel Hill	—	16
Holy Cross	1	51	Edgewood	—	15
Mountain View	2	51	Trinity	1	15
Oakland	4	50	Maplewood	—	15
Rose Hill	4	49	Prospect Hill	4	15
Forest Lawn	2	48	Hollywood	2	14
Sacred Heart	1	48	(Mount) Zion	2	14
Oak Grove	10	47	East Lawn	—	13
Elmwood	7	46	Mount Sinai	—	13
Hillside	7	45	Oak Ridge	2	13
Lakeview	8	42	Resurrection	—	13
Roselawn	—	42	Cedar Grove	4	12
Mount Olivet	6	40	Cedar Lawn	2	12
Resthaven	6	40	Green Hills	1	12
St. Michael	1	40	Mount Olive	1	12
Grandview	2	38	Walnut Grove	2	12
Forest Hill(s)	5	36	Mount Lebanon	—	11
Oaklawn	—	34	Valhalla	1	11
Pine Grove	6	34	Lakewood	2	10
Restlawn	—	32	Total	297	3,431

[1] Collected by author from county and city atlases.
[2] American Cemetery Association, *International Cemetery Directory*, 1967.

181

ing practice over the past century. Several of the most frequently encountered names among modern cemeteries were unknown in the nineteenth century, among them Sunset, Highland, Hillcrest, Roselawn, Resthaven, Oaklawn, Restlawn, and West Lawn. Moreover, many now-familiar items are encountered only once or twice during the earlier period: Forest Lawn, Mountain View, Grandview, Graceland, Lakeside. In the light of the subsequent discussion, the content of such names will be seen to have more than casual significance.

Second, it appears probable that processes of imitation and diffusion are involved in the naming patterns of modern American cemeteries. The names in Table 3 were not reinvented each time they were used but must have been copied from earlier examples. Thus most of the Greenwoods, Forest Lawns, and Arlingtons were inspired by the pioneering enterprises for which they are obviously namesakes. (Why there are so few Mount Auburns is an interesting question. Could it be that the word Auburn simply fails to strike a responsive chord?) Presumably, the initial nineteenth-century naming patterns came from the urban Northeast. During the twentieth century, California and perhaps parts of the South may have become the generators of new ideas.

Third, there appear to be no class or social implications in the names used for American cemeteries, aside from those pertaining to racial, religious, or ethnic affiliation. There may be areal segregation, with the socially and economically superior being interred under more splendid monuments or in mausoleums within larger tracts in more attractive neighborhoods,[24] but the name of the cemetery does not disclose this fact.

PHYSICAL NATURE OF THE AFTERWORLD

Most of the substantive evidence about the physical nature of the American view of the afterworld is given in Table 4, a crude content analysis of the specific portions of American cemetery names. The various references are arranged in four classes: floristic, terrain and hydrology, seasonal and meteorological, and other attributes. The most striking general fact emerging from the table is that in visualizing the American afterworld the namers of our public burial places have laid such emphasis on plant life and terrain. Of the 5,742 items tabulated, 4,498, or some 78 per cent, are concerned with vegetation and matters of topography and hydrology. The catalogue of omitted topics, including fauna, sound, work, and anything urban, will be noted later.

In the popular imagination—to which, one must assume, these names are peculiarly responsive—paradise is a sedately voluptuous locale whose plant cover and surface configuration are ideally beautiful. The particular items of flora and contour that contribute to such a perfected loveliness merit close scrutiny. This can be done either by field inspection or by the study of names, but more fully perhaps via the latter route. The cemetery may or may not materially deliver the promises implicit in its name. While the oaks, roses, chapel, or view of mountain or brook may be there, often such realization is thwarted by physical or economic circumstance. Thus, many a cemetery with crest, view, or -mont in its title is actually quite level—or at least to detect an eminence calls for unusual visual virtuosity—and many a prospect or vista is purely metaphorical. But these are honest, socially acceptable verbal gestures.

The modern American notion of the afterworld is woodland or grassland, or some park-like combination thereof. The nineteenth-century cemetery was emphatically bosky, with the terms *woods, grove, evergreen, forest,* and *sylvan* accounting for 86 per cent of the references to general plant cover. Although the sylvan element is still quite powerful within the current scene, many new cemetery names suggest a much more open landscape. The terms *meadow, prairie, gardens, floral,* and *park* have been coming into vogue. But most impressive has been the widespread adoption of the term *lawn* (never grass or grassy, although a few clovers do appear).

Throughout their history, Americans have been undecided about whether a wooded (and fenced) landscape is preferable to an open grassy (unfenced) sward for residential and other pleasurable purposes.[25] Current cemetery design, responsive to changing tides of fashion, has swung strongly toward the open option, but the swing is hardly irreversible. Indeed, the compromise solution of a park—the interspersion of trees and shrubbery with open lawn and flower bed and the creation of a humanized middle landscape—persists in imaginative literature[26] as well as in toponymy and actual landscape design.

The identity of the plants that are singled out, or ignored, in cemetery names tells us much but also raises more questions than can be answered. In essence, the problem is the degree to which the frequency of plant names in cemetery names matches that of the floristic world of the namers as they experienced it. There are three types of deficiency in our store of facts. First, we know too little about the absolute or relative frequency of various plants in the places inhabited or frequented by the namers of cemeteries, early or recent. The difficulty is compounded by the fact that major alterations of plant cover have occurred almost everywhere in the nation over the past two centuries. Second, we know even less about the flora as perceived: of which plants, wild or domesticated, did the names take particular notice, and to what extent were they able to distinguish one species or genus from another? And, last, what are the psychological connotations of the perceived items, more especially, what are the overtones, good, bad, or indifferent, of the names of such plants?

The term *oak* predominates now as in the past, outnumbering its nearest rival, the maple, by almost four to one, and accounting for more than a third of all plant references. This may simply reflect the high incidence of the genus *Quercus* in much of the countryside. But the oak also symbolizes strength and endurance, and hence immortality; and the word *oak* carries no double meanings. The maple also has no negative attributes, except a much more limited territorial distribution, and it has the distinction of being spectacularly prominent in the symbolically significant autumnal season. Among the other large, areally extensive deciduous species, only the walnut and chestnut are well represented in Table 4, perhaps even over-represented in the case of the chestnut. The rarity or non-incidence of birch, beech, poplar, basswood, gum, locust, or tulip may be explained by restricted range, alien origin, untoward verbal or physical connotation, or some combination thereof. The stately elm is reasonably popular, as might be expected in view of its wide range and lack of derogatory verbal overtones. It is difficult to account for the total absence of the geographically widespread hickory, a tree with many of the same connotations as the oak. Perhaps its relative rarity within urban areas is part of the explanation. The single occurrence of the noble sycamore might be explained by the pun unfortunately implicit in the name. One would also have anticipated greater use of the term *willow*, since it has been so conspicuous in the iconography of American gravestones and in funerary literature. But this may be a case of avoiding any suggestion of mortality in matters nomenclatural.

A different negative effect may operate for the most popular of the evergreen items—the pine—since the verb "to pine" projects an undesirable mood. Consequently, though the genus *Pinus* is as far-flung and as visible as the oak, it is less favored toponymically. The cedar and holly are amply represented within the evergreen category, the cedar possibly because of Scriptural allusions. I was surprised to discover so few cypresses, firs, and junipers, and nary a spruce, larch, or hemlock. Such floristic imbalance may simply bespeak botanical unsophistication on the part of the many Americans to whom all conifers or evergreens are some sort of pine tree. In addition, the toxic reputation of the hemlock may have further weakened its chances. The absence of the yew is noteworthy also, for, although the word has an ambiguous sound (ewe? you?) and the plant some pagan connotations, it is one of the principal ornamental shrubs in our cemeteries and has been of special significance in British churchyards.[27]

Trees are much more prominent in the landscape of the American afterworld than are smaller plants, with the major exception of the rose and the minor exception of the fern. The number of allusions to ivy, clover, woodbine, azalea, boxwood, violet, and similar items (the laurel can be classed as either tree or shrub) ranges from one to four. Among arboreal names, fruit trees receive rather short shrift, with only the olive, orange, and (perhaps) the cherry being noted.

Thus the composite plant cover indicated by cemetery names may be either a natural or a humanized one. In either case it resembles only vaguely most actual landscapes outside the cemetery gates, and even within those grounds the match between name and actuality is far from perfect.[28]

A comparison of the frequency of reference to particular plants in the two periods shown in Table 4 reflects a basic stability in pattern. The enduring popularity of the top seven trees—the oak, maple, pine, elm, cedar, laurel, and walnut—is impressive; but there has also been a dramatic rise in the popularity of the rose, a shrub that thrives best in open, sunny sites. If the list of floristic items has greatly lengthened in recent

TABLE 4

LANDSCAPE REFERENCES AND OTHER ATTRIBUTES OF TERMS USED
IN AMERICAN CEMETERY NAMES, BY NUMBER OF OCCURRENCES

I. Vegetational
a. General Plant Cover

	Pre-1914	1967		Pre-1914	1967
Wood(s)	64	499	Garden(s)	1	11
	37.9%	30.3%	Wildwood	—	10
Lawn	20	491	-hurst	—	9
	11.8	29.8	Meadow	—	9
Grove	50	224	Prairie	—	7
	29.6	13.6	Croft	—	4
Evergreen	17	154	Sylvan	1	4
	10.0	9.4	Desert	—	3
Forest	15	132	Flower	—	2
	8.9	8.0	Glade	—	2
Park	2	56	Green	—	2
	1.2	3.4	Bower	—	1
Floral	—	26	Orchard	—	1
		1.6	Total	170	1,647

b. Specific Plants

	Pre-1914	1967		Pre-1914	1967
Oak	35	348	Holly	3	19
Burr oak	—	4	Olive	2	19
Knotty oak	—	1	Magnolia	—	16
Live oak	—	3	Fern	2	13
Shrub oak	—	1	Willow	1	12
All oak	35	357	Chestnut	2	11
	34.1%	34.5%	Locust	1	11
Rose	6	140	Cypress	2	9
	5.8	13.4	Acacia	—	7
Maple	10	96	Beech	1	7
	9.7	9.2	Ash	—	6
Pine	10	83	Hazel	—	4
	9.7	8.0	Ivy	—	4
Elm	8	68	Linden	1	4
	7.8	6.5	Palm	—	4
Cedar	8	60	Cherry	—	3
	7.8	5.8	Clover	—	3
Laurel	5	36	Fir	—	3
	4.9	3.5	Myrtle	—	3
Walnut	5	24	Woodbine	—	3
	4.9	2.3	Aspen	1	2

TABLE 4 (cont.)

b. Specific Plants (cont.)

	Pre-1914	1967		Pre-1914	1967
Birch	—	2	Cane	—	1
Cottonwood	—	2	Dogwood	—	1
Orange	—	2	Grapevine	—	1
Vine	—	2	Hawthorn	—	1
Acorn	—	1	Juniper	—	1
Alder	1	1	Palmetto	—	1
Arbor Vitae	—	1	Pecan	—	1
Arbutus	—	1	Redwood	—	1
Azalea	—	1	Sycamore	1	1
Berry	—	1	Violet	—	1
Boxwood	—	1	Total	105	1,053
Bush	—	1			

II. Terrain and Hydrology

	Pre-1914	1967		Pre-1914	1967
Hill(s)	53	458	Edge	—	15
	34.4%	25.3%	Mound	3	14
View	25	380	Vale	1	11
	16.2	21.0	Bay	1	10
River	15	129	Knoll	—	10
	9.7	7.1	Cliff	—	6
Crest	—	113	Ocean	—	6
		6.2	Bluff	1	5
Lake	10	87	Sea	—	5
	6.5	4.8	Vista	—	5
Glen	6	76	Mere	—	4
	3.9	4.2	Rock	1	4
Dale	9	71	Summit	—	4
	5.8	3.9	Hilltop	—	3
-mont	4	70	Fountain	—	3
	2.6	3.9	Rolling	2	3
Highland	—	69	Terrace	—	3
		3.8	Overlook	—	2
Ridge	3	64	Slope	—	2
	1.9	3.5	Cove	—	1
Mountain	5	57	Dell	1	1
	3.2	3.1	Den	1	—
Valley	2	37	Falls	—	1
	1.3	2.0	Holm	—	1
Brook	5	29	Pond	1	—
	3.2	1.6	Shore	—	1
Crown	1	19	Spring	1	—
	0.6	1.0	Total	154	1,810

TABLE 4 (*cont.*)

III. Atmosphere, Season, Time of Day

	Pre-1914	1967		Pre-1914	1967
Sunset	—	116	Angelus	—	1
Spring	6	36	Clear	—	1
Sunny	—	19	Northern Lights	—	1
Sky	—	7	Rainbow	—	1
Morning	—	6	Shadow	—	1
Shady	—	6	Total	6	199
Sunrise	—	4			

IV. Other Attributes

a. Color			*b. Compass Direction*		
Green	24	228	West	6	60
Silver	1	25	East	1	41
Golden	—	3	North	5	19
White	—	3	South	3	15
Violet	—	2	Total	15	135
Blue	—	1			
Ebony	—	1			
Emerald	—	1			
Total	25	244			

c. Miscellaneous Attributes

Fair	8	144	Harmony	1	7
Rest	2	110	Harbor	—	4
Hope	11	78	Paradise	—	4
Haven	1	71	Faith	—	2
Pleasant	10	55	Repose	—	2
Grace	1	38	Serenity	—	2
Grand	2	38	Silent	—	2
Home	5	27	Celestial	—	1
Peace	2	23	Concord	1	1
Bel, belle	—	13	Elysian	—	1
Resurrection	—	13	Modern	—	1
Memory	—	11	Providence	—	1
Eden	—	10	Total	46	667
Eternal, eternity	—	8			

years, this is a consequence of the increased number of cemeteries and, in part, of relatively greater population growth in localities with such exotic flora as the magnolia, acacia, and palm.

Something of the same stability may be found in the surface configuration of the American vision of the afterworld. This vision has been, and still is, of a land of rolling hills and highlands, replete with ridges, crests, and knolls and the occasional cliff or bluff, punctuated by valleys, dales, and glens (but nary a bottom or hollow, except for Sleepy Hollow), and by rivers, brooks, and lakes (but hardly any ponds), with distant glimpses of mountain and sea. Evidently there is no room in the stately lexicon of the afterworld for such prosaic, slightly vulgar terms as *creek* or *branch*. Sloping land seems to prevail universally, for references to level terrain are almost nonexistent. It is a land of powerfully visual orientation, almost always with some striking feature to be viewed. Although the precise terminology may change, with the advent of *crest*, *highland*, and *vista*, the basic design is unaltered. The recent popularity of *edge* conveys an ambiguous message, for it may refer to the border between grass and grove or to the lip of an upland prominence.

Remarkably little attention is given to weather, season, or time of day in nineteenth-century cemetery names; the six occurrences of spring are the only pertinent examples. By 1967, however, there was much greater awareness of such phenomena. Spring has grown in popularity, and a few analogues have appeared: morning, sunrise, and resurrection. The sky is being noticed, and it is clear and sunny. The most arresting development, however, is the recent trend toward the adoption of sunset (as an anaesthetic euphemism for death?), a fact that makes the total absence of any reference to the analogous autumn seem illogical and puzzling.

Among the other items and attributes embedded in cemetery names, two are of special geographic interest: hue and compass direction. Green was the solitary color honored in nineteenth-century cemetery names, and the situation had changed but slightly by 1967, when 228 of 244 color references were to green, the others being to such exotic items as silver, golden, violet, and emerald. There is no mention of black and only three, of white. The evolution of the directional references is fascinating.[29] The few from the earlier period appear to be almost randomly distributed, but the 1967 data display a strong predilection for west and east. The pervasive valedictory and resurrectional themes of sunset and sunrise, of death as a long winter sleep from which we shall eventually arise, manifest themselves once again.

The final section of Table 4 is concerned with a miscellany of attributes that cannot be assigned to a single category. But excluding the term *fair*, the equally unspecific *hope* and the expected allusions to Eden and Paradise, two general themes seem to emerge: refuge and tranquility. Thus the afterworld vision is that of a relaxed haven, home, or harbor, one that is pleasant and filled with grace, the seat of harmony, peace, and rest.

Many items are missing from the American view of the afterworld. The lack of several important plants, of autumn, of a great part of the color spectrum, and of numerous other items has already been noted, but there are other voids too. Thus, it is a land totally bereft of fauna; a single reference to elk may or may not be locational. The avoidance of mammals may be explicable; yet, given the symbolic import of the dove or of bird song in general as the embodiment of dawn, spring, hope, and the cyclical continuity of life, several birds' names would surely be fitting. It is an utterly rural domain; the only urban reference I have come across is the poetic Silent City, and the only edifices are the occasional *abbey, chapel, monument,* and *tower,* which are as much at home in the countryside as anywhere. It is highly—and so uncharacteristically for America—nonquantitative in character: Second Home seems to be the only name with any numerical content at all. Nor is size especially valued (another arrantly un-American feature!). The only adjective encountered denoting size is grand, a word having many connotations other than magnitude.

It is, moreover, a land where all the senses but the visual are numb. There is neither sound nor music, except that of chimes; the birds do not sing, and no wind blows. Neither is there mention of anything tactile or olfactory or of food or drink. It is a timeless place without a history. The term *modern* occurs but once, while such designations as *twentieth-century* or *progressive,* which are quite popular among other business enterprises, are totally unknown. Allusions to major events or celebrities are virtually nonexistent. There is a paucity of literary allusions (except for the biblical and for a few Sleepy Hollows). And, finally, it is a land of intense inactivity, where the only industry is remembering. There is absolutely no toponymic evidence for any form of work or play.

THE CHANGING MAP OF THE AFTERWORLD

This, then, is what the evidence of place-names reveals about the envisaged landscape of the American afterworld. It is an elliptical tract of rolling hills and indeterminate size, one that stretches far toward the west and east, but is quite narrow along its north-south axis, and is surrounded at some distance by water and high mountains. It is a monochromatic, evergreen, featuristic land of perpetual spring morning or evening lying under a cloudless, windless, sunny sky, but where brooks and fountains flow nonetheless, and trees, flowering shrubs, and grassy lawns thrive in a park-like ensemble, yet without any animal life. It is a rural place of intense tranquility and silence, where nothing goes on except the enjoyment of the view and reposeful recollection. Concerning the inhabitants of this territory our blurred map legend has nothing to say.

Although the afterworld is usually envisioned as eternal and fixed, our onomastic evidence has been changing over the past hundred years or so and, judging from a perusal of current telephone directories, may well be undergoing revision more rapidly now than ever before. The earlier copies of the map for what is veritably a *terra incognita* are disappointingly fragmentary, but a few scattered conclusions of a geosophical character can be drawn about the kinds of editing this subconscious collective doodle has been undergoing. Our newer versions show a grassier land and one no longer directionless but oriented from west to east, a land much more thickly planted with roses and one where a population of the dead that may have been previously unemployed is now busily engaged in gazing outward and remembering. But, old or new, the American view of the afterworld as expressed by cemetery names is that of an ideal realm far removed from the workaday world of the living. It would be difficult to imagine a greater contrast than that between the gritty actuality of a hurried, disordered land and the calm visual harmony of our posthumous aspirations. Which is the more real?

NOTES

1. In *Human Nature in Geography* (Cambridge: Harvard University Press, 1966), p. 83.
2. Jessica Mitford, *The American Way of Death* (New York: Simon & Schuster, 1963). The fact that public discussion of death generates distinct feelings of discomfort in most Americans has been further brought home to me by audience reactions when this paper was twice presented in an abridged oral version. I was surprised at the amount of nervous laughter, often at quite inappropriate points.
3. William H. Whyte, *The Last Landscape* (Garden City, N.Y.: Doubleday, 1968), p. 240. Interestingly enough, once cemeteries have become well established, they tend to become refuges for the wild or nearly wild fauna of the vicinity and important sites for individual and social recreation. The social and natural ecology of Boston's cemeteries is discussed sympathetically in Jack Ward Thomas and Ronald A. Dixon, "Cemetery Ecology," *Natural History* 82.3 (1973):61–67.
4. For a splendid anthology of such early depictions of the American city, consult John W. Reps, *The Making of Urban America: A History of City Planning in the United States* (Princeton: Princeton University Press, 1965).
5. Three pioneering, but still isolated, efforts in these directions are W. Kephart, "Status after Death," *American Sociological Review* 15 (1950):635–43; W. Lloyd Warner, *The Living and the Dead: A Study of the Symbolic Life of Americans* (New Haven: Yale University Press, 1959), esp. pp. 280–320; and John W. Florin, *Death in New England: Regional Variations in Mortality*, Studies in Geography No. 3 (Chapel Hill: University of North Carolina, Department of Geography, 1971). The possible utility of cemetery data in analyzing social structure is briefly explored in Frank W. Young, "Graveyards and Social Structure," *Rural Sociology* 25.4 (1960):446–50.
6. Notably, Allen I. Ludwig, *Graven Images: New England Stonecarving and Its Symbols, 1650–1815* (Middletown, Conn.: Wesleyan University Press, 1966); Edwin Dethlefsen and James Deetz, "Death's Heads, Cherubs, and Willow Trees: Experimental Archeology in Colonial Cemeteries," *American Antiquity* 31 (1966):502–10, and "Death's Head, Cherub, Urn, and Willow," *Natural History* 76.3 (1967):28–37.
7. Reps, *Making of Urban America*, pp. 325–31.
8. Joe T. Darden, "Factors in the Location of Pittsburgh's Cemeteries," *The Virginia Geographer*, 7.2 (1972):3–8; Donald G. Deane, "The Traditional Upland South Cemetery," *Landscape* 18.2 (1969):39–41; Richard V. Francaviglia, "The Cemetery as an Evolving Cultural Landscape," *Annals of the Association of American Geographers* (hereafter *Annals AAG*) 61 (1971):501–9; John B. Jackson, "From Monument to Place," *Landscape* 17.2 (1967–68):22–26; Fred Kniffen, "Necrogeography in the United States," *Geographical Review* 57 (1967):426–27; David B. Knight, *Cemeteries as Living Landscapes*, Ottawa Branch, Ontario Genealogical Society, Publication 73–8 (Ottawa: 1973); and

Larry W. Price, "Some Results and Implications of a Cemetery Study," *Professional Geographer* 18 (1966):201–7.

9. The most substantial works in this genre are William D. Pattison, "The Cemeteries of Chicago; A Phase of Land Utilization," *Annals AAG* 45 (1955):245–57; and W. G. Hardwick, R. J. Claus, and D. C. Rothwell, "Cemeteries and Urban Land Value," *Professional Geographer* 23 (1971):19–21.

10. The single most important resource for such a study is the Geological Survey's ongoing series of large-scale topographic quadrangles. Some notion of the magnitude of an all-out effort may be gained from the fact that many 7½ minute sheets contain 50 or more cemeteries of one sort or another.

11. It is also feasible to treat the cemetery as an evolutionary phenomenon, to distinguish between the "living" and the "dead" cemetery, a theme perceptively developed by Warner, *The Living and the Dead*, pp. 318–20. In the former case the cemetery enjoys a lively duality, for it not only serves as a repository for the dead but as long as it "is being filled with a fresh stream of the recently dead it stays symbolically a live and vital emblem telling the living of the meaning of life and death" (p. 318). But when the community has ceased to bury its dead in a given graveyard, and it no longer provides visual and moral balm to the mourner, the place becomes truly dead and recedes into the realm of the historic. Personal memories are extinguished, and the cemetery ceases to serve as an instrument for reconciling the living to the unutterable mysteries of mortality. See also Knight, *Cemeteries as Living Landscapes*.

12. The most useful and penetrating accounts of this process are George R. Stewart, *Names on the Land: A Historical Account of Place-Naming in the United States*, rev. ed. (Boston: Houghton Mifflin, 1958), and *American Place-Names: A Concise and Selective Dictionary for the Continental United States of America* (New York: Oxford University Press, 1970).

13. Stewart, *American Place-Names*, pp. xxviii–xxxii.

14. Admittedly Stewart's commendatory names and the proposed new classs of projective names do overlap to a substantial degree, but there is a basic difference between the two groups. The element of puffery, which is basic to the commendatory, may be missing from the projective, since the image contrived by the projective name may or may not be laudatory. Thus, for example, *Sunset Lane Cemetery* is not noticeably commendatory but is projective. Perhaps another, more inclusive class is needed to embrace both types of names.

15. American Cemetery Association, *International Cemetery Directory* (Columbus, Ohio, 1957) and *International Cemetery Directory* (Columbus, Ohio, 1967). These directories include municipal, church-related, fraternal, and ethnic cemeteries as well as commercial enterprises. The main criterion is whether the cemetery is operated in a businesslike fashion with an office and a manager. The feasibility of using telephone directories as primary sources was investigated, but the listings are less exhaustive than those of the A.C.A. The telephone directory entries do, however, have one incidental virtue of more than passing interest: the paid advertisement and its contents. (I am still totally baffled by the Celestial Memory Gardens of Columbia, S.C., which proclaims itself a "Freedom of Choice Cemetery.")

16. A good description of this exuberant source of local geographical information is available in Norman J. W. Thrower, "The County Atlas of the United States," *Surveying and Mapping* 21 (1961):365–73. There is strong regional bias in the areal distribution of these atlases, for they were particularly abundant in the Northeast (most of the counties of New York, Ohio, and Pennsylvania, e.g., are covered quite handsomely), but rare for most of the Southern and Western states. There were few cemeteries to be mapped in the western half of the country before 1900; but in the South, where there must have been many, publication of what was basically a vanity press item was inhibited by a shortage of funds.

17. Only rough conjecture can be ventured regarding the early nomenclature of American burial places, pending the writing of the first comprehensive study of our funerary practices. My impression is that the cemetery was seldom given a name of its own before the early 1800s; it simply shared the name of the church, ethnic group, family, town, or city with which it was associated.

18. Two brief accounts are available. "When a question of a name for the proposed institution came up for consideration, various candidates for the honor were presented. . . . They fixed upon the pleasing and unpretending name which it bears, as appropriate to the wood crowned heights, and as indicating that it should always remain a scene of rural quiet, and beauty, and leafiness, and verdure" (Nehemiah Cleaveland, *Green-Wood Cemetery: A History of the Institution from 1838 to 1864* [New York: Anderson & Archer, 1866], p. 14). "The natural topography of the grounds is admitted by all to be peculiarly beautiful— the gentle undulations, and the grove over the entire subdivision, having suggested the name of 'Graceland' " (*Charter of the Graceland Cemetery (Approved Feb. 22, 1861)* . . . [Chicago: James Barnet, Printer, 1861], p. 6).

19. Because of the great numerical disparity between the two sets of data, this comparison between pre–1914 and 1967 values must be taken with much caution. The same skeptical observation applies to all subsequent diachronic statements in this essay.

20. A parallel development has been noted in the history of American forenames: Wilbur Zelinsky, "Cultural Variation in Personal Name Patterns in the Eastern United States," *Annals AAG* 60 (1970):753.

21. Thus, for example, I have encountered in current South Carolina telephone directories two establishments using the generic designation "biblical gardens." They may have been created or named after the 1967 A.C.A. directory was compiled.

22. I should like to note in passing that the spatial distribution of each term is interestingly uneven, and that the two patterns are quite dissimilar.

23. For example, Edmund Wilson, *Patriotic Gore: Studies in the Literature of the Civil War* (New York: Oxford University Press, 1962), pp. 96–98.

24. Warner, *The Living and the Dead*, pp. 287–99.

25. For a sensitive discussion of this still poorly explored theme, see John B. Jackson, "A New Kind of Space," *Landscape* 18.1 (1969):33–35. The shifting status of the two concepts is a recurrent theme throughout his more recent *American Space: The Centennial Years, 1865–1876* (New York: Norton, 1972). Nehe-

miah Cleaveland, the effusive panegyrist of Brooklyn's Greenwood Cemetery, states the antiforest case with candor and feeling:

> Many of our villages, streets, and homes have become, or are becoming, so densely embowered as to leave small chance for the sun or the air to enter. Clearly this is wrong, unless it can be shown that a stagnant atmosphere— with whole armies of bugs and caterpillars—is promotive of cheerfulness and conducive to health. . . . This inconsiderate and reckless planting of trees and bushes in and around the spots where our dead repose is one of the absurdities of fashion. It is but too often the mere thoughtless copying of an example set by others. In Green-Wood the practice has already caused much inconvenience. . . . The Cemetery grounds which look best at all seasons, and give the highest satisfaction to the eye, are those which most nearly resemble a well-kept lawn. As a general thing, shrubbery and trees, in these little plots, are fatal to neatness. If there be any doubt on this point, let the open lots in Green-Wood be compared with those which are much shaded. (Cleaveland, *Green-Wood Cemetery*, p. 137)

26. This idea is explored in Henry Nash Smith, *Virgin Land: The American West as Symbol and Myth* (Cambridge: Harvard University Press, 1950); Charles L. Sanford, *The Quest for Paradise: Europe and the American Moral Imagination* (Urbana: University of Illinois Press, 1961); Leo Marx, *The Machine in the Garden: Technology and the Pastoral Ideal in America* (New York: Oxford University Press, 1964); Peter J. Schmitt, *Back to Nature: The Arcadian Myth in Urban America* (New York: Oxford University Press, 1969); and J. Wreford Watson, "Image Geography: The Myth of America in the American Scene," *The Advancement of Science* 27 (1970–71):1–9.
27. Vaughan Cornish, *The Churchyard Yew & Immortality* (London: F. Muller, 1946).
28. In many of the more elaborate cemeteries, the various paths and driveways are usually named after trees or flowers. For one especially thorough example, see *The Picturesque Pocket Companion and Visitor's Guide through Mount Auburn* (Boston: Otis, Broadus & Co., 1839).
29. In cases where the reference was locational, e.g. North Hartford or South Bay, the item was not recorded; the table includes compass directions only when the terms appear to be intrinsic to the cemetery.

8

The Geography of Utopia

PHILIP W. PORTER AND
FRED E. LUKERMANN

JOHN K. WRIGHT was an intellectual historian. In his lifelong pursuit of man's scientific and not-so-scientific ideas of nature, environment, and the world, he crossed disciplinary boundaries with ease, following wherever a question drew him, a practice he light-heartedly termed "foolrushery." His interest in the history of ideas and the history of science is evident on every page of his work. His Presidential address, "*Terrae Incognitae:* The Place of the Imagination in Geography," delivered before the Association of American Geographers in December of 1946, is his best statement about the study of geographical knowledge, or *geosophy,* which "covers the geographical ideas, both true and false, of all manner of people—not only geographers, but farmers and fishermen,

We wish to thank our colleague Yi-Fu Tuan for his gracious encouragement and substantive suggestions for this essay. Many people believe that Yi-Fu Tuan comes originally from China. We are convinced that he actually comes from Nature and is Nature's local earth representative. His duties are to observe and record man's views of and responses to environment and nature and to report back. For helpful comments we thank also Ward Barrett, Hildegard Johnson, Ronald Abler, and Joseph Schwartzberg. For editorial help we thank David Lowenthal.

business executives and poets, novelists and painters, Bedouins and Hottentots—and for this reason it necessarily has to do in large degree with subjective conceptions."[1]

The reader will note that Wright's 1946 address informs nearly every essay of this volume. In geography, studies of "perception of environment," "behavioral environment," and "environmental cognition" have come to enjoy increasing popularity in recent years. Such studies have their antecedents in the ideas and examples of Wright and Ralph Hall Brown.[2] The Wright address called for exploration of "the imaginative faculties of geographers and others." One excellent starting point for an examination of man's dreams and imagination is his utopias.

Wright was deeply interested in utopian thought. His older brother, Austin Tappan Wright, wrote the most geographical of utopian novels, *Islandia*. The stimulating bookish environment of their early years in Hanover, New Hampshire, and later in Cambridge (their father was professor of Greek and Latin at Dartmouth and Harvard) must have challenged their young imaginations. Sylvia Wright, Austin Wright's daughter, says that her father originated *Islandia* as a child. "Occasionally he shut my uncle, who was younger, out of Islandia, and my uncle created his own world, Cravay. After my grandfather's death, they discovered that he, too, had mapped an imaginary world."[3]

In this essay honoring John K. Wright, it fits our purpose to use *Islandia* extensively. *Islandia* is no ordinary utopia, though it expresses a decentralist, anti-technological point of view found in some other utopias. It is not merely a plausible place, it is a reality, a view often expressed by those who have read the book. *Islandia* contains some of the most convincing geographical descriptions in utopian literature. John K. Wright, who drew the maps for the published *Islandia*, wrote that when he was making the maps during the spring of 1938, his niece Sylvia "was very meticulous about getting everything exactly right, as though Islandia and the Karain Continent were real—and I tried to play the game with her."[4] Throughout this essay, *Islandia* will serve as a foil for other utopian writings, aiding us as we work toward an understanding of what utopia is.

TYPES OF UTOPIA

As every schoolchild knows, utopia is both no place and a good place. Sir Thomas More in coining the word introduced an essential ambiguity that utopian writers and their critics have puzzled over ever since. Is the good place attainable or must it live forever in the imagination of our hearts? Equally puzzling, what is a good place? This is perhaps the central question in utopian literature. Underlying every utopia is the thought either of the road to perfection or of the return to grace. Man lives in an imperfect world and sees himself as the source of most of its imperfection. What is required to make a perfect world? First, much utopian literature reflects a deep sense of loss. We have been driven from the Garden and long to return. We no longer live harmoniously within nature. Second, much modern utopian writing looks toward the realization of a better world, the creation of the celestial city. In this literature sentiments of nostalgia and loss are replaced by the spirit of progress, the purposeful march toward an ultimate goal.

Most utopian writers can be placed somewhere between the Garden of Eden of Genesis and the New Jerusalem of Revelation. The road connecting the two is history; thus the utopist must normally choose between a journey toward origins and a journey toward man's dreamed-of destination.[5] One goal is biological, the other mineralogical. Eden is a garden, green and pleasant. Indeed, the Lord God was "walking in the garden in the cool of the day" (Gen. 3:8) when Adam and Eve and the serpent were all caught out in their big mistake. The New Jerusalem, however, is dry and completely mineralized.

> The first heaven and the first earth were passed away and there was no more sea. . . . And he that talked with me had a golden reed to measure the city, and the gates thereof, and the walls thereof. And the city lieth four square, and the length is as large as the breadth; and he measured the city with the reed, twelve thousand furlongs. The length and breadth of it are equal. . . . And the building of the walls of it was of jasper, and the city was pure gold, like unto clear glass. And the foundations of the wall of the city were garnished with all manner of precious stones [jasper, sapphire, chalcedony, emerald, sardonyx, sardius, chrysolyte, beryl, topaz, chrysoprasus, jacinth, and amethyst]. . . . And

199

the twelve gates were twelve pearls; every several gate was of one pearl; and the street of the city was pure gold, as it were transparent glass. (Rev. 21:1, 15, 18, 19, 21)

Eden is autarkic and natural; the New Jerusalem geometric and planned. Lewis Mumford's categories—utopias of escape and of reconstruction—are analogous. The utopia of escape functions, in his words, as a "substitute for the external world," whereas in the utopia of reconstruction "the facts of the everyday world are brought together and assorted and sifted, and a new sort of reality is projected back again upon the external world."[6] Elements common to the edenic utopias are a rural agricultural way of life, a generally decentralized settlement pattern and political system, with small towns that may not be permitted to grow beyond a certain size, an active mistrust of the machines and methods of the Industrial Revolution, and a love of nature and natural scenes.

Utopian reconstructionists who see adamic man moving toward the celestial city can be divided into two types: those who aspire to it, and those who dread it. The latter commonly write what may be termed *dystopias*: utopias which, through design or malfunction, are so repressive mentally or physically that they repel. The utopias of the nineteenth century have been largely replaced by dystopias in the twentieth century. Chad Walsh sees this as a trend in the history of ideas with important social, philosophic, and religious implications.[7] Earlier utopias based on religion and science were replaced in the late nineteenth and early twentieth centuries by utopias based on technology and centralization of economic production.

Although reconstructionist utopian and dystopian writers differ in what they view as good, they create worlds that share many common features. Thus, these constructs are urban; they are founded on technology and engineering (psychological, genetic, and social to deal with man; civil, chemical, electrical, and mechanical to deal with environment); they are global and have no effective enemies. People in dystopia exhibit hostility to nature and to what is natural in man. Reconstructionist utopias have achieved an equilibrium condition. When utopia achieves a steady state, history ceases to exist, and the individual is free only insofar as he or she believes and behaves according to the norms established for all. In benevolent utopias, war, poverty, and ignorance have been forever eliminated; whereas in dystopias there is commonly much suffering, brutality, poverty, and fear. Dystopias are anti-images; that is, one must have the positive image of utopia as celestial city before one can have the anti-image of dystopia.

Literature of another kind chronicles the fortunes of attempted utopias, notably the communal experiments that flourished in eighteenth- and nineteenth-century America. These utopias were generally reconstructionist attempts to achieve the celestial city in contemporary life.[8] The historical literature dealing with the development of the American utopian communities and commonweal invariably interrelates utopia, the West, and the Frontier.[9] If one thinks of "West" and "Frontier" as states of mind rather than geographical places, the terms are undoubtedly interrelated. If, however, the frontier is viewed in the context of Turner's generally westward-moving geographic zone, the facts are not congenial. Whether a utopia is fictional or realized, it requires conditions of stability, not an environment of change, in order to flourish. Literary utopias ensure this through isolation. Experimental utopias seek to ensure it not on the Turnerian frontier, but in well-established settled areas where the products of an agrarian and industrial life are marketable (see Fig. 1).[10]

The frontier as state-of-mind, as a journey of purification and as a preparation for the millennium, figured strongly in the thinking of members of experimental communities. J. M. Powell presents some provocative ideas.

> The triggering mechanism [of millennialism] has not yet been explained . . . , but the important implications for migration, resource-appraisal, and settlement evolution should also interest the geographer. . . . Common manifestations of these movements involve the demands of some type of ordeal on the part of the faithful to make them "worthy"—a difficult journey; the building of a settlement in some remote district; the performance of certain rituals and ascetic purifications. Another characteristic is the clear dominance of a visionary leader—messiah or prophet—who evokes the "sense of time" and may even choose the "perfect place."[11]

Preparation for a new life, visionary leadership, and the importance of an arduous journey—all are abundantly present in such movements as Mormonism, Zionism, and the South African Voortrek.

UTOPIAN COMMUNITIES AND THE AMERICAN FRONTIER

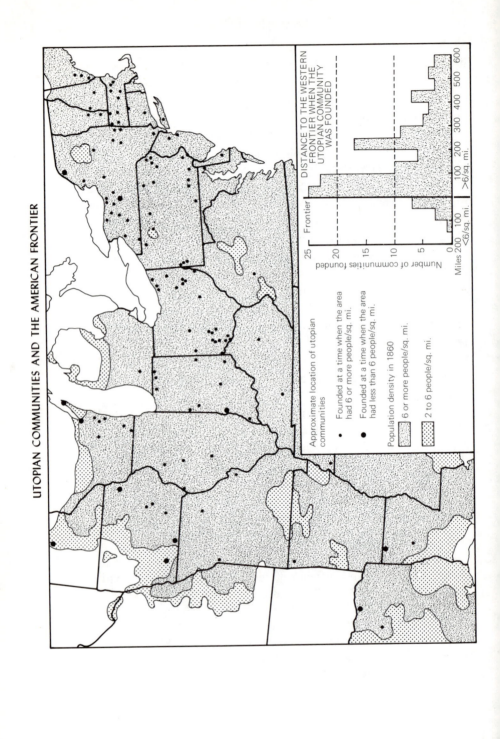

Approximate location of utopian communities

• Founded at a time when the area had 6 or more people/sq. mi.

● Founded at a time when the area had less than 6 people/sq. mi.

Population density in 1860

6 or more people/sq. mi.

2 to 6 people/sq. mi.

DISTANCE TO THE WESTERN FRONTIER WHEN THE UTOPIAN COMMUNITY WAS FOUNDED

Number of communities founded

Frontier

25

20

15

10

5

0

Miles 200 100   >6/sq. mi. 100 200 300 400 500 600

<6/sq. mi.

Whether a utopia's inclination is toward Eden or toward the New Jerusalem, or is an experimental manifestation, it represents a view of man's relation to his world. Utopias are models people create as a way of understanding possible worlds and hence their own world. The idea of utopia as a model for apprehending and controlling the world is explicit in Francis Bacon's *New Atlantis* (1627), the earliest of modern utopias. The noblest institution in the New Atlantis is Salomon's House, an elaborate academy "dedicated to the study of the works and creatures of God." Bacon defined its purpose as follows: "The end of our foundation [Salomon's House] is the knowledge of causes, and secret motion of things, and the enlarging of the bounds of human empire, to the effecting of all things possible."[12] He describes in detail the specialized laboratories and instruments of measurement and experiment and the elaborate division of labor whereby work was assigned and carried out, results codified and evaluated, and further research planned. As Henry Morley put it, "Bacon in his philosophy, sought through experimental

FIGURE 1

Utopian Communities Established Between 1663 and 1860. Map compiled from seven maps in Ronald F. Abler, "The Geography of Nowhere, 1660–1860" (1966).

There is clearly a frontier or at least a backwoods aspect to the establishment of utopian communities in the United States. The map shows the locations of utopian communities started between 1663 and 1860. The small black dots show the 116 communities which, when established, lay within the zone of population density of more than six people per square mile. The larger dots show the eleven communities which, when established, lay outside the zone of more than six people per square mile. The graph summarizes the distance from utopian communities to the westward-moving frontier at the time each community was established. For utopias established during a decade, distance measurements were made to the six-people/sq.-mi. "frontier" as it stood at the end of the decade. Overall, the eleven places established in the "wilderness," averaged 50 miles distance from the six-people/sq.-mi. line. The 116 places established within the settled area, averaged 191 miles distance from the six-people/sq.-mi. line. Nonetheless, 48 utopian settlements, or 41 per cent of the communities established behind the frontier, lay within 100 miles of it at the time they were founded. Abler concluded that the need to buy large contiguous blocks of land at reasonable prices was partly responsible for this proximity to the frontier. (The definition of utopian "communities" sets limits that exclude planned settlements such as Cincinnati, Ohio, or Albion, Illinois, where no "commune" characteristics were present.)

203

science the dominion of men over things, 'for [as Bacon said] nature is only governed by obeying her.' "[13] Salomon's House and the experimental procedure Bacon outlined had great impact on scientific thought in the seventeenth century. The Royal Society was consciously modeled on the research institution of the New Atlantis.[14] We view most utopias as just such Baconian constructs. They are models that encourage one to ask: What are man's ideal relations to his world? How may these relations be secured?

UTOPIA AS PARADIGM

Utopias, whether fictional or experienced, are ways of thinking about the world. As ideal constructs utopias are recorded in every literate culture. In all utopias the notion of the "good" place is primary and pervasive, though what specifically characterizes the good place is variable. The range and variety of utopias and their dichotomous expressions—from utopia to dystopia, Erewhon to Brook Farm, Shaker Colony to Fourier Phalanx, Islandia to Walden Two—wreak havoc with every taxonomy. Every utopia is different at the most detailed descriptive level, yet every utopia is as one at the highest level of abstraction—the ideal. Utopias are probably best understood at the ideal level, studied within the context and methods of the philosophy of science and the history of ideas. Utopias are theories about the human condition.[15]

As social thought, utopia is paradigmatic. That is, a utopia is a generic set of propositions and presuppositions about the world. Therein lies their interest for us as geographers—they are beliefs about the world, not descriptions of it. Utopian thought assumes that the ideal (essence) is reality and that individuals (existence) are stamped out from some all-pervasive generic cookie cutter. Utopian thought assumes that the world, although apparently built up inductively, can be generated deductively through some normative mechanism. It assumes further that the resultant world can be lived inductively; yet we as individuals live by some deductive code. But what, we must ask, are the prevailing norms by which all things, events, and relations utopian are judged? How do specific utopias reflect those norms with reference to location, size, institutions, and codes of living?

Central to every utopian effort is the idea of good, or enforced virtue. Most Christian utopists from Sir Thomas More on have seen mankind achieving oneness with God. A more secular utopia might provide mankind with delicious food, sumptuous palaces, entertainments, and enough sex to fulfill an undergraduate's dreams. But in both sacred and secular utopias something is lacking: the elements of surprise, of risk, of contingency. Something in us fears absolute goodness. We are suspicious that a return to Eden or the attainment of the New Jerusalem would rob life of its interest and worth. Lewis, the narrator in C. S. Lewis's *Perelandra,* catches this dread nicely. Lewis is en route to meet Ransom, who has returned from the moon and Mars, where he conversed with extraterrestrial beings. As he walks the open heath toward Ransom's house with daylight fading fast, Lewis experiences at first the fear of being "drawn in" against his will and better judgment. But after entering Ransom's deserted cottage and realizing that he is in the presence of a non-earthly intelligence, he knows fear of another kind.

> I felt sure that the creature was what we call "good," but I wasn't sure whether I liked "goodness" so much as I had supposed. This is a very terrible experience. As long as what you are afraid of is something evil, you may still hope that the good may come to your rescue. But suppose you struggle through to the good and find that it also is dreadful? . . . Then, indeed, there is no rescue possible: the last card has been played.[16]

Nevertheless, how "good" is defined in a utopia is less important than the consequences of "goodness" for change, equilibrium, time, boundaries, size, location, nature, resources, technology, and work.

UTOPIA AS STEADY STATE AND CLOSED SYSTEM

Features displayed in both Eden and the New Jerusalem are equilibrium and balance. Time, which our Judaeo-Christian heritage made unilinear and forever unfolding, exists only as a closed cycle. This functional, rather than historical, view of time finds expression in Boulding's plea that man define himself as an astronaut on spaceship earth and reject as a model the wasteful cowboy forever moving westward on a frontier of limitless resources.[17]

With rare exceptions, utopias are ahistorical. The author seldom shows how the society managed to transform itself into its current utopian state. In several instances the utopia rises out of the ashes of a terrible war or has been established in virgin country by a displaced people cut off from their past. Not only are the historical origins of utopias usually obscure; but their histories since their founding may be either fragmentary or transformed to serve the state. In Orwell's 1984, history is periodically rewritten by Big Brother to conform with whatever the Party has decided is true. Winston's redemption comes when at last he truly believes according to O'Brien's patient instructions.

Only the disciplined mind can see reality, Winston. You believe that reality is something objective, external, existing in its own right. You also believe that the nature of reality is self-evident. When you delude yourself into thinking that you see something, you assume that everyone else sees the same thing as you. But I tell you, Winston, that reality is not external. Reality exists in the human mind, and nowhere else. Not in the individual mind, which can make mistakes, and in any case soon perishes; only in the mind of the Party, which is collective and immortal. Whatever the Party holds to be truth *is* truth. It is impossible to see reality except by looking through the eyes of the Party. That is the fact that you have got to relearn, Winston. It needs an act of self-destruction, an effort of the will. You must humble yourself before you can become sane.[18]

A world that is perfect needs no history. Indeed, it positively discourages the notion, for history implies change, something with which utopia cannot cope. Because the consequences cannot be foreseen, any change threatens the equilibrium of the system.

In utopia nothing is left to chance. Relations with the outside world, for example, are carefully regulated. Contact between Austin Wright's Islandians and foreigners was strictly controlled by the Hundred Law, which limited the number of foreign residents to one hundred and allowed no one to live there for more than one year in ten. In *The City of the Sun* the older and wiser people "are unwilling that the state should be corrupted by the vicious customs of slaves and foreigners. Therefore they do business at the gates."[19] Zamiatin's world is protected by a high green wall. Indeed D-503, the protagonist (all people are numbered and prefixed by a letter, males by a consonant, females by a vowel), is a mathematician who is building the Integral, a rocket to be launched which will lift a glass substance high and cut the city off from the country once and for all.[20] In Huxley's *Brave New World* an annihilating electric fence separates the happy society from the savages, and in his *Island* the people of Pala deport all unapproved visitors within twenty-four hours.[21]

Utopia cannot survive in proximity to an alternative way of life. The geographical extent of utopia was small when the world remained unknown to European writers and before European power had organized much of the world. More's island *Utopia* was only some two hundred miles across. But as European empires expanded in scope and power, the utopias did too; and since utopists were running out of places to put their imaginary worlds, they had to go underground or resort to outer space or future times. H. G. Wells notes an increase in the size of utopia.

> No less than a planet will serve the purpose of a modern utopia. Time was when a mountain valley or an island seemed to promise sufficient isolation for a polity to maintain itself intact from outward force; . . . but the whole trend of modern thought is against the permanence of any such enclosures. . . . A state powerful enough to keep isolated under modern conditions would be powerful enough to rule the world, would be, indeed, if not actively ruling, yet passively acquiescent in all other human organizations, and so responsible for them altogether. World-state, therefore, it must be.[22]

One writer who has traced the shifting locale of literary utopias found that they tend to lie just beyond the frontiers of man's knowledge.[23] Writers are convinced that utopia cannot withstand normal commerce with the real world. More's *Utopia* (1516) was "somewhere between Brazil and India." Campanella's *City of the Sun* (1602) was on Taprobane (Sri Lanka), whose interior was not yet known to Europeans. Andreae's *Christianopolis* (1619) was on the island of Caphar Salama in "the Ethiopian Sea."[24] Bacon's *New Atlantis* (1627) was placed in the

South Seas, and de Foigny's *La Terre Australe connue* of 1676 was one of several set in that part of the world.[25]

As the world's lands and waters came to be better known to European writers, utopias were shifted underground, as with Holberg's *Niels Klim's Journey under the Ground* (1741), Bulwer-Lytton's *The Coming Race: or the New Utopia* (1871), and Tarde's *Underground Man* (1904). The device persists in Forster's *The Machine Stops* (1928) and Roschwald's *Level Seven* (1959).[26] Access to a number of these utopias was through a hole at the north pole.

The interior of Africa, *terra incognita* to nineteenth-century European writers, was the last terrestrial locale available for utopias. These include Theodor Hertzka's *Freeland—A Social Anticipation* (1891), in which a group of European settlers established themselves in Masailand between Mount Kenya and Mount Kilimanjaro, and Ignatius Donnelly's *Caesar's Column* (1890), whose Swiss community settled in Uganda.[27] Other writers have placed their utopias on the moon or other planets. But the most common modern method is the time dimension, introduced by Edward Bellamy in *Looking Backward*[28] and since carried to wonderful perfection through the time-warps and hyperspaces of science-fiction writers. Although today's utopias may be remote from us, resourceful writers can always get us there or bring "them" here.

Thus far we have been considering abstract attributes of utopia—what time is conceived to be, how utopia relates to neighboring worlds, utopia's size and location. The model a utopist chooses imposes requirements on each of these attributes: time is recursive and ahistorical, borders are strictly maintained to ensure isolation from exogenous sources of contamination, the utopia is located in a remote, inaccessible place. All of these features are requisite to the central concerns of utopia—stability and equilibrium.

THE UTOPIAN ENVIRONMENT

Since man must eat to live and must fashion objects to create a human world about him, the question of resources arises in every utopia. The general issues are man's relations to nature, landscape, and environment, to the resources drawn from that environment, and to technology and work. The model the utopian writer selects imposes constraints on these aspects of utopia if the essential equilibrium is to be maintained. First, let us look at nature and landscape.

One finds in utopias of reconstruction, especially in the dystopian novels, a strong hostility to nature, a disparagement of the physical universe. Chad Walsh finds authors "prone to down-grade the body and fence out untamed nature. . . . Rarely in either utopia or dystopia do you get a sense of awe and reverence towards the miracle of the created universe. What you have is man's imperious mind, lording it over nature."[29] The dystopist tends to focus on urban landscapes and to put positive value on the man-made objects which fill them, such as gleaming glass buildings and fast, clean transport systems. The loathing that modern utopian man feels toward nature is well expressed by D-503, the chronicler of Zamiatin's *We*.

> Soon I reached the road running along the Green Wall. From beyond the Wall, from the infinite ocean of green, there arose toward me an immense wave of roots, branches, flowers, leaves. It rose higher and higher; it seemed as though it would splash over me and that from a man, from the finest and most precise mechanism which I am, I would be transformed into . . . But fortunately there was the Green Wall between me and that wild green sea. Oh, how lovely and divinely limiting is the wisdom of walls and bars! This Green Wall is, I think, the greatest invention ever conceived. Man ceased to be a wild animal the day he built the first wall; man ceased to be a wild man only on the day when the Green Wall was completed, when by this wall we isolated our machine-like, perfect world from the irrational, ugly world of trees, birds, and beasts.[30]

Sensitivity to landscape and nature is a hallmark of the agrarian and decentralist utopias. Some of the finest descriptive geographical writing in utopian literature is to be found in *Erewhon* and *Islandia*. The broad glacial stream beds and rocky gorges of the southern Alps of New Zealand come alive in Butler's narrative.[31] Austin Tappan Wright's sure and observant eye recreates in *Islandia* the Swiss Alps, the university town of Oxford, the flat seascapes of Cape Cod. John Lang's leisurely two-week journey on his horse, Fak, from the City to the Fains' and on to Dorn Island, which introduces the reader to Islandia, is a tour de force of environmental evocation. One does not simply see his landscapes, one experiences them.

> The sky, full of bellying gray and white rain clouds, was an immense dome over my head. The only sounds were the clopping and thudding splashes of the feet of the three horses, the creak of my saddle, the swish of the rain among the trees, and the occasional faint whistle of the wind around the corner of my hat. We passed fields and woods, and gardens of maize or grain, which were wet and green. Through the trees were glimpses of buildings; house, stable, and out-houses, the center of each farm lying in the midst of pastures, meadows, orchards, woods, and market gardens, constantly repeated in varying arrangements. Dorn was a huge huddled figure, so large for his horse as to be slightly funny. My left cheek, where the rain beat upon it, was cool and damp, while the other side of my face was very warm with the exercise of riding. Fak's white coat was pitted and streaked and pointed by the wet. I liked to watch his velvety ears, alert, curious, questioning, while the rest of him walked steadily and mechanically.
>
> Thus an hour passed, wordless and calm, and the world was an immense, spacious, rainy place in the very center of which our train of three horses and two men moved small and alone.[32]

Ofttimes authors treat environment as given. They establish an initial equilibrium in man/environment relations and thereafter ignore these relations. The climate of utopia generally seems to be either an equable given or something totally under man's control. Extreme environmental events are done away with; natural catastrophes do not occur. Just as time is made obsolete in utopia, so are space and a differentiated environment. A. P. Russell proffers a quintessential nineteenth-century utopian climate: Sub-Coelum was "genial and salubrious. Extremes of temperatures were not frequent, and atmospheric violence so rare as to be historical. Seasons of rain and seasons of drouth, to devastate and dessicate, were not known."[33]

The dream of utopists is to annihilate space as well as time. This view was expressed in an article attributed to Samuel Butler.

The ultimatum, the ne plus ultra of perfection in mechanized development . . . [will] be well and effectually completed . . . when all men, in all places, without any loss of time, are cognizant through their senses, of all that they desire to be cognizant of in all other places, at a low rate of charge, so that the back country squatter may hear his wool sold in London and deal with the buyer himself—may sit in his own chair in a back country hut and hear the performance of Israel in Ægypt at Exeter Hall—may taste an ice on the Rakaia, which he is paying for and receiving in the Italian opera house Covent Garden. Multiply instance *ad libitum*—this is the grand annihilation of time and place which we are all striving for.[34]

When an author is explicit about the relations between man and resources in his utopia, his analysis will usually be found wanting. Thomas More gave quite detailed information on population, settlement, land area, acreages cultivated, and crops in his *Utopia*. Darrell Norris, who examined the man-resource assumptions carefully, concluded that More's *Utopia* was geographically and economically unworkable.[35] The crops produced would have fed only 60 per cent of the population. He concluded also that the country was oversupplied with urban places. But utopias should be judged by the spirit of the writing rather than by the practical consequences of the assumptions. The utopist is probably wise not to be explicit in presenting his imaginary world, for our literal interpretation of it will usually subvert his dream.

UTOPIA AND TECHNOLOGY

The treatment of technology and work reflects the requirement that the utopian writer deal with the question of livelihood. In most reconstructionist utopias the triumph of technology makes work either unnecessary or light and interesting. In many dystopias, which, of course, are not examples of achieved perfection, work for many is dull, arduous, demeaning, and pointless. Many nineteenth-century utopias, reacting to the evils of industrialization in Europe and America, look back toward Eden in a mood of loss and show great fear of technology.[36] Inhabitants of the decentralist agrarian utopias of Wright (*Islandia*) and Butler (*Erewhon* and *Erewhon Revisited*) have a deep love of nature and a profound dislike of industrialization and all the organization of space and men it requires. Islandian distrust of technology is made clear in the parliamentary debates between Lord Mora's followers and those of Lord Dorn over the issues of mineral concessions and the construction of railroads and electricity and telegraph lines. The fear of being artificially connected and the special abhorrence of being tied into a permanent structured network are well expressed by Dorna in her discussion with the American, John Lang.

"There would be better roads, schools, libraries, finer public buildings, electric lighting and power, railroads, lots of things. . . ."

She asked me to describe these things, and I was as glowing as I could be.

"But no one may want any of these things," she said. "Of course it is simpler to just press a button to make a light, but all the complications of wires stretched everywhere . . ." She sighed.

"There are two sides to it," I said. "You would get used to wires."

"Never!" she cried with a laugh. "Threads going everywhere tying everyone to someone else!"

"It isn't so bad in practice, Dorna."

"It's not our way," she answered. "And I don't see the gain. We work some of the time to make candles. Someone else would have to make wires and burning things and mills. There would be just as much work."

"But each person could spend more time on one thing."

She shuddered.

"Why should he?"

"You can accomplish more doing one thing. You become more skillful."

"But you touch life in fewer ways."[37]

Erewhonians had rid themselves of the evils of the Industrial Revolution. Butler's earliest experiences of Erewhon include a visit to a village museum.

There were fragments of steam engines, all broken and rusted; among them I saw a cylinder and piston, a broken fly-wheel, and part of a crank, which was laid on the ground by their side. Again there was a very old carriage whose wheels in spite of rust and decay, I could see, had been designed originally for iron rails. Indeed, there were fragments of a great many of our own most advanced inventions; but they seemed all to be several hundred years old, and to be placed where they were, not for instruction, but curiosity.[38]

The consequences of the Industrial Revolution, especially its effects on human labor and well being, inspired many utopian writers to focus attention on economic and technical aspects of production.

UTOPIA AS HISTORICAL FORCE

The way resources, property, and wealth have been treated in some utopias has had significant historical consequences. Bellamy's *Looking Backward* eliminated differences of wealth in an affluent society by carrying then-current economic processes to their logical end. Enterprises got larger and larger through growth and merger until there was but one "universal trust." Big business in fact became the state, which administered the creation and circulation of abundant economic goods and allocated labor mainly on humane and rational grounds. Bellamy's views had immense appeal. Ebenezer Howard, the originator of the garden-city movement and a pioneer in city planning in Great Britain, was inspired by Bellamy's book. Many of Bellamy's ideas were embodied in Howard's influential *Garden Cities of Tomorrow* (1898) and were carried out in garden-city and new-town developments such as Letchworth, Welwyn Garden City, and Stevenage.[39] Bellamy's discussion of the unequal distribution of wealth struck a responsive chord in the minds of many Americans and Europeans at a time when distinctions between rich and poor were becoming increasingly accentuated. Bellamy societies were organized in the United States and Europe. The book, and favorable popular reaction to it, soon inspired a vigorous counterattack, which took the form of utopian rebuttals of *Looking Backward*. Some people feared that Bellamy's proposals might actually be put into practice.

Theodor Hertzka, an economist, presented his utopian ideas in *Free-*

land—A *Social Anticipation*. He sought to resolve the problem of un-equal distribution of wealth through the wide dispersal of property and through joint stock companies and cooperatives. In Austria and Germany alone, nearly a thousand local societies sprang up to put his principles into action.

Australia and New Zealand were in the process of settlement when some of the more influential utopian ideas were being published. J. M. Powell has traced the influence of Henry George on freehold and lease-hold land legislation in Australia.[40] Both Australia and New Zealand, those great "laboratories of social experiment," were hospitable to the cooperative movement and passed legislation to attract religious and national cooperative groups.[41]

ESCAPE TO UTOPIA

Utopia is not sought only in books of fiction and in experimental communities. The promotional literature of travel and tourism, too, is inspired by edenic utopian ideals.[42] Implicit in much of this literature are attitudes toward work and the mundane world. You know the life:

> All your days and nights will be filled with the things you want to do. If you want to do nothing, we'll fill them with peace and quiet. If you're in the mood for good times, for music and parties, we'll show you the way. . . . And every day, four times a day, there will be feasting. . . . All your days and nights filled with good things, shared by good people, too. Your fellow passengers, who have chosen to see the world in a world where nice people are nice to each other. That's the life.

You know the place—Tahiti, for example:

> The sun is up. It's morning—but different from any morning you've ever known before, as you touch down at Papeete to change for the flight to Raiatea. . . . Your plane glides toward a landing. Below you, a shimmering island. White sand. Green palms. A turquoise and sapphire sea. Vivid pinks and purples glimpsed through lush ferns. A thrill sweeps through you. . . .

If Kuoni Escorted Tours has not convinced you, Westours will:

> Laughter mingles with the surge of the Pacific on a coral reef. Water-
> falls flash out into the sunlight from dazzling mountain slopes. Drums
> throb under a canopy of coconut palms and casuarina trees as graceful
> Tahitian girls dance the exuberant *tamure*. Tahiti welcomes you with
> the turquoise of a peaceful lagoon . . . the colors and scent of a mil-
> lion exotic flowers . . . and the friendship of a warm-hearted people
> on the world's happiest of islands.[43]

Consider what a vacation is supposed to be. One escapes the real
world to a setting, often isolated and idyllic, of peace and abundance.
One escapes routine and effectively suspends time. One's identity and
class distinctions may be suspended as on other unreal or ritual occasions, such as Mardi Gras and masked balls.[44] The judge and the janitor
hobnob at the bar while their spouses are teamed up for shuffleboard by
the activities director. Nature, though transformed into a safe environment of beaches, walks, and horse trails, suggests a symbolic return to
Eden. Emphasis is on the out-of-doors—fresh air, sun, sky, salt sea,
woods, fields, and beaches. There is casual near-nudity and a delight in
walking and in being in rural or village settings.

According to Henri Raymond the vacation may have a more narcis-
sistic function. "Whenever we waste time and money during a vacation
it is not simply for relaxation but for reparation—for revenge for the out-
rages perpetrated by our society." Yet the world of work may eventually
seem preferable to the world of indolence. The attitude people have toward their holidays may subconsciously reveal something about their attitude toward utopia. A "vacation always seems like a period of decep-
tion; that is to say, a vacation is a party, a moment of hope which is
destined by nature not to be realized."[45]

PROSPECTS FOR UTOPIA

What general conclusions have we reached regarding utopia? At the detailed descriptive case level of experiment or literary exposition, the question of "norm" seems to be almost totally inappropriate. For example,

the location of utopia fits no single geographical taxonomy: rural, urban, frontier, backwoods, underdeveloped tropics. What can we say about all utopias, attribute by attribute?

The geographer begins to read a utopia with an expectation that the author, who creates a good place out of no place, will create an environment wherein the utopian society will be given meaning. Certain abstract geographical characteristics establish and describe utopias, but they do not explain how they work. Utopias are isolated and have sharply defined, impermeable boundaries. From the sixteenth to the twentieth century, their size has increased and their relative locations have shifted. But these are externalities. What about the geography inside utopia?

Utopian writers are oblivious to, or impatient with, concerns that animate geographers: the concept of resource, the look of the land, the organization of space, the meaning of place, the idea of man in nature and man in landscape, the friction of distance, the economy of location. In finding utopia ahistorical, aspatial within its boundaries, in time-space equilibrium, and with resource problems either willed away or resolved through technology, we begin to perceive utopia's true nature to be the normative model of science.[46]

The relevant question in utopian thought is that of the man-nature-God relation. That question is the utopian paradigm. The prevailing norm in any utopia is a generic proposition about the relation. Sometimes nature (or natural man) is the standard by which all things are judged. The utopians of primitive-escape and perfectionist-reconstruction both postulate that norm—that is, goodness is the achieved, absolute original or final state of nature. Sometimes God-man is the relation examined—either through the process of evolutionary human perfectibility and progress or through the millennialist advent.[47] Sometimes technology is the prevailing norm, as in the technocratic-economic efficiency utopias of the nineteenth century and the dystopias of science fiction.[48] Sometimes the tenets of behavioral psychology are the norm. Utopian models of elaborate reinforcement mechanisms range from contemporary nation states, industrial enterprises, and schools to the medievalism of monastic orders and contemporary sectarian communes. One web envelops them all: man is perfectible down here, up there, or at some station in between.[49] In other cases the norm is political democracy, poetry, or art. Whatever the postulate, it is evident that the norm is a philosophy—a way of looking at life and the world—not life itself. Utopias, as philosophies of nature—that is, the environment of the world—offer important source materials for geographical study.

Islandia has provided occasion for comment on the nature of utopia throughout this essay. In almost every way *Islandia* is the antithesis of the normative model of utopia. It exists in the real world of the first decade of the twentieth century; it is in communication with other countries; it is bordered by German and British protectorates; its people have a profound sense of history, a deeply felt sense of place and the continuity of life; life is lived in real landscapes; the economy functions in a world of particularized resources influenced by the friction of distance. Life there is contingent and emergent. *Islandia* has provided a counterpoint for the normative model of utopia. That *Islandia* is "real," whereas most other utopias are only interesting academic experiments, indicates our skepticism toward utopian perfectionism.

Modern man's recent discovery of spaceship earth and the ecological ethic give a utopian or dystopian flavor to much contemporary writing about man's future. The rapid depletion of nonrenewable resources, radioactive and other pollution of the air we breathe and water we drink, the permanent despoilation of land stripped for coal or covered with concrete have upset the balance of nature and the relation of people to resources.[50] Planet earth is our closed system, our one place. Zero population growth and closed cycles of resource use echo utopia's functional equilibrium, its recursive time. Concern for the development gap between advanced industrial economies and the Third World and calls for world government shift current rhetoric toward the utopian norm. In the world of economic reality, international corporations, many with GNPs and economic and political power exceeding those of all but the largest nations, seem part way to achieving Bellamy's "universal trust," in structure if not in beneficence. It remains to be seen how profound and enduring ecological and one-world beliefs will be; but such thinking, by emphasizing equilibrium, universality, and functionally closed cycles, leads people to evaluate their relations to man and nature in strikingly utopian ways.

John K. Wright commends to us the study of "the geographical ideas, both true and false, of all manner of people." Those who write about the "good place" warrant the scrutiny of geosophers. To define utopia as "a way of looking at the world" is itself a worthy geographical proposition.

NOTES

1. "*Terrae Incognitae*: The Place of the Imagination in Geography," *Annals of the Association of American Geographers* 37 (1947):12.
2. Wright, *The Geographical Lore of the Time of the Crusades: A Study in the History of Medieval Science and Tradition in Western Europe* (New York: American Geographical Society, 1925; New York: Dover, 1965); Brown, *Mirror for Americans: Likeness of the Eastern Seaboard, 1810* (New York: American Geographical Society, 1943).
3. Introduction to Austin Tappan Wright, *Islandia* (1942) (New York: Rinehart, 1958), p. x.
4. Letter from John K. Wright to Hildegard B. Johnson, January 22, 1965.
5. The utopian literature is inexhaustible, but the patience of readers is not. Our essay makes no attempt to be comprehensive. Rather, we have chosen utopias that help to make the points we feel to be important. Our essay examines utopian ideas expressed within the Judaeo-Christian tradition only. For utopian thought in Chinese, Buddist, and Islamic cultures, see Jean Chesneaux, "Egalitarian and Utopian Traditions in the East," *Diogenes*, no. 62 (1968), pp. 76–102. See also the three volumes on Japanese, Chinese, and Indian traditions edited by William Theodore de Bary and entitled *Introduction to Oriental Civilization* (New York: Columbia University Press): *Sources of Japanese Tradition* (1958); *Sources of Chinese Tradition* (1960); *Sources of Indian Tradition* (1958, 1964).
6. In *The Story of Utopias* (New York: The Viking Press, 1922, 1962), p. 15. For representative utopias see also Glenn Robert Negley and J. Max Patrick, *The Quest for Utopia: An Anthology of Imaginary Societies* (New York: H. Schuman, 1952).
7. See *From Utopia to Nightmare* (New York: Harper and Row, 1962), p. 21. Although dystopia is specifically a concept polar to utopia, and is a bad place, it does not require a different theoretical model for purposes of analysis.
8. See Alice Felt Tyler, *Freedom's Ferment: Phases of American Social History from the Colonial Period to the Outbreak of the Civil War* (1944; New York: Harper Torchbook, 1962); Ronald F. Abler, "The Geography of Nowhere: The Location of Utopian Communities, 1660–1860," Ralph H. Brown Collection, Department of Geography, University of Minnesota (Minneapolis, 1966), 26 pp. The experimental utopias of the sixteenth and seventeenth centuries in America were also reconstructionist attempts to achieve the celestial city along lines pro-

posed by More and Campanella, if not by Rabelais. Most of the sixteenth- and seventeenth-century plantings in the New World were inspired by Renaissance and Reformation views on millennialism and the more pervasive Christian thought on "paradise" and "wilderness" which continued to influence the eighteenth- and nineteenth-century experiments. See Norman Cohn, *The Pursuit of the Millennium* (New York: Oxford University Press, 1970); George H. Williams, *Wilderness and Paradise in Christian Thought* (New York: Harper and Bros., 1962); Ernest Lee Tuveson, *Millennium and Utopia* (Berkeley: University of California Press, 1949); J. A. De Jono, *As the Waters Cover the Sea* (Kampen, Neth.: J. H. Koh, 1970); John Leddy Phelan, *The Millennial Kingdom of the Franciscans in the New World* (Berkeley: University of California Press, 1956); Silvio Zavala, *Sir Thomas More in New Spain* (London: The Hispanic and Luso-Brazilian Councils, 1955). For specifically English experiments see W. H. G. Armytage, *Heavens Below* (London: Routledge and Kegan Paul, 1961). For the French, see Frank E. Manuel and Fritzie P. Manuel, *French Utopias* (New York: Free Press, 1966).

9. Representative are Arthur E. Bestor, Jr., *Backwoods Utopias: The Sectarian and Owenite Phases of Communitarian Socialism in America, 1663–1829* (Philadelphia: University of Pennsylvania Press, 1950); Charles Nordhoff, *The Communistic Societies of the United States from Personal Visit and Observation* (New York: Harper and Bros., 1875); Victor L. Parrington, Jr., *American Dreams: A Study of American Utopias* (New York: Russell and Russell, 1964); William A. Hinds, *American Communities and Cooperative Colonies* (Chicago: Kerr and Co., 1908); Mark Holloway, *Heavens on Earth: Utopian Communities in America, 1680–1880* (London: Turnstile Press, 1951).

10. Abler, "Geography of Nowhere," p. 21.

11. "Utopia, Millennium and the Co-operative Ideal: A Behavioural Matrix in the Settlement Process," *The Australian Geographer* 11 (1971):609.

12. In Henry Morley, *Ideal Commonwealths* (London: Colonial Press, 1901), which reproduces Bacon's *New Atlantis*, pp. 118, 129.

13. Ibid., pp. v–vi.

14. See Lewis Mumford, *The Myth of the Machine: The Pentagon of Power* (New York: Harcourt, Brace and Jovanovich, 1970), pp. 105–29; Margery Purver, *The Royal Society: Concept and Creation* (Cambridge: M.I.T. Press, 1967); Nell Eurich, *Science in Utopia* (Cambridge: Harvard University Press, 1967), p. 215. It is understandable that some British historians and historiographers have seen in the founding of the Royal Society the beginning of the modern world. Baconian ideas were also influential, in the broader sense of the "New Philosophy" movement, in the founding and structuring of the American Philosophical Society and the French Académie Royale des Sciences and its predecessors. See M. C. W. Hunter, "The Royal Society and the Origin of British Archaeology," *Antiquity* 45 (1971):113–21, 187–92.

15. The concept of paradigm used here follows the ideas of R. G. Collingwood. He stated that the thought of the society of any period is organized and therefore

explained according to "constellations of absolute presuppositions" held by that society in the period under discussion. See Quentin Skinner, "Meaning and Understanding in the History of Ideas," *History and Theory* 8 (1969):3–53, and his references to R. G. Collingwood (1940), E. H. Gombrich (1960), and T. S. Kuhn (1961, 1962). Also, Michael Krausz, ed., *Critical Essays on the Philosophy of R. G. Collingwood* (Oxford: Clarendon Press, 1972), chapters by Stephen Toulmin, "Conceptual Change and the Problems of Relativity," pp. 201–21; and M. Krausz, "The Logic of Absolute Presuppositions," pp. 221–40. For Toulmin's exposition, see the series of papers and commentary in his *Foresight and Understanding* (New York: Harper and Row, 1961); in R. S. Cohen and M. W. Wartofsky, eds., *Boston Studies in the Philosophy of Science*, vol. 3 (Dordrecht, 1967); and in *Synthèse* 17 (1967):75–99, and 18 (1968):459–63.

16. *Perelandra* (London: Bodley Head, 1943), p. 19.
17. Kenneth E. Boulding, "The Economics of the Coming Spaceship Earth," in Henry Jarrett, ed., *Environmental Quality in a Growing Economy* (Baltimore: Johns Hopkins Press, 1966), pp. 3–14.
18. *1984* (New York: New American Library, 1949), pp. 205–6.
19. Thomas Campanella, *The City of the Sun*, reproduced in Morley's *Ideal Commonwealths*, p. 166.
20. Eugene Zamiatin, *We* (New York: Dutton, 1924).
21. Aldous Huxley, *Brave New World* (London: Chatto and Windus, 1932); *Island* (New York: Harper and Row, 1962).
22. *A Modern Utopia* (London: Nelson, 1905), p. 21.
23. Mary Pfau Lavine, "Geography of Utopia," Ralph H. Brown Collection, Department of Geography, University of Minnesota (Minneapolis, 1966).
24. Quoted in Marie Louise Berneri, *Journey through Utopia* (London: Routledge & Kegan Paul, 1950), p. 108.
25. Bacon, *New Atlantis*; Gabriel de Foigny, *La Terre Australe connue* (Paris: C. Barbin, 1692).
26. Ludvig Holberg, *Niels Klim's Journey under the Ground* (New York: Saxon & Miles, 1845); E. G. E. L. Bulwer-Lytton, *The Coming Race* (Chicago: Donohue, 1871); Gabriel Tarde, *Underground Man* (London: Duckworth, 1904); E. M. Forster, *The Collected Tales of E. M. Forster* (New York: Knopf, 1947); and Mordechai Roschwald, *Level Seven* (London: Heinemann, 1959).
27. Theodor Hertzka, *Freeland—A Social Anticipation* (London: Chatto and Windus, 1891); Ignatius Donnelly, *Caesar's Column* (Chicago: F. J. Schulte, 1890).
28. *Looking Backward* (Boston: Houghton Mifflin, 1888).
29. *From Utopia to Nightmare*, pp. 139–40. We are aware that dystopian, as well as utopian, authors may write satire and that their protagonists may express views that the authors themselves despise. Some authors describe developments they see as undesirable but inevitable. Many dystopian authors do not write about a good or a bad place; they predict a future place. Often it is not possible to distinguish between beliefs and values, or to know whether those expressed by characters in a utopian novel are also those of its author.

30. *We*, pp. 88–89.
31. Samuel Butler, *Erewhon, or Over the Range* (1873), and *Erewhon Revisited Twenty Years Later* (New York: Random House, 1927). Butler had a highly developed eye for landscape, and as a young man he wanted to become a painter. After his return to England from New Zealand he studied art, and some of his pictures were exhibited at the Royal Academy in London.
32. *Islandia*, p. 65.
33. *Sub-Coelum: A Sky-Built Human World* (Boston: Houghton Mifflin, 1893), p. 9. Sub-Coelum must truly have been the perfect utopia, for we find on page 179 that the people did not snore.
34. "From our mad correspondent," *The Press*, Christchurch, New Zealand, Sept. 15, 1863, reprinted in Joseph Jones, *The Cradle of Erewhon* (Austin: University of Texas Press, 1959), pp. 196–97.
35. "More's Utopia, A Geographical Approach," *Geographical Articles* no. 10 (Cambridge: Cambridge University, Department of Geography, 1967), pp. 53–59; and Brian R. Goodey, "Mapping 'Utopia': A Comment on the Geography of Sir Thomas More," *Geographical Review* 60 (1970):15–30.
36. The theme of "Man and the Garden" ties to general themes noted before: millennialism, paradise, wilderness, and frontier. See references cited in notes 8 and 9; and for the American experience in the nineteenth century see Henry Nash Smith, *Virgin Land* (Cambridge: Harvard University Press, 1950); R. W. B. Lewis, *The American Adam* (Chicago: University of Chicago Press, 1955); Arthur K. Moore, *The Frontier Mind* (Lexington: University of Kentucky Press, 1957); Charles L. Sanford, *The Quest for Paradise: Europe and the American Moral Imagination* (Urbana: University of Illinois Press, 1961); Leo Marx, *The Machine in the Garden* (New York: Oxford University Press, 1964); and David W. Noble, *The Eternal Adam and the New World Garden* (New York: Braziller, 1968).
37. Austin Tappan Wright, *Islandia*, pp. 165–66.
38. *Erewhon*, pp. 62–63.
39. Ebenezer Howard, *Garden Cities of Tomorrow* (London: Faber and Faber, 1965), originally titled *Tomorrow: A Peaceful Path to Real Reform* (1898); and R. J. Harrison Church and David Thomas. "Welwyn Garden City, Stevenage and Hampstead: The Development of the Ideas of the Garden City, New Town, and Garden Suburb," *Excursion Guide*, Institute of British Geographers Annual Conference, January 1969, pp. 15–24.
40. J. M. Powell, "The Land Debates in Victoria, 1872–84," *Journal of the Royal Australian Historical Society* 56 (1970):263–80. Henry George, American economist and newspaperman, founded the single-tax movement. In *Progress and Poverty* (1870) he advocated economic reforms to prevent individuals from profiting from unearned increases of land values. George argued that since the community makes land valuable, the community should have the benefit of its value, a result he felt could be achieved by a single tax on land.
41. Powell, "Utopia, Millennium and the Co-operative Ideal," pp. 608–9. Samuel

Butler spent about five years in New Zealand in the then newly established Canterbury settlement. Canterbury was planned and developed according to the colonization principles of Edward Gibbon Wakefield, who promoted settlements in both Australia and New Zealand with the peculiar "utopian" object of preserving the English class system at home and establishing it in new areas overseas. See M. F. Lloyd Prichard, ed., *The Collected Works of Edward Gibbon Wakefield* (Glasgow: Collins, 1968); W. H. G. Armytage, *Yesterday's Tomorrows* (London: Routledge & Kegan Paul, 1968).

42. The utopian ideal is expressed also in the literature of suburban real estate developers, savings institutions, and insurance companies, in the hard-sell promotional brochures for retirement homes in Florida and the Southwest, and in literature from another era—the immigrant letters and the exhortations to "go West."

43. Quotations from Holland America literature on the S.S. *Rotterdam*, from Kuoni Escorted Tours, and from Westours, Inc., 1972–73 announcements.

44. E. R. Leach, "Chronus and Chronos" and "Time and False Noses," *Rethinking Anthropology*, London School of Economics Monographs on Social Anthropology, no. 22 (1961), pp. 124–36.

45. Henri Raymond, "Utopia All-Inclusive," *Landscape* 13.2 (1963–64):7. Pp. 4–7 have several useful observations on the idea of the vacation, which we summarize here.

46. Five analytic studies which treat the general normative presuppositions of utopian thought but are less narrowly focused than the present study are Frank E. Manuel, ed., *Utopia and Utopian Thought* (Boston: Beacon Press, 1967), a Daedalus symposium on the range and variety of utopian thought; Martin G. Plattel, *Utopian and Critical Thinking* (Pittsburgh: Duquesne University Press, 1972), a specifically ideological study; Raymond Ruyer, *L'Utopie et les utopies* (Paris: Presses Universitaires de France, 1950), which treats the utopian "fixations" on regularity, uniformity, authoritarianism, isolation, autarky, and hostility to nature; Joyce Oramel Hertzler, *The History of Utopian Thought* (New York: Macmillan, 1923), a study of utopia as social thought and social idealism from a sociological perspective; and Karl Mannheim, *Ideology and Utopia* (New York: Harcourt, Brace, 1936), an analysis of utopia as political theory.

47. On "progress" see notes 8, 9, and 36 for references. On the eschatological theme of millennialism and the "myth of the return" see Mircea Eliade, "Paradise and Utopia" in Manuel, *Utopia and Utopian Thought*, pp. 260–80, and more broadly, Mircea Eliade, *The Myth of the Eternal Return* (New York: Bollingen Foundation, 1954), reprinted as *Cosmos and History* (New York: Harper, 1959).

48. See especially the study by Mulford Q. Sibley, *Technology and Utopian Thought* (Minneapolis: Burgess, 1971).

49. On the contemporary commune see Rosabeth Moss Kanter, *Commitment and Community* (Cambridge: Harvard University Press, 1972), with commentary and bibliography on communes of the Synanon and Walden Two type. For

background see B. F. Skinner, *Walden Two* (New York: Macmillan, 1948); idem, *Beyond Freedom and Dignity* (New York: Knopf, 1971); and Arthur Koestler, *The Ghost in the Machine* (London: Hutchinson, 1967).

50. See the collection of essays on "The No-Growth Society," *Daedalus* 102.4 (1973).

John Kirtland Wright:
A List of Publications

Prepared by Lynn S. Mullins and Molly Laird
of the American Geographical Society

This bibliography of the publications of John Kirtland Wright is based on a listing compiled by Wright in 1968. It is arranged chronologically by year; within a year the items are listed alphabetically by title. Books reviewed and edited by Wright follow items written by him; within a given year these items are listed alphabetically by author. Before 1951, notes and book reviews contributed by American Geographical Society staff members to the *Geographical Review* were unsigned; such items are indicated by an asterisk. Wright often combined several books in one review article, but each book reviewed is listed separately here. Throughout the bibliography the abbreviation "GR" is used for the *Geographical Review*, and "AGS," for the American Geographical Society.

1908
"Buildings and Parts of Cambridge Commemorated in Longfellow's Poems." *Cambridge* [Mass.] *Historical Society Publications, 3, Proceedings, January 28–October 27, 1908*, pp. 43–47.

1916

"Mt. Lovčen and the Bocche di Cattaro." *Military Historian and Economist* 1:166–69. Includes map by J. K. Wright.

1917

"Belem do Pará." *Military Historian and Economist* 2:47–52. Includes map by J. K. Wright.

1920

*"A Famous Seventeenth Century Map of Italy." GR 10:418.
*"Geographical Conceptions of a Primitive People: Yurok Geography." GR 10:414.
*"Mauritius and Réunion." GR 10:416–17.

1921

*"The Farthest Points Reached by Bartholomeu Dias." GR 11:146–47.
*"French West Africa." GR 11:619–21.
*"Medieval Origins of the Armenian Question." GR 11:446.
*"The Population of Porto Rico." GR 11:140–41.
*"Recent Studies of Glacial Variations in the French Alps." GR 11:301.
*"Three Early Fifteenth Century World Maps in Siena." GR 11:306.
*"Three Mountaineering Books: The Mt. Everest Expedition." GR 11: 449–50.
*"Travel as a Form of Human Enterprise." GR 11:628–29.

---

*Brunhes, Jean, *Géographie humaine de la France*, vol. 1 of *Histoire de la nation française*, ed. Gabriel Hanotaux. 15 vols. Paris: Société de l'Histoire National, 1920. Review, GR 11:430–33.
*Cordier, Henri, *Mélanges d'histoire et de géographie orientales*. 2 vols. Paris: Jean Maisonneuve & Fils, 1914 and 1920. Review, GR 11:638–39.
*Fluss, Max, *Donaufahrten und Donauhandel im Mittelalter und in neueren Zeiten*. No. 22, *Aus Österreichs Vergangenheit*. Prague: A. Haase, 1920. Review, GR 11:640.
*James, W. P., *The Lure of the Map*. 2nd ed. London: Methuen, 1920. Review, GR 11:160.
*Lee, Ida, *Captain Bligh's Second Voyage to the South Sea*. London: Longmans, Green, 1920. Review, GR 11:639–40.
*Leroux, Alfred, *Géographie statistique et historique du pays Limousin depuis les origines jusqu'à nos jours*. Limoges: Imprimerie et Librairie Limousines, 1919. Review, GR 11:637–38.
*Le Strange, G., trans., *The Geographical Part of the Nuzhat-al-Qulūb composed by Hamd-Allāh Mustawfi of Qazwīn in 740 (1340)*, E. J. W. Gibb

Memorial Series, Vol. 23. Leyden: E. J. Brill, 1919. Review, GR 11:457.
*Markham, C. R., *The Lands of Silence: A History of Arctic and Antarctic Exploration*. Cambridge: University Press, 1921. Review, GR 11:641–42.

1922
*"British Enterprise in Northern Baluchistan." GR 12:498–99.
*"The Exploration of Mts. Kilimanjaro and Kenya." GR 12:494–96.
"Notes on the Knowledge of Latitudes and Longitudes in the Middle Ages." *Isis* 5:75–98.
*"Some Recent Studies in the History of Australian Exploration." GR 12: 499–501.

---

*Freshfield, D. W., *The Life of Horace Benedict de Saussure*. London: Edward Arnold, 1920. Review, GR 12:519–20.

1923
*"Aboriginal Geography of New York State and City." GR 13:133.
Aids to Geographical Research: Bibliographies and Periodicals, Research Series no. 10. New York: AGS [American Geographical Society], 243 pp. Rev. ed.: *Aids to Geographical Research: Bibliographies, Periodicals, Atlases, Gazetteers and Other Reference Books*, Research Series no. 22. New York: Published for American Geographical Society by Columbia University Press, 1947, 331 pp. (with Elizabeth T. Platt).
*"The 'Bibliographie géographique' and Two Other Bibliographical Aids of Value to the Geographer." GR 13:480–81.
*"Changes in the Nile Delta and Lower Nile; the Delta Lake Fisheries." GR 13:618–20.
*"Chinese Geography of the West in Antiquity." GR 13:311–13.
*"The Draining of the Zuider Zee." GR 13:617–18.
*"Modern Australia and Recent Studies in Australian Discovery and Exploration." GR 13:473–75.
"The Mount Everest Expeditions of 1921 and 1922." GR 13:620–23.
*"The Northern Sea Route to Siberia and the Norilsk Coal Region." GR 13:309–11.
*"Physical Geography at the Court of the Emperor Frederick II." GR 13: 141–42.
*"Recent Studies in Medieval Moslem Geography." GR 13:630–31.

---

*Bonnerot, Jean, *Les Routes de France*. Paris: H. Laurens, 1921. Review, GR 13:149–50.
*Bryce, James, *Memories of Travel*. New York: Macmillan, 1923. Review, GR 13:482–83.

*Dainelli, Giotto, *La Regione balcanica: Sguardo d'insieme al paese e alle gente.* Florence: Soc. An. Editrice "La Voce," 1922. Review, GR 13:315–16.

*Danckwortt, P. W., *Sibirien und seine wirtschaftliche Zukunft.* Leipzig: B. G. Teubner, 1921. Review, GR 13:314–15.

*Lacroix, A., and Daressy, G., *Dolomieu en Égypte (30 Juin 1798–10 Mars 1799),* Mémoires Présentés à l'Institut d'Égypte, vol. 3. Cairo: Institut Français d'Archéologie Orientale, 1922. Review, GR 13:654.

*Maull, Otto, *Griechisches Mittelmeergebiet.* Breslau: Ferdinand Hirt, 1922. Review, GR 13:315–16.

*Mesick, J. L., *The English Traveller in America, 1785–1835.* New York: Columbia University Press, 1922. Review, GR 13:655.

*Ortroy, Ferrand van, *Bio-bibliographie de Gemma Frisius, Fondateur de l'École belge de géographie.* . . . Mémoires, Classe des Lettres et des Sciences Morales et Politiques, ser. 2, vol. 11. Brussels: Académie Royale de Belgique, 1920. Review, GR 13:325–26.

*Philby, H. St. J. B., *The Heart of Arabia: A Record of Travel & Exploration.* 2 vols. London: Constable, 1922. Review, GR 13:484–85.

*Roget, S. R., ed., *Travel in the Two Last Centuries of Three Generations.* London: T. Fisher Unwin, 1921. Review, GR 13:655.

*Vidal de la Blache, P., *Principes de géographie humaine publiés d'après les manuscrits de l'auteur par Emmanuel de Martonne.* Paris: Armand Colin, 1922. Review, GR 13:144–46.

1924
*"The Agrarian Problem in Sicily." GR 14:144–45.

*"Chronological Records of the Nile Floods and Changes in the Nile Delta in the Middle Ages." GR 14:312–13.

*"Cotton Raising in Sicily." GR 14:473.

*"The Development of Italian East Africa." GR 14:148–50.

*"The Earliest Known Printed Map Showing America." GR 14:318–19.

*"Early Topographical Maps: Geographical and Historical Value as Illustrated by the Maps of the Harrison Collection." GR 14:426–32.

Early Topographical Maps: Geographical and Historical Value as Illustrated by the Maps of the Harrison Collection of the American Geographical Society. Library Series no. 3. New York: AGS, 38 pp.

*"The Economic and Political Status of Russia in 1923." GR 14:651.

*"Exploration in Papua." GR 14:654–55.

*"The First Separate Map of Pennsylvania." GR 14:305–6.

*"The Forests of Northern European Russia." GR 14:306–7.

*"The Geographical Position of Budapest." GR 14:646.

*"Geography and Proposed Territorial Reorganization in Italy." GR 14: 471–73.
*"Geography in Literature." GR 14:659–60.
*"The Geography of Dante." GR 14:319–20.
*"The Gradual Filling In of the Crater of Vesuvius." GR 14:308–10.
*"Indian Migration within the British Empire." GR 14:152–53.
*"An Irrigation and Hydro-electric Project in Sardinia." GR 14:473–74.
*"Italian Cartography of the Sixteenth and Early Seventeenth Centuries and a Sixteenth Century Description of Italy." GR 14:146–47.
*"Military Tunnels in the Glaciers of the Ortler." GR 14:474–75.
*"The Political and Economic Importance of the North Arabian Desert." GR 14:151–52.
*"The Political Significance of Abyssinia." GR 14:147–48.
*"A Proposed Atlas of Natural Calamities." GR 14:153–54.
*"Recent Investigations of the Currents of the Western Mediterranean." GR 14:310.
*"Recent Studies in the Geography of Coal Resources." GR 14:316–18.
*"A Regional Division of France, 1790." GR 14:144.
*"The Reports of the Eighth Italian Geographical Congress." GR 14:320–21.
*"Some Recent Geographical Bibliographies with Special Reference to North America." GR 14:643–44.
*"Some Recent Maps of Central Asia." GR 14:652–54.
*"Statistics on the New Baltic States." GR 14:143–44.
*"The Study of Maps." GR 14:656–57.
*"The View from Mont Blanc: Switzerland As Seen from the Air." GR 14: 644–45.

---

*Abernethy, T. P., *The Formative Period in Alabama, 1815–1828.* Publ. no. 6, Historic and Patriotic ser. Montgomery: Alabama State Department of Archives and History, 1922. Review, GR 14:673–74.
*Bruce, C. G., and others, *The Assault on Mount Everest,* 1922. New York: Longmans, Green, 1923. Review, GR 14:324–25.
*Coy, Owen C., *California County Boundaries: A Study of the Division of the State into Counties. . . .* Berkeley: California Historical Survey Commission, 1923. Review, GR 14:674–75.
*———, *The Genesis of California Counties.* Berkeley: California Historical Survey Commission, 1923. Review, GR 14:674–75.
*Curzon, G. N., *Tales of Travel.* New York: George H. Doran, 1923. Review, GR 14:672–73.
*Freeman, Lewis R., *The Colorado River: Yesterday, To-day and To-morrow.* New York: Dodd, Mead, 1923. Review, GR 14:326.

*Freshfield, D. W., *Below the Snow Line*. London: Constable, 1923. Review, GR 14:672–73.
*Gaurier, Ludovic, *Études glaciaires dans les Pyrénées Françaises et Espagnoles de 1900 à 1909*. Pau: Garet-Haristoy, 1921. Review, GR 14: 670–71.
*Gennep, Arnold van, *Traité comparatif des nationalités*. vol. 1, *Les Éléments extérieurs de la nationalité*. Paris: Payot, 1922. Review, GR 14: 667–68.
*Moritz, Bernhard, *Arabien: Studien zur physikalischen und historischen Geographie des Landes*. Hanover: Heinz Lafaire, 1923. Review, GR 14: 174.
*Pidal, Pedro, and Zabala, J. F., *Picos de Europa: Contribución al estudio de las montañas españolas*. Madrid: Club Alpino Español, 1918. Review, GR 14:670–71.
*Saint-Saud, A. d'A., *Monographie des Picos de Europa (Pyrénées Cantabriques et Asturiennes)*. Paris: Henry Barrère, 1922. Review, GR 14:670–71.
*Schrader, F., *Massif de Gavarnie et du mont Perdu*. Paris: Henry Barrère, 1914. Review, GR 14:670–71.
*Sorre, M., *Les Pyrénées*. Paris: Armand Colin, 1922. Review. GR 14:670–71.
*Thalamas, A., *Étude bibliographique de la géographie d'Ératosthène*. Paris: Marcel Rivière, 1921. Review, GR 14:333–34.
*————, *La Géographie d'Ératosthène*. Paris: Marcel Rivière, 1921. Review, GR 14:333–34.

1925

*"Cartographic Tendencies in the Seventeenth and Eighteenth Centuries." GR 15:672–74.
*"Chinese Migrations." GR 15:144–45.
*"The Economic Geography of Katanga." GR 15:485–86.
*"Former Caravan Routes through the Libyan Desert." GR 15:142–43.
The Geographical Lore of the Time of the Crusades: A Study in the History of Medieval Science and Tradition in Western Europe. Research Series no. 15. New York: AGS, 563 pp.; reprint ed., New York: Dover Publications, 1965.
*"Geographical Research and the Tropics." GR 15:670–71.
*"Geography among the Babylonians and Egyptians." GR 15:152–53.
*"Geography and Railroad Consolidation." GR 15:496–98 (with O. M. Miller).
*"The Geography of the Routes of Migration of the European White Stork." GR 15:316.

"The History of Geography: A Point of View." *Annals of the Association of American Geographers* 15:192–201.
*"The Human Geography of Africa before European Colonization." GR 15:484–85.
*"Materials for the Geographical Study of American Ports." GR 15:654–55.
*"Medieval Jewish Travelers in the Orient." GR 15:318–19.
*"Notes on the Arctic Coast of Canada." GR 15:300–301.
*Obituary of Henri Cordier. GR 15:500–501.
*"The Oceanography of Barentz Sea and the Climate of Northern Europe." GR 15:147–48.
*"The Place Names of France." GR 15:658–59.
*"Recent Exploration of the Laguna Iberá, Argentine Republic." GR 15: 481–82.
*"Recent Studies of State and County Boundaries in the Western United States." GR 15:303–4.
*"Steppes and Deserts; the Desert Vegetation of Tunisia." GR 15:140–41.
*"The Temperature of Ground and Surface Waters in the United States." GR 15:655–56.
*"Travel in the Middle Ages." GR 15:671–72.
*"What is a Desert?" GR 15:151–52.

---

*Agostini, A. M. de, *I miei Viaggi nella Terra del Fuoco.* Turin: De Agostini, 1923. Review, GR 15:680–81.
*Buchan, John, *The Last Secrets: The Final Mysteries of Exploration.* London: Thomas Nelson, 1923. Review, GR 15:167–68.
*Buxton, P. A., *Animal Life in Deserts: A Study of the Fauna in Relation to the Environment.* London: Edward Arnold, 1923. Review, GR 15:170–72.
*Cebrian, Konstantin, *Geschichte der Kartographie: Ein Beitrag zur Entwicklung des Kartenbildes und Kartenwesens. I. Altertum. I. Von den ersten Versuchen der Länderabbildung bis auf Marinos und Ptolemaios.* Geographische Bausteine no. 10. Gotha: Justus Perthes, 1923. Review, GR 15:169.
*Charlesworth, M. P., *Trade-Routes and Commerce of the Roman Empire.* Cambridge: University Press, 1924. Review, GR 15:510–11.
*Farrer, Reginald, *The Rainbow Bridge.* London: Edward Arnold, 1922. Review, GR 15:502–3.
*Gerstenberg, Kurt, *Ideen zu einer Kunstgeographie Europas.* Bibliothek der Kunstgeschichte, vol. 48–49, ed. Hans Tietze. Leipzig: E. A. Seemann, 1922. Review, GR 15:694–95.
*Gregory, J. W., and Gregory, C. J., *To the Alps of Chinese Tibet: An Account of a Journey of Exploration up to and among the Snow-Clad

Mountains of the Tibetan Frontier. Philadelphia: Lippincott, 1924. Review, GR 15:502–3.
*Haushofer, Karl, and März, Josef, *Zur Geopolitik der Selbstbestimmung: Südostasiens Wiederaufstieg zur Selbstbestimmung; Das Schicksal überseeischer Wachstumsspitzen.* Munich: Rösl, 1923. Review, GR 15:340–41.
*Haverfield, F., *The Roman Occupation of Britain: Being Six Ford Lectures.* Oxford: Clarendon Press, 1924. Review, GR 15:510–11.
*Kent, Rockwell, *Voyaging Southward from the Strait of Magellan.* New York: Putnam, 1924. Review, GR 15:680–81.
*Leaf, Walter, ed., *Strabo on the Troad, Book XII, Chap. I.* . . . Cambridge: University Press, 1923. Review, GR 15:512–13.
Map of Roman Britain. Southampton: Ordnance Survey, 1924. Review, GR 15:510–11.
*Nissen, N. W., *Die südwestgrönländische Landschaft und das Siedlungsgebiet der Normannen.* Abhandlungen aus dem Gebiet der Auslandskunde, vol. 15, ser. C, Naturwissenschaftliche, vol. 5. Hamburg: Hamburgische Universität, 1924. Review, GR 15:685–86.
*Ronaldshay, Earl of, *India: A Bird's-Eye View.* Boston: Houghton Mifflin, 1924. Review, GR 15:677–78.
*———, *Lands of the Thunderbolt: Sikkim, Chumbi & Bhutan.* Boston: Houghton Mifflin, 1924. Review, GR 15:677–78.
*Ward, F. Kingdon, *The Mystery Rivers of Tibet: A Description of the Little-Known Land.* . . . Philadelphia: Lippincott, 1923. Review, GR 15:502–3.
———, *The Romance of Plant Hunting.* London: Edward Arnold, 1924. Review, GR 15:502–3.
Zeitschrift für Geopolitik, ed. K. Haushofer. Berlin-Grunewald: Vowinckel, 1924. Review, GR 15:340–41.

1926
*"Altitude and Settlement in North America." GR 16:136.
*"Aviation and Geography." GR 16:672–73.
*"The Chaparral and Desert Vegetation of California." GR 16:310–11.
*"The Completion of the Sennar Dam." GR 16:139–40.
*"The Deltas of Italian Rivers." GR 16:660–61.
*"The Earliest Known Maps." GR 16:668–69.
*"The English Search for a Northwest Passage in the Time of Queen Elizabeth." GR 16:330.
*"Erosion by Solution and Fill." GR 16:334.
*"Geographical Literature and 'Philosophic' Ideas in France under the Ancien Régime." GR 16:671–72.

*"The Geography of Makalla." GR 16:317.
*"The Geography of Sardinia." GR 16:498–99.
*"Hanno's Voyage on the West Coast of Africa." GR 16:661–62.
*"Homeric Geography." GR 16:669–71.
*"Human Habitations in the Massif des Baronnies." GR 16:313–15.
*"The Non-Chinese Peoples of Kansu." GR 16:319–20.
"A Plea for the History of Geography." *Isis* 8:477–91, reprinted with revisions in John K. Wright, *Human Nature in Geography: Fourteen Papers, 1925–1965* (Cambridge: Harvard University Press, 1966), pp. 11–23.
*"Rainfall and Population in Kansas, Nebraska, and Dakota." GR 16:135–36.
*"The Revolution in Transportation." GR 16:136–37.
*"Some Recent Mountaineering Expeditions and Studies." GR 16:149–51.
*"Some Recent Mountaineering Publications." GR 16:667–68.
*"Twenty-Second Annual Meeting of the Association of American Geographers." GR 16:330–32.

---

*Battye, J. S., *Western Australia: A History from Its Discovery to the Inauguration of the Commonwealth.* New York: Oxford University Press, 1924. Review, GR 16:164–66.
*Brunhes, Jean, *La Géographie humaine.* 3 vols. Paris: Félix Alcan, 1925. Review, GR 16:519.
*Hassert, Kurt, *Australien und Neuseeland geographisch und wirtschaftlich.* Perthes Kleine Völker und Länderkunde zum Gebrauch im praktischen Leben, vol. 12. Gotha: Friedrich Andreas Perthes, 1924. Review, GR 16:164–66.
*Price, A. G., *The Foundation and Settlement of South Australia 1829–1845: A Study of the Colonization Movement. . . .* Adelaide: F. W. Preece, 1924. Review, GR 16:164–66.
*Roberts, S. H., *History of Australian Land Settlement (1788–1920).* Melbourne: Macmillan and Melbourne University Press, 1924. Review, GR 16:164–66.

Musil, Alois, *The Northern Heǧâz: A Topographical Itinerary.* Oriental Explorations and Studies, no. 1, ed. J. K. Wright. New York: AGS, 374 pp.

1927

*"De Filippi's Explorations in the Himalaya, Karakoram, and Chinese Turkestan: A Review." GR 17:138–42.
*"Explorations in Sinai." GR 17:677–78.
*"The Islands of the Blessed and Atlantis." GR 17:505–6.

*"Jodocus Hondius' World Map on Mercator's Projection, 1608." GR 17: 682–83.
"Northern Arabia: The Explorations of Alois Musil." GR 17:177–206.
*Obituary of Eduard Brückner. GR 17:684–85.
*"Place Names and Plant Geography Illustrated from the Vicinity of Munich." GR 17:492.
*"Some Recent Geographical Bibliographies, with a Special Reference to the History of Geography." GR 17:683–84.
*"The Sultanate of Muscat and 'Oman." GR 17:494.
*"Three Recent Books on the Alps and Mountaineering." GR 17:671–72.
*"Two Icelandic Cartographers." GR 17:334–35.

---

*The Approach towards a System of Imperial Air Communications: Memorandum by the Secretary of State for Air. . . . London: H. M. Stationery Office, 1926. Review, GR 17:686–87.
*Cheesman, R. E., In Unknown Arabia. London: Macmillan, 1926. Review, GR 17:344–45.
*Erskine, Beatrice (Mrs. Stuart), The Vanished Cities of Arabia. London: Hutchinson, 1925. Review, GR 17:513–14.
*Goodrich-Freer, A. (Mrs. A. H. Spoer), Arabs in Tent and Town: An Intimate Account of the Family Life of the Arabs of Syria, Their Manner of Living in Desert and Town. . . . London: Seeley Service, 1924. Review, GR 17:513–14.
*Grosser Luftverkehrs-atlas von Europa. Berlin: Verlag für Börsen und Finanzliteratur, 1927. Review, GR 17:686–87.
*Harrison, Paul W., The Arab at Home. New York: Thomas Y. Crowell, 1924. Review, GR 17:513–14.
*Kunhenn, Paul, Die Nomaden und Oasenbewohner Westturkestans. Langendreer: Heinrich Pöppinghaus, 1926. Review, GR 17:514–15.
*Lawrence, T. E., Revolt in the Desert. New York: George H. Doran, 1927. Review, GR 17:691–92.

Musil, Alois, Arabian Deserts: A Topographical Itinerary. Oriental Explorations and Studies, no. 2, ed. J. K. Wright. New York: AGS, 631 pp.
———, The Middle Euphrates: A Topographical Itinerary. Oriental Explorations and Studies, no. 3, ed. J. K. Wright. New York: AGS, 426 pp.

1928
*"Afghanistan in Transformation." GR 18:507–8.
*"Changes in the Frontier of the French Language since 1806." GR 18: 505–6.
*"The Decline of Transhumance in Rumania." GR 18:150.

*"Geographical Aspects of the Tourist Industry in Italy." GR 18:504–5.

The Geographical Basis of European History. Berkshire Studies in European History. New York: Henry Holt, 140 pp.; reissued by American Geographical Society, 1943.

*"Geography of the Odyssey." GR 18:157–58.

*"The Italian Occupation of Fezzan in 1914." GR 18:506–7.

The Leardo Map of the World, 1452 or 1453, in the collections of the American Geographical Society. Library Series no. 4. New York: AGS, 74 pp.

*"Medieval Transportation and Travel." GR 18:158–59.

*"Movements of Population in Calabria." GR 18:150–51.

*"Notes on the Climate of the Sahara." GR 18:507.

*"The Port of Alexandria." GR 18:329–30.

*"Publication of the La Vérendrye Documents." GR 18:159.

*"Three Recent Ecological Studies of Geographical Interest." GR 18:511–12.

*"Two Recent Geographical Studies of Rural India." GR 18:680–81.

---

*Atkinson, Geoffroy, La Littérature géographique française de la Renaissance: Répertoire bibliographique. Paris: August Picard, 1927. Review, GR 18:702.

*Benedetto, Luigi Foscolo, Marco Polo: Il Milione. Florence: Leo S. Olschki, 1928. Review, GR 18:521–22.

*Buchanan, Angus, Sahara. New York: Appleton, 1926. Review, GR 18:516.

*Charignon, A. J. H., ed., Le Livre de Marco Polo. Peking: Albert Nachbaur, 1924. Review, GR 18:521–22.

*Dondore, D. A., The Prairie and the Making of Middle America: Four Centuries of Description. Cedar Rapids, Iowa. Torch Press, 1926. Review, GR 18:163–64.

*Fite, Emerson D., and Freeman, Archibald, A Book of Old Maps Delineating American History from the Earliest Days down to the Close of the Revolutionary War. Cambridge: Harvard University Press, 1926. Review, GR 18:339–40.

*Friederici, Georg, Der Charakter der Entdeckung und Eroberung Amerikas durch die Europäer. Stuttgart: Friedrich Andreas Perthes, 1925. Review, GR 18:162–63.

*Gautier, E. F., L'Islamisation de l'Afrique du Nord: Les Siècles obscure du Maghreb. Paris: Payot, 1927. Review, GR 18:514–16.

*Gottschalk, Paul, The Earliest Diplomatic Documents on America: The Papal Bulls of 1493 and The Treaty of Tordesillas Reproduced and Translated. . . . Berlin: Paul Gottschalk, 1927. Review, GR 18:701.

*Humphreys, Arthur L., *Old Decorative Maps and Charts*. London: Halton & Truscott Smith, 1926. Review, GR 18:339–40.

*Jessen, Otto, *Die Strasse von Gibraltar*. Berlin: Dietrich Reimer, 1927. Review, GR 18:347–48.

*Komroff, Manuel, ed., *The Travels of Marco Polo [the Venetian]*. 2nd ed. New York: Boni & Liveright, 1926. Review, GR 18:521–22.

*Parks, George B., ed., *The Book of Ser Marco Polo the Venetian Concerning the Kingdoms and Marvels of the East*. New York: Macmillan, 1927. Review, GR 18:521–22.

*Penzer, N. M., ed., *The World Encompassed and Analagous Contemporary Documents Concerning Sir Francis Drake's Circumnavigation of the World*. London: Argonaut Press, 1926. Review, GR 18:340–41.

*Robertson, John W., *Francis Drake and Other Early Explorers Along the Pacific Coast*. San Francisco: Grabhorr Press, 1927. Review, GR 18:340–41.

Sir Francis Drake's Voyage Round the World 1577–1580. London: Bernard Quaritch, Oxford University Press, and Kegan Paul, Trench, Trubner, 1927. Review, GR 18:340–41.

The Travels of Marco Polo the Venetian. London: J. M. Dent, 1926. Review, GR 18:521–22.

*Wagner, Henry R., *Sir Francis Drake's Voyage Around the World: Its Aims and Achievements*. San Francisco: John Howell, 1926. Review, GR 18:340–41.

Musil, Alois, *Palmyrena: A Topographical Itinerary*. Oriental Explorations and Studies, no. 4, ed. J. K. Wright. New York: AGS, 367 pp.

———, *Northern Neǧd: A Topographical Itinerary*. Oriental Explorations and Studies, no. 5, ed. J. K. Wright. New York: AGS, 368 pp.

———, *The Manners and Customs of the Rwala Bedouins*. Oriental Explorations and Studies, no. 6, ed. J. K. Wright. New York: AGS, 712 pp.

1929

*"The Demarcation of the Boundary between Jubaland and Kenya." GR 19:509–10.

*"The Economic Regions of France." GR 19:505–6.

*"Man and Nature in Central Arabia." GR 19:510–11.

*"The Need for a Sound Land Policy in the United States." GR 19:669–70.

"New England." GR 19:479–94.

*"A Recent Study of Urban Geography in Sweden." GR 19:506–7.

*"Research in Agriculture and Land Utilization in New England." GR 19:324–25.

*"Some Recent Field Studies of Highland Peoples in Europe." GR 19:154–56.
"The Study of Place Names: Recent Work and Some Possibilities." GR 19:140–44.
*"Urban Development in South America." GR 19:674–75.
*"Variations in and Possible Disappearance of Lake Chad." GR 19:157–58.

*Hedin, Sven, *Auf grosser Fahrt: Meine Expedition mit Schweden, Deutschen und Chinesen durch die Wüste Gobi*, 1927–28. Leipzig: F. A. Brockhaus, 1929. Review, GR 19:694–96.
*Hoskins, H. L., *British Routes to India*. New York: Longmans, Green, 1928. Review, GR 19:520–21.
*Lattimore, Owen, *The Desert Road to Turkestan*. London: Methuen, 1928. Review, GR 19:694–96.

1930
*"The Aspect and the Place Names of Palestine." GR 20:511–12.
*"Cotton Manufacturing in the South and in New England." GR 20:322–23.
*"The Density of Population of Belgium, Luxembourg, and the Netherlands." GR 20:157–58.
*"The Duke of the Abruzzi's Recent Explorations in Abyssinia." GR 20:159–60.
*"The High Atlas; the Eastern Alps." GR 20:336–37.
*"Is the Summit of Mont Blanc in France?" GR 20:509.
*"The Mecca Pilgrimage and the Arab World." GR 20:514–15.
*"Movements of the Jewish Population during the Last Century." GR 20:515–16.
*"New Maps of the Dodecanese and Their Geographical Interest." GR 20:157.
*"The Portolan Chart of Angellino de Dalorto, 1325." GR 20:340–41.
*"A Recent Geographical Study of the Vicinity of Fiume." GR 20:331–32.
*"Rural Depopulation in Virginia." GR 20:507.
*"Trading Areas in the United States." GR 20:506–7.

*Blanchard, Raoul, *Asie Occidentale*; Grenard, Fernande, *Haute Asie*. Géographie Universelle, vol. 8. Paris: Armand Colin, 1929. Review, GR 20:527–28.
*Kende, Oskar, *Geographisches Wörterbuch: Allgemeine Erdkunde*. 2nd ed. Leipzig: B. G. Teubner, 1928. Review, GR 20:175–76.

*Nunn, George E., *Origin of the Strait of Anian Concept*. Privately printed, Philadelphia, 1929. Review, GR 20:353–54.
*Passarge, Siegfried, *Das Judentum als landschaftkundlich-ethnologisches Problem*. Munich: J. S. Lehmann, 1929. Review, GR 20:352–53.

1931
*"Fisheries of the Great African Lakes." GR 21:494.
*"Geography and Taxation in the United States." GR 21:489–90.
*"The Measurement of Snowfall in Mountain Regions." GR 21:500.
*"Mexican Immigration to the United States." GR 21:316–17.
*"Sir Aurel Stein's 'Innermost Asia' and Supposed Climatic Changes in Central Asia." GR 21:321–24.
*"Some Recent Linguistic Studies of Geographical Interest." GR 21:500–501.
*"Some Recent Studies of African Rainfall." GR 21:493–94.
*"The Tsetse Fly in the Sudan and in Tanganyika Territory." GR 21:672–73.

---

*Carruthers, Douglas, ed., *The Desert Route to India: Being the Journals of Four Travellers by the Great Desert Caravan Route between Aleppo and Basra 1745–1751*. Hakluyt Society, *Works*, 2nd ser., no. 63. London: Printed for the Hakluyt Society, 1929. Review, GR 21:351–52.
*Gautier, E. F., *Moeurs et coutumes des Musulmans*. Paris: Payot, 1931. Review, GR 21:687–88.
Hermann Wagner Gedächtnisschrift: Ergebnisse und Aufgeben geographischer Forschung. Petermanns Mitteilungen, Ergänzungsheft no. 209, 1930. Review, GR 21:349–51.
*Hobbs, Samuel Huntington, Jr., *North Carolina: Economic and Social*. Chapel Hill: University of North Carolina Press, 1930. Review, GR 21:357.
*Stevens, Henry N., ed., *New Light on the Discovery of Australia as Revealed by the Journal of Captain Don Diego de Prado y Tovar*. London: Henry Stevens, Son & Stiles, 1930. Review, GR 21:176.

1932
*"Primitive Cartography." GR 22:491–92.
*"The Probable Origin of Alphabetic Writing." GR 22:158–59.
"Sections and National Growth: An Atlas of the Historical Geography of the United States." GR 22:353–60.
*"Sixteenth Century Cartography of the Atlantic Coast of Canada." GR 22:329.

*"Two Recent Geographical Bibliographies." GR 22:330.
"Voting Habits in the United States: A Note on Two Maps." GR 22:666–72.

---

*Almagià, Roberto, comp., *Monumentae Italiae cartographica: Riproduzioni di carte generali e regionali d'Italia del seculo XIV al XVII.* Florence: Istituto Geografico Militare, 1929. Review, GR 22:173–75.
Atlante internazionale del Touring Club Italiano. 3rd ed. Milan: Touring Club of Italy, 1929. Review, GR 22:173–75.
Atlante statistico italiano, pt. 1: Natalità, mortalità, densità della popolazione. Rome: Istituto Centrale di Statistica del Regno d'Italia, 1929. Review, GR 22:173–75.
*Austin, Stephen F., *Three Manuscript Maps of Texas; with Biographical and Bibliographical Notes by Carlos E. Castañeda . . . and Early Martin, Jr.* Privately printed, Austin, Texas, 1930. Review, GR 22:351–52.
*Biggar, H. P., *A Collection of Documents Relating to Jacques Cartier and the Sieur de Roberval.* Publications of the Public Archives of Canada, no. 14. Ottawa: Published . . . under the Direction of the Keeper of the Records, 1930. Review, GR 22:506–7.
*Dutton, E. A. T., *Kenya Mountain.* London: Jonathan Cape, 1930. Review, GR 22:169–70.
*Lattimore, Owen, *High Tartary.* Boston: Little, Brown, 1930. Review, GR 22:168–69.
*Martin, Lawrence, ed., *The George Washington Atlas.* Washington, D.C.: United States George Washington Bicentennial Commission, 1932. Review, GR 22:502.
Rural Vermont: A Program for the Future. Burlington: Vermont Commission on Country Life, 1931. Review, GR 22:504.
*Stokes, I. N. Phelps, and Haskell, Daniel C., *American Historical Prints: Early Views of American Cities, etc., From the Phelps Stokes and Other Collections.* New York: New York Public Library, 1932. Review, GR 22:702–3.
*Thomas, Bertram, *Arabia Felix: Across the "Empty Quarter" of Arabia.* New York: Charles Scribner's Sons, 1932. Review, GR 22:333–35.
*Tyrell, J. B., ed., *Documents Relating to the Early History of Hudson Bay.* Publications of the Champlain Society, no. 18. Toronto: Champlain Society, 1931. Review, GR 22:506–7.

Paullin, Charles Oscar, *Atlas of the Historical Geography of the United States,* edited with Introduction by J. K. Wright. Washington, D.C.: Carnegie Institution and AGS, 162 pp., 166 pls.

1933

"The Changing Geography of New England," in *New England's Prospect: 1933*. Special Publication no. 16, ed. J. K. Wright. New York: AGS, pp. 459–76.

*"The Columbus and Magellan Concepts of South American Geography." GR 23:145–46.

*"Explorations of Philby, Rutter, and Sadek Bey in Arabia." GR 23:332–33.

*"Geography of the Reindeer." GR 23:683–84.

*"Michigan in Prehistoric Times." GR 23:134–35.

*"New Edition of the George Washington Atlas." GR 23:488–89.

*"A New Population Map of the United States." GR 23:133–34.

*"A New Series of Studies of Latin American Cultures." GR 23:504–5.

*"The Physiographic Regions of Arabia." GR 23:331–32.

*"Population and Censuses of 1790 and Earlier." GR 23:505–6.

*"The Rainfall of Turkey." GR 23:330–31.

"Regions and Landscapes of New England," in *New England's Prospect: 1933*. Ed. J. K. Wright. New York: AGS, pp. 14–49.

*"Some Geographical Studies Made for Cosimo de' Medici." GR 23:146–47.

*"Some Recent Studies of the Lapps." GR 23:672–73.

*"The Vote by Counties in the Presidential Election of 1932." GR 23:323–24.

---

*Anderson, Andrew Runni, *Alexander's Gate, Gog and Magog, and the Inclosed Nations*. Publication no. 12 (Monograph no. 5). Cambridge, Mass.: Medieval Academy of America, 1932. Review, GR 23:350–51.

*Andrews, Fannie Fern, *The Holy Land under Mandate*. Boston: Houghton Mifflin, 1931. Review, GR 23:507–8.

*Bentwich, Norman, *A Wanderer in the Promised Land*. New York: Charles Scribner's Sons, 1933. Review, GR 23:507–8.

*Burgy, J. Herbert, *The New England Cotton Textile Industry: A Study in Industrial Geography*. Baltimore: Waverly Press, 1932. Review, GR 23:161–62.

*Fleg, Edmond, *The Land of Promise* (trans. from the French by Louise Waterman Wise). New York: Macauley, 1933. Review, GR 23:507–8.

*Karpinski, Louis C., *Bibliography of the Printed Maps of Michigan, 1804–1880*. . . . Lansing: Michigan Historical Commission, 1931. Review, GR 23:165.

*———, *Historical Atlas of the Great Lakes and Michigan*. Ibid., 1931. Review, GR 23:165.

*Marchi, Luigi de, *Memorie scientifiche 1883–1932*. Padua: Dott, 1932. Review, GR 23:525–26.

*Rouček, Joseph S., *Contemporary Roumania and Her Problems: A Study in Modern Nationalism*. Stanford, Calif.: Stanford University Press, 1932. Review, GR 23:516–17.
*Smith, George Adam, *The Historical Geography of the Holy Land*. 25th ed. New York: Ray Long & Richard R. Smith, 1932. Review, GR 23: 507–8.
*Stevenson, Edward Luther, trans. and ed., *Geography of Claudius Ptolemy*. New York: New York Public Library, 1932. Review, GR 23:351–52.
*Ubach, Bonaventura, *El Gènesi*. Montserrat (Spain): Monestir de Montserrat, 1929. Review, GR 23:507–8.

New England's Prospect: 1933. Special Publication no. 16, ed. with Foreword by J. K. Wright. New York: AGS, 502 pp.

1934
*"The Geography of Rural Settlements." GR 24:502–4.
*"Historical Geography at Recent International Congresses." GR 24:504–5.
*"Mountaineering in Scotland and in the Northeastern United States Contrasted." GR 24:148–49.
*"Population Changes in Three Massachusetts Counties." GR 24:326–27.
*"Some Recent German Geographical Works of Comprehensive Scope." GR 24:674–76.
*"Studies of Colonial Connecticut." GR 24:657–58.

Atlante internazionale del Touring Club Italiano. 4th ed. Milan: Touring Club of Italy, 1933. Review, GR 24:162–63.
Beaglehole, J. C., *The Exploration of the Pacific*. London: A. & C. Black, 1934. Review, *Saturday Review of Literature* 11 (Dec. 29):393.
*Dougherty, Raymond Philip, *The Sealand of Ancient Arabia*. Yale Oriental Series: Researches, vol. 19. New Haven: Yale University Press, 1932. Review, GR 24:510–12.
*Fawcett, C. B., *A Political Geography of the British Empire*. Boston: Ginn, 1933. Review, GR 24:507–8.
*Gane, Douglas M., *Tristan da Cunha: An Empire Outpost and Its Keepers*. London: George Allen & Unwin, 1932. Review, GR 24:166–67.
*Gaussen, Henri, *Géographie des plantes*. Collection Armand Colin (Section de Géographie), no. 152. Paris: Armand Colin, 1933. Review, GR 24:172–73.
*Gilbert, E. W., *The Exploration of Western America, 1800–1850: An Historical Geography*. Cambridge: University Press, 1933. Review, GR 24: 158–59.

*Helfritz, Hans, *Chicago der Wüste*. Berlin: Reimar Hobbing, 1932. Review, GR 24:510–12.

*Jones, Clarence Fielden, *Manual to Accompany American History and Its Geographic Conditions*. Boston: Houghton Mifflin, 1933. Review, GR 24:159.

Landesplanung im engeren mitteldeutschen Industriebezirk. . . . Merseburg: Verlag der Landesplanung für den engeren mitteldeutschen Industriebezirk, 1932. Review, GR 24:162–63.

*Meulen, D. van der, and Wissman, H. von, *Hadramaut: Some of Its Mysteries Unveiled*. Printed for the Trustees of the "De Goeje Fund," no. 9. Leyden: E. J. Brill, 1932. Review, GR 24:510–12.

Mitchell, J. L., *Earth Conquerors: The Lives and Achievements of the Great Explorers*. New York: Simon and Schuster, 1934. Review, *Saturday Review of Literature* 11 (Dec. 29):393.

*Philby, H. St. J. B., *The Empty Quarter; Being a Description of the Great South Desert of Arabia Known as Rubʻ al Khali*. New York: Henry Holt, 1933. Review, GR 24:510–12.

*Prenant, Marcel, *Géographie des animaux*. Collection Armand Colin (Section de Géographie), no. 153. Paris: Armand Colin, 1933. Review, GR 24:172–73.

*Semple, Ellen Churchill, *American History and Its Geographic Conditions*. Boston: Houghton Mifflin, 1933. Review, GR 24:159.

*Stamp, L. Dudley, and Beaver, Stanley H., *The British Isles: A Geographic and Economic Survey*. London: Longmans, Green, 1933. Review, GR 24:507–8.

*Wehrli, M., *Neue Völker- und Sprachenkarte von Europa* (1:10,000,000). Bern: Kümmerly & Frey, 1932 [?]. Review, GR 24:163–64.

*Wolfram, Georg, and Gley, Werner, eds., *Elsass-Lothringer Atlas*. Frankfort: Elsass-Lothringen Institut, 1931. Review, GR 24:162–63.

*Youssouf Kamal, *Monumenta cartographica Africae et Ægypti*. Cairo, 1926–32. Vol. 1, *Époque avant Ptolémée*, 1926; vol. 2, *Ptolémée et époque gréco-romaine and Atlas antiquus et index*, 1928, 1932, 1933; vol. 3, *Époque Arabe*, 1930, 1932. Review, GR 24:175–76.

1935
"The Exploration of the Fiord Region of East Greenland," in *The Fiord Region of East Greenland*, by Louise A. Boyd and others. Special Publication no. 18, ed. J. K. Wright. New York: AGS, pp. 317–57.

*"Forest Conservation Under the Venetian Republic." GR 25:683.

*"The Fourteenth International Geographical Congress, Warsaw, 1934." GR 25:142–48.

*"The Iraq-Mediterranean Pipe Lines." GR 25:503.

*"Italian Colonization in Libya; The Jebel Nefusa." GR 25:495–96.
*Obituary of Curtis Fletcher Marbut. GR 25:688.
*"The Origin of the Rural Landscapes of France." GR 25:679–80.
*"Rain Makers and Drought." GR 25:491–92.
*"The Solar Climate of the French Riviera." GR 25:681–82.
"Some Broader Aspects of the History of Exploration: A Review." GR 25: 317–20.
*"Some Geographical Aspects of Tourism." GR 25: 507–9.
*"Two Eighteenth-Century Maps of the Philippine Islands." GR 25:686–87.
*"Two Fundamental Geographical Inventions." GR 25:511.
*"The Wends in Germany and Texas." GR 25:509–10.

---

*Arctowski, H., ed., *Zbiór prac póswięcony przez Towarzysto Geograficzne we Lwowie Eugenjuszowi Romerowi w 40-lecie jego twórczósci naukowej (Collection of Studies Dedicated by the Geographical Society of Lwów to Eugene Romer in Commemoration of His Forty Years of Scientific Work)*. Lvov: Ksiaznica Atlas, 1934. Review, GR 25:175–76.
Bradley, J. H., *Autobiography of the Earth*. New York: Coward-McCann, 1935. Review, *New York Times Book Review*, Oct. 27, p. 4.
Outhwaite, Leonard, *Unrolling the Map: The Story of Exploration*. New York: Reynal & Hitchcock, 1935. Review, *New York Times Book Review*, Feb. 24, p. 1.
*Rathjens, Carl, and Wissmann, Hermann v., *Landeskundliche Ergebnisse*. Rathjens- v. Wissmannsche Südarabien Reise, vol. 3. Hamburg: Friederichsen, de Gruyter, 1934. Review, GR 25:521–22.
*Raswan, Carl R., *The Black Tents of Arabia: My Life amongst the Bedouins*. London: Hutchinson, 1935. Review, GR 25:522–23.

---

*Boyd, Louise A., and others, *The Fiord Region of East Greenland*. Special Publication no. 18, ed. J. K. Wright. New York: AGS, 369 pp.

1936
"The Diversity of New York City: Comments on the Real Property Inventory of 1934." GR 26:620–39.
*"The Eruption of Mt. Pelée, 1929–1932." GR 26:499.
"A Method of Mapping Densities of Population, with Cape Cod as an Example." GR 26:103–10.
*"A Note on Ethiopia." GR 26:150–53.

---

*Blanchard, Raoul, and Crist, Raymond E., *A Geography of Europe*. New York: Henry Holt, 1935. Review, GR 26:518–20.

*Bogardus, J. F., *Europe: A Geographical Survey*. New York: Harper & Bros., 1934. Review, GR 26:518–20.
*East, W. Gordon, *An Historical Geography of Europe*. London: Methuen, 1935. Review, GR 26:520.
*Hernández-Pacheco, Eduardo, *Síntesis fisiográfica y geológica de España*. Trabajos Museo Nacional de Ciencias Naturales, Ser. Geológica no. 38. 2 vols. Madrid: 1934. Review, GR 26:517–18.
*Odum, Howard W., *Southern Regions of the United States*. Chapel Hill: University of North Carolina Press, 1936. Review, GR 26:692–93.
*Robinson, Edgar Eugene, *The Presidential Vote, 1896–1932*. Stanford, Calif.: Stanford University Press, 1934. Review, GR 26:516–17.
*Shackleton, Margaret Reid, *Europe: A Regional Geography*. London: Longmans, Green, 1934. Review, GR 26:518–20.
*Van Valkenburg, Samuel, and Huntington, Ellsworth, *Europe*. New York: Wiley, 1935. Review, GR 26:518–20.

McBride, George McCutchen, *Chile: Land and Society*. Research Series no. 19, ed. J. K. Wright. New York: AGS, 408 pp.

1937
*"The Classification and Cataloguing of Geographical Materials." GR 27: 688–89.
*"Meeting of the Population Association of America." GR 27:158–59.
"Some Measures of Distributions." *Annals of the Association of American Geographers* 27:177–211.
*"Some Recent Publications in the Field of Medieval Geography." GR 27: 686–87.
*"Two New Encyclopedias." GR 27:689–90.
*"The Use of Building Materials in Poland." GR 27:674–75.

Allt för Allas Världsatlas. Stockholm: Åhlén & Åkerlunds, 1931–34. Review, GR 27:161–63.
Atlas de France. Paris: Comité National de Géographie, 1933–37. Review, GR 27:161–63.
Atlas Niedersachsen. Oldenburg (Germany): Gerhard Stalling, 1934. Review, GR 27:161–63.
Atlas Republiky Československé (*Atlas de la République Tchécoslovaque*). Prague: L'Académie Tchèque, Éditions Orbus, 1935. Review, GR 27: 161–63.
*Pomfret, J. E., *The Geographic Pattern of Mankind*. Century Earth Science Series. New York and London: Appleton-Century, 1935. Review, GR 27: 133.

*Stieler Grand Atlas de géographie moderne. 10th ed. Gotha: Justus Perthes, 1934–37. Review, GR 27:161–63.

Taylor, Griffith, Environment and Nation: Geographical Factors in the Cultural and Political History of Europe. Chicago: University of Chicago Press, 1936. Review, American Historical Review 42:700–702.

*Wirtschafts- und verkehrsgeographischer Atlas von Pommern. Stettin (Poland): Ostsee, 1934. Review, GR 27:161–63.

Heidel, William Arthur, The Frame of the Ancient Greek Maps. Research Series no. 20, ed. J. K. Wright. New York: AGS, 141 pp.

1938

"The American Geographical Society, New York City, N.Y." Appalachia 22:134–35.

*"Classifications of Regions of the World." GR 28:499.

*"A Dictionary of English Place Names." GR 28:326–27.

"Geographical Sections and American Political History as Illustrated by Certain Maps in The Atlas of the Historical Geography of the United States." Compte Rendus du Congrès International de Géographie, Varsovie, 1934, vol. 4, Travaux de la Section IV–VI et Communications aux Séances Spéciales, pp. 103–7.

"Geography and the Study of Foreign Affairs." Foreign Affairs 17:153–63.

*"Growth of European Knowledge of the Red Sea and the Indian Ocean." GR 28:163.

"Problems in Population Mapping," in Notes on Statistical Mapping, with Reference to the Mapping of Population Phenomena. Mimeographed Publication no. 1, ed. J. K. Wright. New York: AGS and Population Association of America, pp. 1–18.

*"Vegetation and Land Use in the Pennine Alps." GR 28:152.

Bowman, Isaiah, ed., Limits of Land Settlement: A Report on Present-Day Possibilities. New York: Council on Foreign Relations, 1937. Review, American Historical Review 43:827–29.

*Hitti, Philip K., History of the Arabs. London: Macmillan, 1937. Review, GR 28:166–67.

*Krische, Paul, Mensch und Scholle: Kartenwerk zur Geschichte und Geographie des Kulturbodens. Berlin: Deutsche Verlagsgesellschaft, 1936. Review, GR 28:174–75.

*Thomas, Bertram, The Arabs: The Life Story of a People Who Have Left Their Deep Impress on the World. Garden City, N.Y.: Doubleday, Doran, 1937. Review, GR 28:166–67.

John K. Wright Bibliography

Antevs, Ernst, *Rainfall and Tree Growth in the Great Basin*. Special Publication no. 21, ed. J. K. Wright. New York: AGS and Carnegie Institution, 97 pp.

*Boyd, Louise A., *Polish Countrysides: Photographs and Narrative*. Special Publication no. 20, ed. J. K. Wright. New York: AGS, 235 pp.

Forbes, Alexander, *Northernmost Labrador Mapped from the Air*. Special Publication no. 22, ed. J. K. Wright, New York: AGS, 255 pp.

Wright, John K., and others, *Notes on Statistical Mapping, with Special Reference to the Mapping of Population Phenomena*. Mimeographed Publication no. 1, ed. J. K. Wright. New York: AGS and Population Association of America, 37 pp.

1939

Descriptive Catalogue of an Exhibit of Maps, Photographs, Instruments and Other Materials of Geographical Interest at the House of the American Geographical Society. New York: AGS, 45 pp.

*"Geographical Studies in Bulgaria." GR 29:678–79.

*"London, A Primate City." GR 29:332–33.

*"Natural Landscape Factors of the Ozark Province." GR 29:670.

*" 'The Pattern of Urban Growth.' " GR 29:138–39.

*"A Report on Urbanism in the United States." GR 29:139–40.

*"Timber-Line Studies in the Rocky Mountains and on Mount Washington." GR 29:328.

---

*Antonius, George, *The Arab Awakening: The Story of the Arab National Movement*. Philadelphia: Lippincott, 1939. Review, GR 29:514.

*Collingwood, R. G., and Myres, J. N. L., *Roman Britain and the English Settlements*. Oxford History of England. Oxford: Clarendon Press, 1937. Review, GR 29:524–25.

*Kimble, George H. T., *Geography in the Middle Ages*. London: Methuen, 1938. Review, GR 29:696–97.

*Simpson, Sir John Hope, *Refugees: Preliminary Report of a Survey*. Issued under the auspices of the Royal Institute of International Affairs, London. New York: Oxford University Press, 1938. Review, GR 29:161–62.

*Stefansson, Vilhjalmur, *Unsolved Mysteries of the Arctic*. New York: Macmillan, 1939. Review, GR 29:352.

Price, A. Grenfell, *White Settlers in the Tropics*. Special Publication no. 23, ed. J. K. Wright. New York: AGS, 311 pp.

246

1940

*"America's First Globe Maker." GR 30:145–46.

*"The Text and Maps of Ptolemy's 'Geography.'" GR 30:504.

"The World in Maps: The American Geographical Society's Exhibition." GR 30:1–18.

---

*Adams, Frank Dawson, *The Birth and Development of the Geological Sciences*. Baltimore: Williams & Wilkins, 1938. Review, GR 30:701–2.

*Albion, Robert Greenhalgh, *The Rise of New York Port, 1815–1860*. New York: Charles Scribner's Sons, 1939. Review, GR 30:337–38.

*Dainelli, Giotto, *Atlante fisico-economico d'Italia*. Milan: Consociazione Turistica Italiane, 1940. Review, GR 30:340–42.

Lattimore, Owen, *Inner Asian Frontiers of China*. Research Series no. 21, ed. J. K. Wright. New York: AGS, 585 pp.

1941

"Certain Changes in Population Distribution in the United States." GR 31:488–90.

*"Columbus, Professor Morison, and 'The American Neptune.'" GR 31:337–38.

*"Geologic History of the Presidential Range." GR 31:676–77.

*"The Location and Size of Population Centers." GR 31:683–84.

"Man and Time in Ancient Rome: The Population, Dwelling Houses, and Streets of Imperial Rome." GR 31:659–60.

*"National Congress on Surveying and Mapping." GR 31:684–85.

"The Netherlands Territories," in *The European Possessions in the Caribbean Area: A Compilation of Facts . . .* , by Raye R. Platt, John K. Wright, John C. Weaver, and Johnson E. Fairchild. Map of Hispanic America Publication no. 4, ed. J. K. Wright. New York: AGS, pp. 70–85.

*"The 'Worst' Weather in the World." GR 31:503–4.

---

*Earle, E. M., and McKee, Samuel, Jr., *Earle-McKee American History Series* (set of ten maps). New York: Rand McNally, 1939–1940 [?]. Review, GR 31:702–3.

Hartshorne, Richard, *The Nature of Geography: A Critical Survey of Current Thought in the Light of the Past*. Lancaster, Pa.: Association of American Geographers, 1939. Review, *Isis* 33:298–300.

*Michell, H., *The Economics of Ancient Greece*. New York: Macmillan, 1940. Review, GR 31:701–2.

*Riesenberg, Felix, *Cape Horn*. New York: Dodd, Mead. 1939. Review, GR 31:527–28.
Stefansson, Vilhjalmur, *Ultima Thule: Further Mysteries of the Arctic*. New York: Macmillan, 1940. Review, *American Historical Review* 46:854–56.
*Wu, Aitchen K., *Turkestan Tumult*. London: Methuen, 1940. Review, GR 31:169.

Platt, Raye R., Wright, John K., Weaver, John C., and Fairchild, Johnson E., *The European Possessions in the Caribbean Area*. Map of Hispanic America Publication no. 4, ed. J. K. Wright. New York, AGS, 116 pp.

1942
"Geography for War and Peace." *American Scholar* 12:118–22.
"Map Makers Are Human: Comments on the Subjective in Maps." GR 32: 527–44. Reprinted in John K. Wright, *Human Nature in Geography: Fourteen Papers, 1925–1965* (Cambridge: Harvard University Press, 1966), pp. 33–52.
"Pacific Islands." GR 32:481–86.

---

*Morison, Samuel Eliot, *Admiral of the Ocean Sea: A Life of Christopher Columbus*. 2 vols. Boston: Little, Brown, 1942. Review, GR 32:682–84.

1943
"Americans Grow Map-Minded." *American Mercury* 57 (1943):331–38.
*"Amish Community and Ocean City: Two Sociological Studies." GR 33: 494–96.
*"Areas of the United States, 1940." GR 33:494.
*"Corsica, Turbulent Isle." GR 33:152–53.
*"The Forests of French North Africa." GR 33:154–55.
The Geographical Basis of European History. Reprint Series no. 4. New York: AGS, 110 pp.; reprint of book originally published in 1928.
"Where History and Geography Meet: Recent American Studies in the History of Exploration," *Proceedings of the Eighth American Scientific Congress* 9:17–23. Reprinted in Wright, *Human Nature in Geography* (Cambridge: Harvard University Press, 1966), pp. 24–32.
*"White Influence in New Guinea and Fiji." GR 33:672–74.

---

*Penrose, Boies, *Urbane Travelers 1591–1635*. Philadelphia: University of Pennsylvania Press, 1942. Review, GR 33:520–21.
*Stefansson, Vilhjalmur, *The Friendly Arctic: The Story of Five Years in Polar Regions*. New York: Macmillan, 1943. Review, GR 33:688–89.

*———, *Greenland*. Garden City, N.Y.: Doubleday, Doran, 1942. Review, GR 33:688–89.

1944

"Discovery and Exploration," Chap. 3 in *The Pacific World: Its Vast Distances, Its Lands and the Life upon Them, and Its Peoples*. Ed. Fairfield Osborn. New York: W. W. Norton, pp. 29–38.

*Geographical Foundations of National Power, sec. 1, pt. 1, *The Great Powers*. Army Services Manual M 103–1. Washington, D.C.: U.S. Government Printing Office, 152 pp. (with Derwent Whittlesey and Dorothy Good).

*"Geography," in U.S. Office of War Information, *A Handbook of the United States of America: Pertinent Information about the United States and the War Effort*. London: Hutchinson, pp. 52–56 (with J. C. Weaver).

"Human Nature in Science." *Science*, n.s., 100:299–305. Reprinted in Wright, *Human Nature in Geography* (Cambridge: Harvard University Press, 1966), pp. 53–67.

"Introduction," in *Military Maps and Air Photographs: Their Use and Interpretation*, by A. K. Lobeck and Wentworth J. Tellington. New York: McGraw-Hill, pp. ix–x.

Obituary of Douglas Wilson Johnson. GR 34:317–18.

*"A Proposed Atlas of Diseases." GR 34:642–52.

"The Terminology of Certain Map Symbols." GR 34:653–54.

"Training for Research in Political Geography." *Annals of the Association of American Geographers* 34:190–201.

---

*Atlas of World Maps for the Study of Geography in the Army Specialized Training Program. Army Services Manual M-101. Washington, D.C.: U.S. Government Printing Office, 1943. Review, GR 34:672–74.

*Greenhood, David, *Down To Earth: Mapping for Everybody*. New York: Holiday House, 1944. Review, GR 34:674–75.

*Harrison, Richard Edes, *Look at the World: The Fortune Atlas for World Strategy*. New York: Alfred A. Knopf, 1944. Review, GR 34:672–74.

*Howe, Henry F., *Prologue to New England: The Forgotten Century of the Explorers*. New York: Farrar & Rinehart, 1943. Review, GR 34:346–48.

*Lobeck, A. K., and Tellington, Wentworth J., *Military Maps and Air Photographs: Their Use and Interpretation*. New York: McGraw-Hill, 1944. Review, GR 34:675–76.

*Olschki, Leonardo, *Marco Polo's Precursors*. Baltimore: Johns Hopkins Press, 1943. Review, GR 34:169–70.

*Olson, Everett C., and Whitmarsh, Agnes, *Foreign Maps*. New York: Harper & Bros., 1944. Review, GR 34:675–76.

*Palsits, Victor Hugo, ed., *Narrative of American Voyages and Travels of Captain William Owen, and Settlement of the Island of Campobello in the Bay of Fundy 1766–1771.* New York: New York Public Library, 1942. Review, GR 34:346–48.
*Peattie, Roderick, *How to Read Military Maps.* New York: George W. Stewart, 1942. Review, GR 34:675–76.
*Putnam, William C., *Map Interpretation with Military Applications.* New York: McGraw-Hill, 1943. Review, GR 34:675–76.
*Raisz, Erwin, *Atlas of Global Geography.* New York: Global Press, 1944. Review, GR 34:672–74.
*Spykman, Nicholas John, *The Geography of the Peace.* Institute of International Studies, Yale University. New York: Harcourt, Brace, 1944. Review, GR 34:672–74.

1945
*Ball, John, *Egypt in the Classical Geographers.* Cairo: Survey of Egypt, 1942. Review, GR 35:166–67.
*Lord, Clifford L., ed., *The Atlas of Congressional Roll Calls,* vol. 1, *The Continental Congresses and the Congresses of the Confederation, 1777–1789.* Prepared by the Historical Records Survey, New York City, 1938–39; New Jersey, 1940–42. Cooperstown, N.Y.: New York State Historical Association, 1943. Review, GR 35:342–43.
*Pohl, Frederick J., *Amerigo Vespucci: Pilot Major.* New York: Columbia University Press, 1944. Review, GR 35:340–41.
*Wroth, Lawrence C., *The Early Cartography of the Pacific.* Papers, vol. 38. New York: Bibliographical Society of America, 1944. Review, GR 35:505–6.

1946
*"Falmouth, Massachusetts: A Resort Community." GR 36:490–91.
*Obituary of Alois Musil. GR 36:686–87.

1947
Aids to Geographical Research: Bibliographies, Periodicals, Atlases, Gazetteers, and Other Reference Books. Research Series no. 22. 2nd ed. (1st ed., 1923.) New York: Published for American Geographical Society by Columbia University Press, 331 pp. (with Elizabeth T. Platt).
"Terrae Incognitae: The Place of the Imagination in Geography," *Annals of the Association of American Geographers* 37:1–15. Reprinted in Wright, *Human Nature in Geography* (Cambridge: Harvard University Press, 1966), pp. 68–88.

*Munch, Peter A., *Sociology of Tristan da Cunha*. Results of the Norwegian Scientific Expedition to Tristan da Cunha 1937–1938, no. 13. Oslo: Norske Videnskaps-Akademi, 1945. Review, GR 37:691–93.

1948

"The Educational Functions of the Geographical Societies of the United States." *Journal of Geography* 47:165–73.
*"Some Recent Arabian Explorations and Studies." GR 38:146–48.

---

*Aubert de la Rüe, E., *L'Homme et le vent*. Géographie Humaine, 16. Paris: Gallimard, 1940. Review, GR 38:166–67.
*Capot-Rey, Robert, *Géographie de la circulation sur les continents*. Géographie Humaine 20. Review, GR 38:166–67.
*Monod, Théodore, *L'Hippopotame et le philosophe*. 2nd ed. Paris: René Juilliard, 1946. Review, GR 38:521–22.
*Olschki, Leonardo, *Guillaume Boucher: A French Artist at the Court of the Khans*. Baltimore: Johns Hopkins Press, 1946. Review, GR 38:172–73.

1949

"Communication" [re "geosophy"]. *Annals of the Association of American Geographers* 39:47.
"The Sixteenth International Geographical Congress, Lisbon, 1949." GR 39:482–87.

1950

"Highlights in American Cartography, 1939–1949." *Comptes Rendus du Congrès International de Géographie, Lisbonne, 1949*, vol. 1, Actes du Congrès, Travaux de la Section I, pp. 303–14.
"The Society's Beginnings." GR 40:350–52.
"Some Boyhood Memories of William M. Davis." *Annals of the Association of American Geographers* 40:179–80.

---

*Kurath, Hans, *A Word Geography of the Eastern United States*. Studies in American English, I. Ann Arbor: University of Michigan Press, 1949. Review, GR 40:510–12.

1951

"The Field of the Geographical Society," in *Geography in the Twentieth Century: A Study of Growth, Fields, Techniques, Aims and Trends*. Ed. Griffith Taylor. New York: Philosophical Library, pp. 543–65 (2nd ed., 1953; 3rd ed., 1957).

1952

"The American Geographical Society: 1852–1952." *Scientific Monthly* 74: 121–31.

"British Geography and the American Geographical Society, 1851–1951." *Geographical Journal* 118:153–67.

Geography in the Making: The American Geographical Society, 1851–1951. New York: AGS, 437 pp.

Obituary of W. L. G. Joerg. GR 42:482–88.

"Protean Geography." GR 42:175–76.

"Who Invented the Hydraulic Lock?" GR 42:312.

---

*Report of the Commission on the International Map of the World, 1:1,000,000. VIIth General Assembly, XVIIth International Geographical Congress, Washington, August 8–15, 1952, ed. J. K. Wright. Washington, D.C.: International Geographical Union, 32 pp.

1953

"The Open Polar Sea." GR 43:338–65. Reprinted in Wright, *Human Nature in Geography* (Cambridge: Harvard University Press, 1966), pp. 89–118.

Evans, E. Estyn, *Mourne Country.* Dundalk: Dundalgar Press, 1951. Review, GR 43:298–99.

Gilbert, Edmund W., "Seven Lamps of Geography: An Appreciation of the Teaching of Sir Halford J. Mackinder." *Geography* 36 (1951):21–43. Review, GR 43:130–31.

1954

"AAG Programs and Program-Making, 1904–1954," *Professional Geographer* 6.6:6–11.

"A Geographical Note" [on Hastings-on-Hudson], in *Know Your Village.* Hastings on Hudson, N.Y.: League of Women Voters, pp. 6–7.

American Geography: Inventory and Prospect. Published for Association of American Geographers, ed. Preston E. James and Clarence F. Jones; consulting editor, J. K. Wright. Syracuse, N.Y.: Syracuse University Press, 590 pp.

1955

" 'Crossbreeding' Geographical Quantities." GR 45:52–65.

Obituary of Samuel Whittemore Boggs. GR 45:130–31.

Obituary of Lawrence Martin (with William O. Field). GR 45:587–88.

Hammond, Harold Earl, *A Commoner's Judge: The Life and Times of Charles Patrick Daly*. Boston: Christopher Publishing House, 1954. Review, GR 45:604–5.

Sanger, Richard H., *The Arabian Peninsula*. Ithaca, N.Y.: Cornell University Press, 1954. Review, GR 45:457–58.

1956

"From 'Kubla Khan' to Florida." *American Quarterly* 8:76–80. Reprinted in Wright, *Human Nature in Geography* (Cambridge: Harvard University Press, 1966), pp. 119–23.

Stewart, George R., *American Ways of Life*. Garden City, N.Y.: Doubleday, 1954. Review, GR 46:139–40.

The World Map of Richard of Haldingham in Hereford Cathedral, Circa A.D. *1285, with memoir by* G. R. Crone. *Reproductions of Early Manuscript Maps*, III. London: Royal Geographical Society, 1954. Review, GR 46:150.

1957

"American Communities." GR 47:126.

A World Geography of Forest Resources. American Geographical Society Special Publication no. 33, ed. Stephen Haden-Guest, J. K. Wright, and Eileen M. Teclaff. New York: Ronald Press, 736 pp.

1958

"The Heights of Mountains: An Historical Notice." Special Libraries Association: Geography and Map Division, *Bulletin* no. 31, pp. 4–15. Reprinted in Wright, *Human Nature in Geography* (Cambridge: Harvard University Press, 1966), pp. 140–53.

[History of Egypt to 1952] in *Egypt: A Compendium*, by Raye R. Platt and Mohammed Bahy Hefny, with contributions from John Kirtland Wright and David Lowenthal. New York: AGS, pp. 1–48.

Buchanan, R. H., ed., *Ulster Folklife*. Belfast: Committee on Ulster Folklife and Traditions, vol. 2 (1956). Review, GR 48:586–87.

East, W. Gordon, and Moodie, A. E., eds., *The Changing World: Studies in Political Geography*. Yonkers-on-Hudson, N.Y.: World Book, 1956. Review, GR 48:288–89.

Evans, E. Estyn, *Irish Folk Ways*. New York: Devin-Adair, 1957. Review, GR 48:586–87.

1959

"Isaiah Bowman, 1878–1950." National Academy of Sciences, *Biographical Memoirs*, 33:39–51 (with George F. Carter).

"Some British 'Grandfathers' of American Geography," in *Geographical Essays in Memory of Alan G. Ogilvie*, ed. R. Miller and J. Wreford Watson. London: Nelson, pp. 144–65.

Cruickshank, Helen Gere, ed., *John and William Bartram's America: Selections from the Writings of the Philadelphia Naturalists*. American Naturalists Series, vol. 4. New York: Devin-Adair, 1957. Review, GR 49:150.

Harper, Francis, ed., *The Travels of William Bartram: Naturalists Edition*. New Haven: Yale University Press, 1958. Review, GR 49:150.

The Map of Great Britain Circa A.D. 1360 Known as the Gough Map. *Royal Geographical Society Reproductions of Early Manuscript Maps, IV; Bodleian Library Map Reproductions, I*. London: Royal Geographical Society and Bodleian Library, 1958. Review, GR 49:453–54.

Paassen, C. van, *The Classical Tradition of Geography*. Groningen: J. B. Wolters, 1957. Review, GR 49:300–302.

1960

"Geography and History Cross-Classified." *Professional Geographer* 12.5: 1–3.

"Map" [sections of article], *Encyclopedia Britannica* (1966), 14:827, 834–37.

James, Preston E., ed., *New Viewpoints in Geography*. Twenty-Ninth Yearbook. Washington, D.C.: National Council for the Social Studies, 1959. Review, GR 50:446–48.

1961

"Daniel Coit Gilman, Geographer and Historian." GR 51:381–99. Reprinted in Wright, *Human Nature in Geography*, pp. 168–87.

"Introduction," in *A History of Exploration from the Earliest Times to the Present Day*, by Sir Percy Sykes. New York: Harper & Bros., Harper Torchbooks/The Academy Library, pp. xv–xxxviii.

Life Pictorial Atlas of the World. New York: Time, 1961. Review, *New York Herald Tribune*, October 15, p. 8.

1962
"Miss Semple's 'Influences of Geographic Environment': Notes toward a Bibliobiography." GR 52:346–61. Reprinted in Wright, *Human Nature in Geography* (Cambridge: Harvard University Press, 1966), pp. 188–204.

Lunny, Robert M., *Early Maps of North America*. Newark: New Jersey Historical Society, 1961. Review, GR 52:618–19.

Stamp, L. Dudley, ed., *A Glossary of Geographical Terms*. London: Longmans, 1961. Review, *Geographical Journal* 128:71–73.

1963
"The Lost World of Cape Canaveral, 1911." *Harper's Magazine* 227 (November):67.

"Wild Geographers I Have Known." *Professional Geographer* 15.4:1–4.

1964
"A Night in a Burnt Region." *Appalachia*, n.s. 30:76–77.

Baker, J. N. L., *The History of Geography*. Oxford: Basil Blackwell, 1963. Review, GR 54:597–99.

1965
The Geographical Lore of the Time of the Crusades: A Study in the History of Medieval Science and Tradition in Western Europe. (Reprint of 1925 ed.) New York: Dover, 563 pp.

"J. Franklin Jameson and the Atlas of the Historical Geography of the United States," in *J. Franklin Jameson: A Tribute*, ed. Ruth Ann Fisher and W. L. Fox. Washington, D.C.: Catholic University Press, pp. 66–79.

"The Northern Mahoosucs, 1910–1911: Terra Incognita." *Appalachia*, n.s. 31:626–54.

Crombie, A. C., ed., *Scientific Change: Historical Studies in the Intellectual, Social, and Technical Conditions for Scientific Discovery and Technical Invention*. . . . New York: Basic Books, 1963. Review, GR 55:137–39.

Destombes, Marcel, ed., *Mappemondes* A.D. *1200–1500: Catalogue Preparé par la Commission des Cartes Anciennes de l'Union Géographique Internationale*. Imago Mundi, Suppl. no. 4. Amsterdam: N. Israel, 1964. Review, *Geographical Journal* 131:571–72.

Marsh, George Perkins, *Man and Nature*, ed. David Lowenthal. Cambridge: Harvard University Press, Belknap Press, 1965. Review, *Vermont History* 33:353–54.

Rowley, Virginia M., *J. Russell Smith: Geographer, Educator, and Conservationist.* Philadelphia: University of Pennsylvania Press, 1964. Review, GR 55:614–15.

1966
"Foreword," in *Maps of the Ancient Sea Kings: Evidence of Advanced Civilization in the Ice Age,* by Charles H. Hapgood. Philadelphia: Chilton Books, pp. ix–x.
Human Nature in Geography: Fourteen Papers, 1925–1965. Cambridge: Harvard University Press, 361 pp. Previously unpublished, in addition to the Introduction and Epilogue, are "What's 'American' about American Geography?" revision of a paper read at the Columbia University Seminar on American Civilization, New York, 1956, pp. 124–39; "On Medievalism and Watersheds in the History of American Geography," revision of a paper read at the Columbia University Seminar on American Civilization, New York, 1960, pp. 154–67; "Notes on Measuring and Counting in Early American Geography," pp. 205–49; and "Notes on Early American Geopiety," pp. 250–85.
"Panorama from the Pinnacle (Acorn Hill)." Lyme, N.H.: Lyme Historians (with Vivian Piper and Lucy King; drawings by John K. Wright).

Skelton, R. A., Marston, Thomas E., and Painter, George D., *The Vinland Map and the Tartar Relation.* New Haven: Yale University Press, 1965. Review, GR 56:452–54.

1968
"Marcel Aurousseau in the 'Twenties: Geographer and Traveller," *Meanjin Quarterly* (Brisbane) 27:418–21.
"Mysterious Islands: The Wright Papers in the Dartmouth Library," *Dartmouth College Library Bulletin,* n.s. 9:42–54.
"The View from Thetford Hill, Vt. (940 ft.)," drawing by J. K. Wright. Thetford, Vt.: Thetford Academy.

Forthcoming
Wright, John K., "Distributors and Distributees." Geography Publications at Dartmouth, no. 9, 248 pp. (with Fred E. Lukermann and Philip W. Porter).

Index

257

Index

Mendoza, Antonio de, 48
Mercator, Gerhardus, 76
Mexico, 48–49, 52, 56
Meyer, Alfred H., 154, 162
Michigan, University of, 154
Miami Valley (Ohio), 154
Middle West, 108, 126
Milton, John, 41
Minnesota, University of, 67
Missouri River, 125, 130
Missouri, University of, 67
Mitchell, Thomas, 56
Mitford, Jessica, 171
Montana, 134
Monticello (Virginia), 98
More, Thomas, 199, 205, 207, 211
Morison, Samuel Eliot, 44, 67
Morley, Henry, 203
Morris, Ralph C., 133
Morse, Jedidiah, 64
Motley, John Lothrop, 97, 121
Mumford, Lewis, 200
Murray River (Australia), 46

National Academy of Sciences, 65
Nebraska, 123, 128
New Atlantis (Bacon), 203, 207
New England, 150, 153, 157
New Hebrides, 56
New Mexico, 48, 50, 52, 134
New Zealand, 213–14
Niagara Falls, 103
Nicholson, Norman L., 156
Niels Klim's Journey under the
  Ground (Holberg), 208
Niger River, 46
Nile River, 104
Nilsson, Martin P., 17
1984 (Orwell), 206
Norris, Darrell, 211
North Carolina, University of, 67

Oakeshott, Michael, 73–74
Ohio, 104
Old Santa Fe Trail (Inman), 122

Oliphant, Laurence, 95
Ontario, 156
Oregon Trail, 130
Orinoco Basin, 55
Ortelius, 76
Orwell, George, 206
O'Sullivan, John Louis, 94

Paine, Thomas, 94
Park, Mungo, 46
Parkins, Almon E., 155
Parkman, Francis, 77, 121
Parrish, Randall, 121, 125, 126
Passarge, Siegfried, 154
Pattison, William D., 172
Paulding, James K., 93
Paxson, Frederic L., 121, 129–30,
  138
Pearl, Valerie, 89
Pecos, Valley of the, 50
Pennsylvania State University, 67
Perelandra (Lewis), 205
Pericles, 24
Peru, 56
Peter Martyr, 53
Pillars of Hercules, 44
Piranesi, Giambattista, 98
Pizarro, Francisco, 56
Pliny, 20
Polo, Marco, 56
Polo family, 54
Pounds, Norman J. G., 157, 159
Powell, J. M., 201, 214
Powell, John Wesley, 128, 130
Prescott, William Hickling, 121
Prester John, 53–55
Price, Larry W., 172
Prince, Hugh C., 89
Pytheas, 44

Quirós, Pedro Fernandez de, 56

Raleigh, Walter, 56
Raymond, Henri, 215
Reimmichls Volkskalender, 28

261